Political Legitimacy in Asia

Palgrave Series on Asian Governance

Series editors:
Michael Wesley, Lowy Institute for International Policy, Australia
Patrick Weller, Griffith University, Australia

Published by Palgrave Macmillan:

Dissident Democrats: The Challenge of Democratic Leadership in Asia
Edited by John Kane, Haig Patapan, and Benjamin Wong

China's "New" Diplomacy: Tactical or Fundamental Change?
Edited by Pauline Kerr, Stuart Harris, and Qin Yaqing

Corruption and Money Laundering: A Symbiotic Relationship
By David Chaikin and J. C. Sharman

India-Pakistan: Coming to Terms
By Ashutosh Misra

China Engages Global Health Governance: Responsible Stakeholder or System-Transformer?
By Lai-Ha Chan

Political Legitimacy in Asia: New Leadership Challenges
Edited by John Kane, Hui-Chieh Loy, and Haig Patapan

POLITICAL LEGITIMACY IN ASIA
NEW LEADERSHIP CHALLENGES

Edited by

*John Kane, Hui-Chieh Loy, and
Haig Patapan*

POLITICAL LEGITIMACY IN ASIA

First published in 2011 by
PALGRAVE MACMILLAN®
in the United States—a division of St. Martin's Press LLC,
175 Fifth Avenue, New York, NY 10010.

Where this book is distributed in the UK, Europe and the rest of the world,
this is by Palgrave Macmillan, a division of Macmillan Publishers Limited,
registered in England, company number 785998, of Houndmills,
Basingstoke, Hampshire RG21 6XS.

Palgrave Macmillan is the global academic imprint of the above companies
and has companies and representatives throughout the world.

Palgrave® and Macmillan® are registered trademarks in the United States,
the United Kingdom, Europe and other countries.

ISBN: 978–0–230–33753–4

Library of Congress Cataloging-in-Publication Data

    Political legitimacy in Asia : new leadership challenges / edited by
John Kane, Hui-Chieh Loy, and Haig Patapan.
       p. cm.—(Palgrave series on Asian governance)
    Includes index.
    ISBN 978–0–230–33753–4 (alk. paper)
      1. Legitimacy of governments—Asia. 2. Asia—Politics and
government—1945– I. Kane, John, 1945 Apr. 18– II. Loy, Hui-Chieh,
III. Patapan, Haig, 1959–

JQ24.P66 2011
320.95—dc23
                                               2011019054

A catalogue record of the book is available from the British Library.

Design by Newgen Imaging Systems (P) Ltd., Chennai, India.

First edition: November 2011

10 9 8 7 6 5 4 3 2 1

Printed in the United States of America.

Contents

ACKNOWLEDGMENTS

This book has its origins in the international workshop *The Search for Legitimacy in Asia*, held at the National University of Singapore on 27–28 July 2009. We thank all those who took part in the workshop, especially the discussants for their thoughtful comments and helpful suggestions. Papers from the workshop were subsequently published in a special issue of the journal *Politics and Policy* (38 [3] [June 2010]).

We gratefully acknowledge the editors of *Politics and Policy*, Emma R. Norman and David Mena Alemán, as well as Associate Editor Riccardo Pelizzo, for their warm generosity, encouragement, and support. We also thank John Wiley & Sons, Inc., for permission to reproduce material from the special issue of the journal.

After this publication we came to the conclusion that recent changes warranted a reconsideration of the evolving nature of legitimacy in the countries examined in the special issue. In addition, to provide a more comprehensive picture of the dynamics of legitimacy in Asia we thought it necessary to examine other countries in the region. Accordingly, we invited new contributions on Taiwan, the Philippines, and Korea. As a result we believe this book provides an extensive, rich, and contemporary account of the evolving foundations of legitimacy in Asia.

Finally, we are pleased to acknowledge the research assistance of Lee Morgenbesser and Jonathan Sim, and more generally, the Department of Philosophy, National University of Singapore, the Griffith Asia Institute and the Centre for Governance and Public Policy, Griffith University, and the Australian Research Council Discovery Funding Scheme for their support on this project.

CHAPTER 1

Introduction

John Kane, Hui-Chieh Loy, and Haig Patapan

In this book we explore the theory and practice of political legitimacy through a detailed examination of 11 countries in East Asia: China, Japan, Vietnam, Indonesia, Malaysia, Thailand, Singapore, Burma, the Philippines, South Korea, and Taiwan. Sixteen years ago, Muthiah Alagappa (1995, 4) noted that "[d]espite its centrality, political legitimacy in developing countries has seldom been studied explicitly." Alagappa's (1995) edited book, *Political Legitimacy in Southeast Asia: The Quest for Moral Authority*, richly addressed this deficit with studies of seven countries in South East Asia—Malaysia, Singapore, the Philippines, Burma, Thailand, Indonesia, and Vietnam. Reflecting on that work, we cannot help but be struck by the changes that have taken place in the decade-and-a-half since its publication. It is not simply the subsequent economic boom and crisis or the inevitable transformations in each country that draws our attention. It is the increasing importance of Asia in an international context and, by implication, the challenges and opportunities such internationalization presents to each country in the region. How the balance of threats and opportunities inherent in such changing circumstances will work out depends in no small part upon the capacity of nations to manage both their internal politics and their relations with one another, factors that are highly interdependent in a globalized environment.

As the chapters in this book reveal, among the principal challenges facing political leaders in East Asia are challenges to their own governmental legitimacy. These chapters also disclose great complexity in the way legitimacy issues play out in particular contexts and circumstances. As is seen from the cases examined, the grounds of domestic legitimacy are often shifting and are deeply contested by various societal actors and sectors, creating highly intricate and sometimes volatile political dynamics. This domestic complexity is exacerbated by the subtle or direct influences of external forces originating in the international community, many members of which are far from indifferent to the internal political arrangements of their fellows. In fact, the increasing economic integration fostered by a globalizing age has not made the issue of political legitimacy any less salient; if anything, economic integration has made the issue more pressing and more difficult to manage diplomatically. The concluding chapter of this book argues, indeed, that the overly simplistic (and contradictory) views regarding legitimacy that the Western international order fostered over several centuries have provided inadequate conceptual formulations for dealing with the on-the-ground complexities of less-than-democratic developing nations. As developing nations become increasingly entangled in the international economic order, this lack becomes an issue in a way that it was not when the world was sharply ideologically divided, as a glance at history reveals.

The immediate post–World War II world order was characterized by two parallel lines of development: the entrenchment of liberal democratic politics and capitalistic economic development within the countries that formed what we know as "the West," and patterns of increasingly open reciprocal trade between Western nations. This order, endorsed by the hegemonic authority and backed by the economic power of the United States, was originally intended to be universally inclusive but soon confronted the realities of the Cold War. Instead of a truly global order, there was established instead a clearly delimited liberal, democratic, and capitalistic bloc opposed by a communistic one, each with its own ideas about political and economic development. These blocs formed two "worlds," each competing for influence and natural resources among the developing nations of the so-called Third World. The last, whether they leaned toward one of the two blocs or tried desperately to maintain a policy of nonalignment, remained for the most part as severely dependent on external powers as many of them had formerly been on colonial masters.

The logic of these international arrangements was shattered by the collapse and breakup of the Soviet Union in the 1980s and 1990s, posing new doubts and questions for all parties. The main issue facing members of the triumphant First World was whether their unity had been founded on anything more than the now defunct common fear of the communist enemy, or whether it was based upon deeper cultural, economic, and political connections conducing to peaceful interdependence (Mearsheimer 2001). Contrary to the expectations of many, the liberal order survived and prospered (at least until the recent financial shocks to the system), buoyed by strains of neoliberal revivalism (Ikenberry 2006). The question for former members of the communist bloc (including China) and for Third World countries generally was less *whether* to join this thriving order than *on what terms* to join it. In fact, the astonishingly rapid rise of China as an industrial power since the early 1980s, the steadier ascent of India, the natural resource-based revival of post–Soviet Russia, and the eagerness of many Latin American and African countries to join the great game confirmed the continuing vitality and potential of capitalistic development under globalizing conditions.

Yet enhanced economic multipolarity sharpened the issue of whether or how far the liberal international order could accommodate nonliberal, authoritarian states without deforming its own nature. More crucially, it challenged the capacity of that order to foster peaceful interdependence among its expanding membership without cracking under the strain of conflicting relations. Liberal theory had over many centuries, and *a fortiori* during the Cold War, propounded the thesis that economic modernization and democratization went hand-in-hand—if not quite immediately, sooner or later. That thesis was now under practical challenge from one of the largest players in a game that had suddenly become more complicated and consequential for all the parties involved.

The Case of Asia

It is against this background that we place our study of legitimacy in contemporary East Asia, a region that has experienced remarkable economic development in the post–World War II era. It is home to the economic powerhouse of Japan, the four Asian Tigers of South Korea, Taiwan, Hong Kong, and Singapore, and the feverishly developing People's Republic of China. It also includes Thailand, Malaysia, Indonesia, and the Philippines whose gains—though more modest when compared with the previously mentioned countries—have been far from negligible. It is not too much to say that East Asia in the second half of the twentieth century witnessed possibly the greatest leap from poverty to material plenty in mankind's history for a considerable proportion of the world's population. Yet such rapid economic development has confronted the governments of these Asian countries with difficult questions regarding the nature and sources of their own legitimacy.

The problem is that some Asian regimes have pursued capitalistic development while wishing to maintain traditional forms of political control. For these, the Soviet breakup provided an object lesson: it showed that radical change had to be very carefully managed and continuity of rulership adequately justified. But any justification was inherently problematic if participation in the liberal international order required abandoning old ideological positions that were based precisely on resistance to the developmental logic of that order. Profound questions concerning the maintaining or altering of political identities were necessarily involved. The risk was that a failure to legitimize rule under new directions would lead to political turmoil and regime collapse or, worse, cause a destructive external projection of nationalistic passions into conflicts that could destroy the developing international order.

The rulers of contemporary Asian nations faced fateful choices analogous to those faced by Japan—one of its own members—when it industrialized in the late nineteenth and early twentieth centuries. Japan's options lay between the liberal internationalism championed by the Americans and the competitive imperialism that characterized European power relations. Japanese liberals ultimately lost out to aggressive militarist-imperialists, who subsequently led the nation into a disastrous Pacific War (Buruma 2004). Though the political and economic conditions for such competitive imperialism no longer hold, there remain serious differences between nations within the Asia-Pacific region, and potential flashpoints for conflict manifestly exist. An expanded liberal internationalist order that includes Russia, China, Japan, India, Pakistan, and many other nations with small reason to trust one another, and often with histories of conflict, must inevitably be a more delicate one than an order founded principally on the postwar U.S.-European alliance. The new order is one characterized by a peculiar mix of cooperative interdependence and competitive rivalry under conditions of imperfect trust, in which old-fashioned regional balances of power will remain important into the foreseeable future, thus presenting inherent dangers of imbalance.

The fact is that Asian nations have entered the liberal international order for the sake of encouraging their own rapid growth, but not all of them have done so on classical liberal terms. Some have sought the material benefits of scientific and capitalistic development and internationalization while resisting pressures toward political reform in liberal democratic directions. The success of the Asian economies has, in effect, issued a challenge to the traditional Western view that the liberalization of economics and the liberalization of politics are mutually supportive and necessarily correlated. One might object that this challenge was already laid down years ago by Lee Kwan Yew's Singapore (whose own legitimacy problems are treated in this issue). But it is one thing for a small island to play successfully at the margins of the international arena—aided by at least a show of democratic forms—and quite another when the most populous and fastest growing country on earth tries to take the same route. Some of the more combative Western thinkers have sounded the alarm over this development. Robert Kagan (2008) warns that Western democracies must wake from their dream of inevitable progress toward a world of liberal states living in peaceful and prosperous coexistence and understand that "history has returned" with a vengeance, propelled by the ambition, pride, and fear of competitive, mutually suspicious and potentially hostile nation-states. The leaders of nations, such as China and Russia, he claims, *believe* in autocracy and see liberal democracy as a destabilizing threat. The international liberal order does not imply progress for them but oppression, and their foreign policy must, therefore, include the defense of autocracy itself against the combined forces of democracy.

Whatever one thinks of such an argument, the latent enmity it portrays between democratic and autocratic states must surely be complicated, to say the least, by the depth of the mutual economic entanglement between these states. Kagan (2008) emphasizes the threat to the West while underplaying the dangers courted by the autocracies themselves. There is no doubt that the latter wish to benefit economically from the international order while insulating their politics from its liberal tendencies, but it is important to understand the magnitude of the challenge they face, which is more than just a practical one. Their deeper problem is that the ideologies that served them in former times, and which were a central component of their claim to political legitimacy, will not bear the weight imposed by their participation in capitalistic forms of development. The payoff for such development is, of course, a rapidly rising standard of living for populations and access to the culture of Western liberalism and consumerism. But this means that autocratic regimes have tacitly or explicitly abandoned former ideological justifications and, in effect, tied themselves to economic performance as a central plank of their legitimacy.

One obvious problem with this is that economic growth is usually very uneven, creating deep and problematic social cleavages, and also subject to sudden recessions or reversals. The 2008 global financial crisis, caused initially by mortgage defaults in the United States, and swiftly transmitted to Europe and then to China and Asia, demonstrates how deeply intertwined are all national and regional economies (decoupling theses notwithstanding), and how vulnerable any regime must be to sudden shock. In the absence of any other strong planks of legitimation, economic crises can easily become crises of political legitimacy. The example is again provided by Japan (the inclusion of whose case in this book may seem at first surprising), whose superimposed constitutional democracy concealed a *de facto* one-party state that ran into a serious and prolonged legitimacy crisis when economic progress slowed drastically.

Current Asian regimes, as is demonstrated by the chapters in this book, are quite aware of this problem and address it by outlining other justifications for their continued rule. Their struggles to establish new or renovated grounds for their own political legitimacy is a topic, we believe, that repays serious attention. Centrally at stake, arguably, is the question of whether the international order will largely shape the internal politics of member regimes or whether, alternatively, the internal politics of regimes will attenuate the liberal nature of the order with unpredictable and possibly dangerous consequences for international relations.

A Theoretical Challenge

Though legitimacy is a central and crucial concept of political life, it is nevertheless a problematic, even a controversial one for some scholars, who doubt that it is either valid or useful for understanding the politics of different societies. An objection typically raised is that legitimacy is so deeply "embedded" a concept that it is impossible to say which way causation goes (does political support create legitimacy, or do perceptions of legitimacy generate support?), making it uselessly tautological for analytical purposes.

Another objection (arguably a variant of the same) concerns the supposed difficulty of distinguishing the *source* of legitimacy from the *object* of legitimation (e.g., is a king's monarchical authority both the source and object of legitimation?). Furthermore, how exactly are we to measure legitimacy, and what are we to take as the indicative criteria of genuine legitimacy? Should we attend to people's expressed attitudes or to their behavior, and in either case how do these align with the procedural forms taken to confer legitimacy in various regimes?[1]

The problem with such criticisms is that they conflate theoretical and sociological approaches and arguments. Few political science concepts would survive such critique. Consider, for example, the concept of "power," central to modern political science. Power also seems too deeply embedded and problematically causal for us to know whether it is a dependent or an independent variable. Is a leader's power a function of his or her capacity to lead or of the willing acquiescence of the led (see Kellerman 2008)? Power as a concept also seems susceptible to charges of tautology—powerful people have power. Power seems to conceal a crucial moral dimension marking the difference between calculated obedience due to fear, and willing obedience expressing genuine consent. Finally, attempts to measure power are dogged by familiar problems about exactly what is being measured and how. These difficulties with power—and one could list similar ones for, say, authority—do not commonly lead analysts to suggest that these concepts be discarded. Neither should we seek to discard legitimacy. We believe the real problem for social scientists is the inherently normative nature of the concept, which makes some prefer to do without it altogether, or to replace it with concepts more purely descriptive and hence measurable, for example, "political support." This is a forlorn hope if political support and legitimacy are always crucially, however confoundingly, intertwined.

Readers of this collection will be repeatedly struck by the continuing force of Rousseau's dictum that goes to the heart of the legitimacy question: "The strongest man is never strong enough to be master all the time, unless he transforms force into right and obedience into duty" (Rousseau 1968, Book I, Chapter 3). It *is* possible, as our outlier case of Burma demonstrates, to rule by sheer force for some considerable time, but even in Burma the desperate, ever-failing attempts of the military junta to found its rule on something larger and finer attests to the importance of legitimacy and the costs incurred by its lack. And this is the reason that we feel it worthwhile investigating the subject at some length. Whatever the reservations of social scientists and theorists, questions of legitimacy and illegitimacy are of vital concern for people involved in political action. It is apparent in the chapters on individual countries in this collection that issues of legitimacy, and related concepts of authority and justice, emerge quite naturally from within the self-representations of the political actors themselves.

The peculiar complexity of the concept of legitimacy is a consequence precisely of its location at the problematic juncture of morality and power. It is impossible to understand modern Western political systems without appreciating the central role that debates over legitimacy played in their often conflicted historical development. Readers of this collection will see how older sources of legitimacy in various contemporary Asian countries vie politically (and confusingly) with newer ones, as in the complex interaction between the Thai monarchy and Thai democracy, or in the attempts of the Chinese and Vietnamese communist parties to replace or reinforce ideological sources of legitimacy with performance-based or nationalistic ones, or in the struggle of Malaysians to alter ethnic community norms in a democratic direction while confronting the rising Islamist agenda of one particular political party. The principal focus of these dramas of political legitimacy is generally that entity we call "the state," yet nearly all modern states, and especially those of Southern Asia, have borders that enclose distinct, overlapping, and often inimically opposed communities, which do not uniformly accept the legitimacy of the state or its governors. Even in a more homogenous nation, such as Japan, state leaders face the repeated necessity of establishing, reestablishing, and maintaining their legitimacy in the face of steeply declining public trust. And, as we adverted to above, in addition to the problem of shoring up internal legitimacy, leaders must have regard to the external legitimacy of their state within an international order upon which, in a globalizing world, they are deeply dependent.

Some theorists might argue that the real issue is less legitimacy and more the manner in which self-conscious elites "manufacture consent" among populations through media control of "public opinion" and virtual propaganda (Fried 1997; Herman and Chomsky 1988). Of course, it is an empirical matter whether, how, and to what extent such manipulation occurs, but the fact that elites feel they must make such efforts to secure the consent of the people is itself a testament to the central importance of legitimacy. The point is that legitimacy matters very much to people, both elites and masses, for a great deal hangs on how successfully legitimacy claims are established and defended, or alternatively how they are criticized and demolished. If the political scientist wants to be faithful to political phenomena, then, he or she must treat the concept seriously.

The Search for Legitimacy

Given our stress on the global nature of the international order, it might be asked why we should focus on East Asia in particular. No doubt it would be as valid to look at issues of legitimacy thrown up in Latin America, which is also undergoing significant change, or Eastern Europe, or even contemporary Africa. One compelling reason for choosing East Asia, however, is the intrinsic significance of the region itself. The Asia-Pacific is the crucible in which many of the most consequential dramas of rising and declining powers will be played out over the coming decades. East Asia also encompasses an intriguing array of disparate large and small powers struggling to adapt to change and/ or to fend it off. Practical limitations of space have meant that otherwise fascinating case studies have not been included—we have set aside North Korea, Cambodia, and Laos.[2] Nevertheless, the countries we have chosen provide an analytically broad spectrum for understanding the different factors that may be said to shape and influence legitimacy in Asia.

The countries we have chosen to study are China (whose rising star obscures many difficult challenges); Japan (whose faltering "miracle" caused a legitimacy crisis); Vietnam (another formerly communist country entering the international fold but bearing a history of enmity with both the West and China); Thailand (a never-colonized, only fitfully democratic kingdom whose monarch still plays a vital role); Indonesia (recently and apparently successfully transitioned from military to democratic rule); Malaysia (with its ethnic nationalism and idiosyncratic style); Singapore (whose elitist technocratic model charms the Chinese and yet has apparently shallow foundations); Burma (a military dictatorship generally disliked but pragmatically supported by its larger neighbors); the Philippines (revealing a tension between the promise of democratic rule and the reality of instability and corruption); South Korea (where a succession of military regimes finally gave way to a democratically elected government); and Taiwan (claimed to be the first Chinese democracy). These countries present fascinating opportunities for exploring the theoretical and practical contours of legitimacy as they become manifest in very different but regionally related contexts.

What sort of things do these cases reveal about legitimacy? First, they demonstrate that there is no single basis for legitimacy sufficient on its own to fully justify rule, a fact underlined by the transnational dimension to which we referred above. Domestic ideas of legitimacy are invariably shaped by or formed in reaction to influential international conceptions, and arguments for legitimacy typically draw upon multiple sources, both traditional and new. What we see from the chapters presented is that legitimacy is, in each country, contingent, cumulative, dynamic, and constantly contested: the insufficiency of any one ground, or set of grounds, requires constant recourse to other, still never-quite-sufficient, bases of legitimation. Second, this constant contestation means that legitimacy issues are seldom settled once and for all. They may become most obvious during crises, as in coup-prone Thailand, or during crucial elections, as recently in Malaysia and the Philippines, but it is clear from the chapters that the search for legitimacy may be extended over a few or even many decades—as in Thailand itself, or in post-Mao China, Vietnam, South Korea, Taiwan, or Japan. Third, it is clear, too, that fear or compulsion is never sufficient on its own to secure a regime. We have already noted this with regard to Burma, whose erstwhile socialist military authority tried to rehabilitate a quasi-monarchic authority to legitimate its rule before turning to elections, but the judgment applies to all cases.

We do not wish to anticipate the reader's own judgment by providing a comprehensive assessment of the insights to be gained from the rich and detailed examinations of each country. It may be useful, however, if we note some major themes that emerge from a synoptic overview of all the chapters. These themes concern three of the most obvious modern foundations for legitimacy: performance, nationalism, and democracy.

Performance

Performance is by no means the simple, one-dimensional concept that it is often taken to be. As has been argued in a recent book on legitimacy, performance is an essential and irreducible element of *any* conception of legitimacy (Gilley 2009). Performance ranges from simple security and safety, to economic prosperity, to preservation of cultural values, to safeguarding national pride and prestige, and to guarantees provided by constitutionalism, rule of law, and transparency. It is to be expected, then, that all the countries examined will rely on some sort of performance criteria as a foundational basis for legitimacy. Even the Burmese junta justifies its own coercive rule on such a criterion, namely the army's unique capacity to hold together a country riven by ethnic conflicts.

Vietnam's reassessment of its communist ideology was driven by perceived failures of performance in economic matters, and all the countries we examine have entered the international trading order to seek improvement in this area. Yet, as noted above, problems occur if governments focus too narrowly on a single dimension, performance included. While Singapore has, to a remarkable extent, made economic performance (secured by technocratic competence) its preeminent basis for legitimacy, it has also turned from time to time to "Asian values" or nationalism to bolster its rule. Modern Japan, by contrast, was founded almost exclusively on economic performance (as its famous label "Japan

Inc." illustrates), with the result that there was little else for the moribund ruling Liberal Democratic Party (LDP) to fall back on when that performance declined.

Another very important factor in the failure of the LDP regime in the eyes of Japanese—and one that recurs in the following pages as a prime factor undermining legitimacy in all countries—was the revelation of large-scale corruption among elites. Corruption is universally interpreted by populations as failure of performance of the most offensive kind.[3] One of the large questions for the new China and other Asian nations—which have also placed many of their eggs in the economic development basket and are plagued by official corruption—is whether they can perform sufficiently across the board to avoid the LDP's fate (Chu et al. 2008).

One problem in basing legitimacy upon performance is that the latter is contingent upon changing times and altered expectations. Thaksin's reforms to secure performance in Thailand, for example, appear to have strengthened the case for legitimacy based on constitutionalism and popular sovereignty. Many important shifts, however, are not deliberately intended. The very success of a country in economic development inevitably causes large changes in its population, notably by creating a broad middle class with better education, more familiarity with the wider world, new demands, new dissatisfactions, and more sophisticated ways of making those demands and dissatisfactions felt. This dynamic can be seen playing itself out in South Korea. On the one hand, the industrial programs initiated by the authoritarian regimes (in the 1960s and 1970s) brought about rapid economic growth, enhancing the legitimacy of those regimes. But on the other hand, the same developments dissolved the agricultural sector, creating a disaffected pool of unskilled labor and urban poor who eventually became crucial opponents of these same regimes. Consequently, development-oriented regimes must be quite flexible and creative in consolidating fresh bases of legitimacy if they are to stay ahead of the game and show themselves sufficiently responsive to such changes.

Nationalism

All the states examined here have employed nationalism to various degrees to support their legitimacy. Nationalist appeals are typically founded upon ethnicity, language, history, or tradition and are employed to create a sense of solidarity among often quite disparate populations. Nationalism is, of course, a modern ideology closely attached to the phenomenon we call the "nation-state," an ideology that has proved immensely powerful yet also dangerous. Although nationalism lost much of its intellectual respectability after the wars of the twentieth century, the appeal to nationalist passions remains an enduring temptation for rulers, especially when other sources of legitimacy are failing. Leaders who can successfully cast themselves as representing and defending the nation, especially during security scares, are generally assured of support. But the dangers of this are twofold, one internally focused, the other externally.

States that resort to ethnic nationalism—for instance, the Han in China, the Malays in Malaysia, the Burmese in Burma, the Thai in Thailand, and the Kinh in Vietnam—appeal to only one section of the population, which, even if it is by far the largest one, automatically excludes significant and often disgruntled minorities (Brown 2008). In some cases ethnic nationalism is augmented with religion—for example, Buddhism in Thailand and Burma, Islam in Malaysia and Indonesia, and Shinto in Japan—which compounds the problem for citizens who are adherents of other religions. Appeals to a glorious history—for example, the ancient civilization of China—may or may not reinforce division, depending on how such appeals are couched. But given that the borders of modern states are often the arbitrary products of history, generally enclosing multiple ethnicities and religions, ethnic nationalism is usually a recipe for internal division, sometimes conflict and, in the extreme case, separatism. Such forms of nationalism are, in other words, often vehicles for the oppression and domination of minority groups by majorities. It is to avoid such appearances or realities that some regimes—for example, Indonesia and Singapore—stress the multiethnic makeup of their states, appealing to the concept of a "neutral state" that serves all its members regardless of ethnicity, language, or religion. Fostering the heritage of Confucianism in some East Asian societies has also been argued to be a nondivisive means of encouraging loyalty to the state (Chaibong 2004).

When states refuse to play the ethnic nationalism card, there is little internal role left for nationalist ideology to perform (although we should not underestimate how effectually the prospect of national greatness plays among Chinese citizens as they contemplate their future with renewed pride). Yet the possibility of an external role for nationalism always remains. Nationalism is typically employed most effectively against other nations in situations of tension or conflict. There is a perennial temptation for rulers to stir up such tensions or exploit any that accidentally arise for the sake either of promoting internal unity or pursuing certain domestic or foreign policy objectives. One may point to the calculated provocations of Japan's ultranationalists when they obliged Japanese leaders to visit the Yasukuni Shrine with its buried war criminals, raising predictable outcries from China and Korea. Over the past decades, the Chinese government has alternately inflamed anti-U.S. nationalist sentiment (e.g., over the bombing of the Chinese embassy in Belgrade during the Kosovo crisis in 1999, and over the downed U.S. spy-plane in 2001) and then ruthlessly doused it when it decided good relations with the United States mattered to China's welfare. Indeed, the passionate and volatile nature of nationalist sentiment makes it an always dangerous tool, for its effects may easily become counterproductive or uncontrollable.

Democracy

Democracy represents the most recent challenge to legitimacy in Asia, having gained force from the demise of communism and the opportunities of rapid growth and prosperity created by the liberal international order. As noted above, however, a number of states have sought the material benefits of scientific and capitalistic development and internationalization while resisting pressures toward political reform in liberal democratic directions. Singapore, China, and Vietnam are our most prominent examples (though even in these countries "democratic" reforms of some kind have been instituted in possibly reluctant acknowledgment of their legitimating force).

Other countries have embraced democracy somewhat haphazardly or imperfectly (Chang, Chu, and Huang 2006; Winichakul 2008). Thailand is a problematic example where the promise of democracy has been undermined by competing ideas of legitimacy based on the trinity of "nation, religion, king" (*chart, sasana, phramahakasat*). So is Malaysia, where the rule of law is deeply uncertain but where recent elections seemed to challenge traditional ethnonationalist politics. Meanwhile the military rulers of Burma have been struggling for two decades to devise a new constitution that would institutionalize the army's political role. They effectively forfeited any claim to democratic legitimacy, however, when, confident of their own victory, they held free and fair elections in 1990 that were won by Aung San Suu Kyi's National League for Democracy, which the junta promptly suppressed. The 2011 elections, however questionable, appear to be another attempt at founding legitimacy on democratic grounds.

It is ironic that the Burmese junta's model of an ideal constitution is that of Suharto's Indonesia, now abandoned in Indonesia itself.

Indonesia indeed has proved to be an unexpected and spectacular success, managing not just to dismantle a dictatorial military regime but to combine a moderate Islamic culture with a democratic one, thanks in large measure to the wise judgment of its leaders. The cases of the Philippines, Taiwan, and South Korea show the increasing dominance of democratic principles. Democratic legitimacy, though dogged by clientelism, lack of performance, and corruption, has since the 1986 "people power revolution" been firmly established in the Philippines. In the case of South Korea, some five decades of authoritarian rule by a succession of military regimes eventually gave way to democratically elected government. Taiwan has been effectively democratic since the Nationalist or Kuomintang regime sought to contest elections in the 1980s. And, finally, there is the peculiar case of Japan, which has to all appearances been a functioning democracy under an American-imposed constitution since 1947, yet whose public politics were little more than a façade for a tightly ordered oligarchic-bureaucratic state. As the Japan chapter in this book shows, Japan is now facing a challenge from a more genuine form of popular sovereignty.

Democratization as a conscious goal of the Western powers was seriously discredited after the Iraq War. Yet, as the Obama administration realizes now, it is impossible for a U.S. president dealing with nondemocratic partners wholly to ignore the democratic legitimacy argument, often framed in terms of safeguarding of human rights. This certainly complicates relations that are, in many other respects, coming ever closer, but the dance of subtle or overt pressure and resistance is likely to continue long into the future. The way this contest over legitimacy proceeds at the international level, and its interaction with domestic politics, is a topic addressed in the last chapter of this book. It is one that demonstrates the importance and inescapability of the concept of legitimacy and the value of reevaluating the way we define it.

Conclusion

Understanding the struggles over legitimacy in particular cases requires nuanced exploration of the ways in which a country articulates and tries to resolve its own search for legitimacy. In this brief overview, we have focused on performance, nationalism, and democracy as major factors in contention throughout East Asia. The country studies that follow reveal many other factors, confirming the complex, conflicted, and dynamic nature of legitimacy claims in the region. We, therefore, recommend the thoughtful, finely textured analyses gathered in this book as a necessary and valuable step toward a better understanding of the politics of legitimacy in Asia.

Notes

1. For a discussion of the theoretical limitations to the concept see generally Alagappa (1995), Schaar (1981), Barker (1990), Beetham (1991), and Gilley (2009).
2. For a recent examination of some of the countries not included see Kane, Patapan, and Wong (2008).
3. For an essay noting the same phenomenon in Latin America, see Seglison (2002).

References

Alagappa, Muthiah. 1995. *Political Legitimacy in Southeast Asia: The Quest for Moral Authority.* Stanford: Stanford University Press.

Barker, Rodney S. 1990. *Political Legitimacy and the State.* Oxford: Oxford University Press.

Beetham, David. 1991. *The Legitimation of Power.* London: Macmillan.

Brown, David. 2008. "The Ethnic Majority: Benign or Malign?" *Nations and Nationalism* 14: 768–788.

Buruma, Ian. 2004. *Inventing Japan: 1853–1964.* New York: Modern Library.

Chaibong, Hahm. 2004. "The Ironies of Confucianism." *Journal of Democracy* 15: 93–107.

Chang, Yu-tzung, Yun-han Chu, and Min-hua Huang. 2006. "The Uneven Growth of Democratic Legitimacy in East Asia." *International Journal of Public Opinion Research* 18: 246–255.

Chu, Yun-han, Michael Bratton, Marta Lagos, Sandeep Shastri, and Mark Tessler. 2008. "Public Opinion and Democratic Legitimacy." *Journal of Democracy* 19: 74–87.

Fried, Amy. 1997. *Muffled Echoes: Oliver North and the Politics of Public Opinion.* New York: Columbia University Press.

Gilley, Bruce. 2009. *The Right to Rule: How States Win and Lose Legitimacy.* New York: Columbia University Press.

Herman, Edward S., and Noam Chomsky. 1988. *Manufacturing Consent.* New York: Pantheon Books.

Ikenberry, G. John. 2006. *Liberal Order and Imperial Ambition.* Cambridge, UK: Polity Press.

Kagan, Robert. 2008. *The Return of History and the End of Dreams.* New York: A. A. Knopf.

Kane, John, Haig Patapan, and Benjamin Wong, eds. 2008. *Dissident Democrats: The Challenge of Democratic Leadership in Asia*. New York: Palgrave Macmillan.

Kellerman, Barbara. 2008. *Followership: How Followers Are Creating Change and Changing Leaders*. Boston, MA: Harvard Business School Press.

Mearsheimer, John J. 2001. *The Tragedy of Great Power Politics*. New York: W. W. Norton.

Rousseau, Jean-Jacques. 1968. *The Social Contract*. Harmondsworth, UK: Penguin.

Schaar, John H. 1981. *Legitimacy in the Modern State*. New Brunswick, NJ: Transaction Books.

Seglison, Mitchell A. 2002. "The Impact of Corruption on Regime Legitimacy: A Comparative Study of Four Latin American Countries." *The Journal of Politics* 64: 408–433.

Winichakul, Thongchai. 2008. "Toppling Democracy." *Journal of Contemporary Asia* 38: 11–37.

CHAPTER 2

Reclaiming Legitimacy in Postrevolutionary China: Bringing Ideology and Governance Back In

Heike Holbig

Introduction

The contemporary politics of China reflects an ongoing effort by the ruling Chinese Communist Party (CCP) to reclaim the right to rule in light of the consequences of economic development, international pressures, and historical change. China stands out within the Asian region for the relative success the regime has achieved in that effort. While the CCP does face challenges to its legitimacy, those challenges are for the most part defeated by regime claims. In some respects, China is a classically Asian case: a democratic opposition struggles against the rational-legal and economic performance claims of the regime.

Most measurements find that in the post-1989 period, the party had succeeded in rebuilding its popular legitimacy. Gilley (2006), using both attitudinal and behavioral data at the aggregate level, finds that China was a "high legitimacy" state in comparative perspective from the late 1990s to early 2000s, ranking thirteenth out of 72 states considered, and second in Asia only to Taiwan. Other quantitative measures report similar results (Chen 2004; Wang, Z. 2005). Such findings are based on mean-centered models of measurement. However, the CCP's own attempts to measure its legitimacy tend toward a more disaggregated micro-level approach that is more concerned with variance. Based upon observations about how it deals with seemingly insignificant "mass incidents" and how it studies their potential effects, the CCP appears to look for nodes of legitimacy crisis, in both social and geographic spaces, perhaps on the view that delegitimation can occur quickly as a result of "mass incidents" or other forms of mass mobilization triggering a cascade of preference shifts (Zhang 2009).

The CCP's perception of the brittleness of high mass legitimacy is not unreasonable. In a country the size of China one must engage in substantive geographical (which region?), institutional (which institutions?), and popular (which groups?) complexification (Schubert 2008, 196). When one does this, one recognizes that China has *both* high overall legitimacy *and* serious legitimacy fissures if only because of its size and complexity. If high national average legitimacy can easily crumble in the face of a particular localized crisis, then China's size and complexity as a nation suggest the party is right to be worried about even seemingly minor threats to its legitimacy.

In popular and even many academic discussions, the reasons for regime legitimacy in China are reduced to two main factors: economic growth and nationalism. "China's regime retains authority by means of patriotism and performance-based legitimacy" says Roskin (2009, 426). Pan writes that "the government has grown expert at...rallying nationalist sentiment to its side...[while] the extended boom has enhanced the party's reputation" (2008, 323). Laliberté and Lanteigne write that the CCP's claims to legitimacy "in a nutshell, are encapsulated in the notion that only the CCP is able to ensure economic growth, provide social stability, and defend national sovereignty" (2008, 8).

There is a good factual basis for this claim: the importance attached to economic growth and nationalism has remained high in a World Values Survey (WVS) question asking people to cite "the most important goal for the country," accounting for a combined 73% of responses in 2007 (down slightly from 87% when the question was first asked in 1990). Yet a closer examination of the search for legitimacy in China reveals the importance of two additional clusters of legitimacy sources: (1) ideology and the collective social values that it supports as well as, more recently, culturalism; (2) governance, including the ways in which the regime has been able to define the terms "democracy" and "human rights" in ways that support its existing performance and values.

After a brief outline of the historical dimension of the CCP's legitimacy, the chapter analyzes the various sources of legitimacy. Focusing on developments during the reform period and particularly during the past decade, the aim is to elaborate the relative importance of these sources shifting over time as well as inherent dilemmas and limitations. We do not challenge the importance of growth and of nationalism. However, we believe that they are insufficient to explain the legitimation of the

CCP regime. The key to the party's search for legitimacy, we believe, lies in understanding its ability to construct and influence the subjective values and meanings against which its performance is measured. There has been a clear shift in emphasis from the economic-nationalistic approach to an ideological-institutional approach.

Communist Party Legitimacy in History

The legitimacy of Chinese Communist Party has always been contested and often explicitly rejected by significant portions of China's population. The Civil War that preceded the CCP's victory in 1949 reflected a profoundly divided population. Eastman described the situation as "little...support...on the Nationalist side; some... support...on the Communist side" (1984, 88). Millions fled from China (including 1 million to Hong Kong alone, of whom 385,000 remained by 1954) rather than submit to communist authority. Peterson calls the flight from communist rule in China "one of the largest refugee flows in world history" (2008, 172). Within the country, counterinsurgency operations continued until 1951 in Han areas. Anti-CCP insurgents captured 31 of 79 county capitals in the southwest province of Guizhou in 1950 before finally being crushed in "bandit suppression" campaigns by the end of 1951 (Brown 2007, 114). Tibet and Xinjiang were subdued by force.

In its earliest years, from 1949 to 1956, it was generally assumed (although difficult to prove) that the People's Republic of China (PRC) successfully established its legitimacy through revolutionary ideology and myths, and through concrete performance—ending civil conflict, controlling inflation, and rebuilding the economy. With the excesses of the antirightist campaign of 1956, rising inner party conflicts, and then the disastrous Great Leap Famine of 1959–1961, that legitimacy began to ebb. The internecine violence of the Cultural Revolution, launched in 1966, further degraded CCP legitimacy, despite Mao's hopes that it would reinvigorate social support. By 1976, party leaders believed that the party's popular standing was at an all-time low.

The reform era, and particularly the revival of reforms after the Tiananmen Crackdown in 1989 with its devastating effects on party legitimacy, can be seen as an attempt to rebuild legitimacy along postrevolutionary lines. The motivations were primarily domestic. This effort accelerated with the collapse of communism throughout Eastern Europe and in the Soviet Union. Other external events—the rise of human rights interventionism, the Kuomintang's loss of power in

Taiwan in 2000, and entry into the World Trade Organization—are variously cited by Chinese party analysts in explaining the heightened attention to the party's moral authority over society. No less important, the changing nature of Chinese society—the development of a large private sector, the disappearance of an industrial proletariat, and sharp intergenerational shifts in values—put the party on guard.

The quest for legitimacy was made explicit in 2004 when the party admitted in a document following a high-level plenum that "[our] ruling status is not inborn, nor is it something fixed for eternity." As a member of the Shanghai party committee research arm put it, "if we do not...prevent and overcome the threat of legitimacy crisis, living only by the old dictum that 'anyone can rule by force alone' then it is not inconceivable that we will follow the same path as the Soviet Union" (Zhou, S. 2006, 250–251). Shambaugh calls the 2004 declaration "probably the most important" party document since the 1978 plenum decision that launched the reform movement (Shambaugh 2008, 124).

In the years following, an intensive debate emerged within the party's intellectuals on the explicit question of legitimacy. The number of articles on the question of party legitimacy in a representative sample of 36 party school journals rose from just 14 in 2002 to a peak of 84 in 2006. Of the 168 articles that dealt with the topic of regime legitimacy in party school journals, university journals, and public policy journals we studied between 2003 and 2007, 30% warned of a legitimacy crisis (*hefaxing weiji*) looming for the CCP, while a larger proportion (68%) warned about some form of legitimacy challenge, threat, problem, or weakness (*tiaozhan, weixie, wenti, ruodian*, etc.). Only a few scattered voices among hard-line party ideologues pointed out that Marxist parties should *by definition* not be debating their own legitimacy because "raising the question of whether China should still be led by the CCP" could have "serious negative consequences" (Xin 2005). This in turn has provided the basis for a constant and restless striving to adjust, change, modify, and sometimes radically alter aspects of public policy and state institutions in order to conform to the perceived demands of legitimacy. Reclaiming legitimacy is at the center of contemporary Chinese politics.

Economic Growth and Nationalism

Growth and nationalism, as mentioned, are widely cited among outside analysts as the main sources of legitimacy in China. No doubt, as the WVS question shows, they matter. But the WVS data also shows that they are probably declining in importance, and both face inherent dilemmas.

There is a view widely shared among analysts in China that economic growth in particular, while providing a short-term fillip to party legitimacy, was, like revolutionary legitimacy, bound to be exhausted. This was because it is generating its own problems (inequalities, environmental degradation, etc.), creating rising expectations, and fuelling shifts in social values and political culture. Indeed, Chinese elites have worried for years about the fleeting nature of economic success, which is aggravated by the increasing dependence on the global market. Samuel Huntington's "King's dilemma," translated as "performance dilemma" (*zhengji kunju*), was borrowed as starting point for a critical analysis of the first two decades of economic reforms. It was argued that party rule would come under growing pressure as the satisfaction of material needs would breed nonmaterial ones, such as demands for political participation and pluralization, and as social inequalities fuelled a sense of injustice (Gilley and Holbig 2009).

The relationship between growth and regime legitimacy is not an obvious one. Economic growth and material well-being are highly abstract notions for the individual, notions that are usually experienced by way of intertemporal, interpersonal, interregional, and international comparison. This is to say, economic success is not per se a source of regime legitimacy; instead, it has to be framed in ways conducive of positive subjective perceptions of the regime, for example, as competent, efficient, fair, committed to the realization of the common interest while avoiding publicly manifest partiality or bias, capable of selectively embracing the benefits of globalization while defending national interests on a complex international terrain, and so on.

According to the same logic, economic crises should not be regarded as an immediate threat to regime legitimacy, bringing down autocrats once the growth falls—again, the emergence of legitimacy deficits depends on how the crisis is framed by the incumbent regime. Nevertheless, the CCP is aware of both the fleeting and the subjective nature of growth-based legitimation. It has constantly to struggle to maintain this source of legitimacy. Not unsurprisingly it has devoted major efforts to search for alternative legitimacy sources.

Nationalism as a legitimation strategy also faces inherent dilemmas. The role of Chinese nationalism since the 1990s has been illustrated widely in the international media—a phenomenon that has its source in the growing disenchantment with the West in the wake of the Soviet collapse (Barmé 1995). Anti-Western and anti-Japanese outbursts have been common. In the field of Chinese studies, scholars have discussed how much of this nationalist sentiment is state-sponsored (rooted in the official cultivation of a well-behaved "patriotism" and national sovereignty instrumentalized by the Chinese party-state as an ersatz ideology), and how much is popular nationalism (resulting, among other factors, from the uncertainties produced by the pluralization and marketization of social life, ruptures in the process of socialization and the building of personal identities, mounting pressures in the fields of education and employment, and the ensuing sensibility toward nationalistic myths). Most authors agree that present-day nationalism is a complex mixture of both state and popular nationalism, where mechanisms of top-down and bottom-up mobilization are closely interrelated (Barmé 1995; Unger 1996; Gries 2004; Zhao 2004; Link 2008; Friedman 2008; Wang, G. 2008).

Due to this complex interplay of top-down and bottom-up mechanisms of mobilization, the leveraging of nationalism as a source of regime legitimacy is an inherently problematic strategy. The Chinese leadership is well aware of this. Wan Jun from the Central Party School, for example, regards the resort to nationalism in China as a double-edged sword. While nationalist sentiments may hold a positive potential for regime legitimation and social mobilization, they can easily grow out of control and cause a destructive mentality of aggression. Particularly in a multiethnic state such as China, he warns, nationalist aspirations may not enhance social cohesion but rather subvert China's fragile national unity (Wan 2003). The construction of the People's Republic of China as a multiethnic nation-state, with all its contested national identities and territorial disputes, is a most illuminating example of the disruptive character inherent in the claim for national sovereignty as a source of legitimation (Beetham 1991, 121–135). Repeated outbursts of ethnic conflicts in areas inhabited by Tibetan, Uigur, and other minorities bear witness to this inherent dilemma of nationalism, as do the ongoing irritations in the international arena.

Indeed, as the waves of nationalist ire raging against the United States, Japan, and Western Europe mentioned above have shown, the Chinese government's vulnerability to external and internal interferences has been growing over the past decade (Jia 2005). Overseas Chinese living in the West and having direct access to U.S. and European media played an unprecedented role in 2008 as patriotic "interpreters" of the alleged anti-Chinese publicity found in these countries in the wake of the Tibet protests, the earthquake in Sichuan province and the Olympics. Their involvement presents a highly volatile element that could easily turn against decisions made by the same regime under different conditions.

The interplay between state nationalism and popular nationalism, between top-down and bottom-up mechanisms of mobilization, has been further complicated in the past few years by the increasingly prominent role played by the so-called New Left in China. Despite the heterogeneity of this group, it has become possible over the past few years to identify the New Left as a hotbed of increasingly self-assured, if not aggressive, forms of elite-sponsored nationalism. Some scholars have become quite outspoken in their criticism of what they regard as the hegemony of "Western" values, concepts, and institutions, such as democracy, human rights, the free market theories, the Washington consensus. In the wake of the 2008 events, various prominent scholars started to publicly question the universality of "universal values" claimed by the West (Zhou, X. 2008).

While proestablishment members of the New Left clothe their criticism in rather vague and sweeping language and avoid naming specific persons or countries, the authors of a recent national bestseller published in March 2009 with the title *Unhappy China: The Great Time, Grand Vision and Our Challenges* cross the limits of political correctness by naming names all over (probably one reason for the book becoming a bestseller). The book presents a collection of essays from scholars and journalists raging against foreign adversaries such as U.S. hegemonism and its allies, particularly Sarkozy and Merkel. First and foremost, however, the authors lash out against "political elites, government economists, cultural elites, editors-in-chief and even some military chiefs" at home who are accused of buying the mistaken belief of neoliberals that "the West would care for and reward China if it humbly accept the world's criticisms" and employing an overly soft approach toward the United States and Western Europe (Song, Q. 2009). Among others, prominent Chinese intellectuals and writers with liberal outlooks or Western educational background, as well as liberal Chinese media groups with internationally acknowledged track records of progressive investigative journalism, are derided as naive lackeys of Western and "universal values." The "grand vision" the book outlines instead is that "with Chinese national strength growing at an unprecedented rate, China should stop debasing itself, recognize the fact that it has the power to lead the world and break away from Western influence" (Song, Q. 2009).

As its rhetoric reveals, this New Left nationalism caters to the tastes of a chauvinistic and increasingly vengeful nationalism among parts of China's urban youth, while at the same time formulating trenchant criticisms of the political, intellectual, and business elites who are accused of corruption, egotism, technocratic arrogance, moral decay, and, most viciously, of blackguards betraying their country's national interests. Thus, it's not only liberal intellectuals who come under attack, but also the "establishment" at large.

The End of the "End of Ideology"

The underlying question of legitimacy is where the common expectations, or evaluative norms, on which legitimacy is judged come from. Since social norms are plural and contested, how do certain ones emerge as dominant? What are the norms that create the sense of political community, the expectations of political culture, and basis of performance evaluations?

In authoritarian systems, the solution to the problem of normative pluralism is ideology. In communist party regimes, Beetham argues, ideology has to provide the normative foundation for the rightful source of political authority; to justify the government's performance in the light of the "common interest"; and to serve as a stimulus to mobilize popular consent or, at least, assent (Beetham 1991, 2001).

Contrary to the proposition of an "end of ideology" that allegedly paralleled the collapse of the Soviet Union and the ensuing "end of history," the CCP has never discontinued its reliance on ideology as a crucial source of regime legitimacy. The alleged "pragmatism" of Deng Xiaoping has been less about an abandonment of ideology than about its constant renovation. Party theorists have clearly acknowledged the challenges to socialist ideology resulting from the reform period—the fading memories of the revolution, the discrediting experiences of Maoism, the decay of Soviet communism, economic globalization, the import of Western culture, technology, and the Internet (e.g., Sun and Sun 2003; cf. also Gilley and Holbig 2009). However, the answer to these challenges has been to refurbish the old-fashioned image of Marxism and breathe new life into worn-out socialist tenets.

Heeding the words of Deng Xiaoping who, after the Tiananmen Massacre of 1989, reflected that "our biggest mistake was in the area of education, in particular ideological and political education" (Deng 1989), his successors Jiang Zemin and Hu Jintao have invested much conceptual energy and large sums of money to modernize the party's ideology. Faced with the loss of power of Taiwan's ruling Kuomintang in early 2000, the party leadership under Jiang Zemin came forward with an explicit strategy to adapt its dominant ideology to a changing environment. Jiang Zemin's controversial concept of "Three Represents" signalled that the CCP was about to redefine its formerly proletarian social base and cast its lot with the newly affluent segments of society (Lewis and Xue 2003).

At the same time, the concept was advertised as the core of an ideological reconstruction of the CCP's legitimacy as ruling party. The right to rule was not claimed any longer with reference to the CCP's long revolutionary history and socialist dogmas, but instead by emphasizing the innovativeness of party theory and the vitality of the CCP resulting from its ability to reform itself from within. Despite strong resistance from inside and outside the CCP that denounced the Three Represents—particularly the official invitation of private entrepreneurs into the communist party—as "muddle-headed," betraying the party's nature as vanguard of the working class, even as "capitalist fascist dictatorship," the formula entered the party constitution in November 2002 as legacy of the retiring CCP general-secretary and most recent manifestation of the party's innovative spirit.

When Hu Jintao took over from Jiang Zemin as party chief in late 2002, he faced the daunting challenge of putting an end to the ideological controversies surrounding the Three Represents. Besides announcing a temporary ban on discussions of the issue in the media, in party organizations and in academic circles in summer 2003, he engineered a subtle reinterpretation of the formula's elitist connotations. The essence of the Three Represents was now interpreted in official discourse as "establishing a party that is devoted to the public interest and governing for the people" (*Renmin Ribao*, July 2, 2003; cf. Holbig 2009).

Upholding this claim of innovativeness, Hu Jintao (and his advisors) came forward with a more theoretical concept of his own. The first was the "Scientific Outlook on Development," introduced in early 2004 as a grand strategy of "comprehensive, coordinated, and sustainable development" (*Renmin Ribao*, January 12, 2004, March 27, 2004; cf. Holbig 2009). With this concept, the new leadership distanced itself from the growth-only mentality of the first two decades of economic reforms and instead promised to balance economic development with social and ecological concerns. This was followed closely by another formula, the "Harmonious Socialist Society," which was innovative in explicitly acknowledging the existence of social tensions and claiming to tackle their root causes that were increasingly perceived as a risk to social stability and to the political legitimacy of CCP rule. Hu stated that a Harmonious Socialist Society was "essential for consolidating the party's social foundation to govern and achieving the party's historical governing mission" (*Renmin Ribao*, June 27, 2005).

Moving beyond mere rhetoric, the CCP under Hu Jintao invested heavily in political campaigns and scholarly ventures. The most well-known and costly was probably the campaign to "preserve the party's progressive nature" launched in early 2005, in fact the broadest and most systematic inner party education campaign since the start of economic reforms. In the course of 18 months, all 70 million party members were supposed to prove their loyal commitment to the party's cause by equipping themselves with the most recent developments of "Sinicized Marxism" and socialist party theory (*Renmin Ribao*, October 15, January 1, 2005). Another example is the new Academy of Marxism founded in late 2005 under the auspices of the Chinese Academy of Social Sciences. To fulfill its mission—the theoretical innovation of Marxism and compilation of new Marxist textbooks catering to the tastes of younger generations—the Academy received hundreds of millions in RMB (Xinhua News Agency, 26.12.05).

Our analysis of more than 200 articles published in party school organs and scholarly journals between 2004 and 2008 revealed that the majority of authors dwelt on the important role of ideological adaptation and innovation that are seen as *the* prerequisite of relegitimating party rule ideology (Gilley and Holbig 2009). For Lu Ailin of Henan's Zhongyuan Industrial College, who is one of the most prolific writers in contemporary China on party legitimacy, ideology is the "key factor for public identification with the political authority" (2005, 2006). A 2008 article in the journal *Qiushi* (Seeking Truth), the CCP's top party theory organ, argued that in China as elsewhere, ideology serves as a cohesive force of parties worldwide. Socialist ideology should not be regarded as signalling only a remote ideal, but as a practical means to satisfy people's actual needs under the conditions of social transformation. If the party wants to maintain its ideology-based legitimacy, therefore, it has to take stringent measures to restore social justice and harmony—otherwise, increasing social injustice could lead to an identity crisis or even to a legitimacy crisis (Nie and Hu 2008).

In today's China, efforts to mobilize ideological commitment are focused on political elites, particularly on Communist Party cadres who form the rank and file of the administrative staff at all levels of party, state, and military hierarchies. The ideological commitment of these elites can be used as a test of political loyalty vis-à-vis the regime and publicized as representing the consent of the whole populace based on doctrines of the Communist Party as "vanguard" of the masses.

However popular consent is framed, the multiple tasks official ideology has to shoulder create an ongoing need for ideological adaption and reform in order to sustain an "ideological hegemony" (Sun 1995, 16), which contributes to political and social stability. At the same time, it causes a particular vulnerability of socialist systems. Compared to other authoritarian regime types, they are much more easily thrown out of balance once reforms extend beyond the communist grand tradition and the ruling ideology is unravelled (Gore 2003). The debate among Chinese party theorists and scholars confirms the precarious role of ideological reform as the "Achilles Heel" of regime legitimacy that, in turn, allows us to understand the continuous and enormous investments made by the CCP leadership to constantly adapt its ideology to a changing domestic and international environment (Holbig 2009).

Culture and Its Competing Reinventions

According to U.S. scholar Sun Yan, ideology in China has important nationalist and culturalist underpinnings: "the Chinese concern for ideological and conceptual adaptation," she argues, "is related to the national search for identity and resurrection that has faced the nation since its confrontation with the West in the last century. Not incidentally, the reconceptualization of socialism is frequently linked with the question of 'cultural reconstruction'—the reconstruction of Chinese cultural values—in academic and political discussions" (Sun 1995, 18).

Culturalism can be identified as an alternative strategy to legitimize party rule in China that has gained increasing currency over the past decade. While the reference here is not the claim for national sovereignty but the claim to represent the legacy of cultural tradition(s) of society and, with it, its cultural identity, nationalism and culturalism bear a strong structural similarity in that they are subject to a complex interplay between bottom-up and top-down mechanisms of mobilization. Parallel to the party-state's strategic ambiguity toward nationalist aspirations, we find quite ambivalent attitudes of the CCP leadership toward the revival of numerous traditional elements of "Chinese culture" that could be observed in the reform period. The renaissance of Confucianism is a most illustrative case in point. John Makeham, who in his recent book analyzed its role in contemporary academic discourse, may be right that "the widely held view that the promotion of Confucianism in contemporary China is orchestrated by the Party-state and its functionaries is untenable" (2008, 7). Indeed, the renewed interest in Confucianism since the early 1980s seems to have originated inside various quarters of society without evident initiative (though with the silent toleration) by the central and local authorities. However, starting in 1986, we find the party-state reacting toward these bottom-up initiatives by attempting to regain at least discursive hegemony over what seems to have been perceived as an increasingly uncontrolled proliferation of "low" and "high culture" interpretations of Confucianism and to reframe them in ways compatible with the CCP's claims toward legitimate rule.

Within only a few years after the end of the Cultural Revolution's iconoclastic campaigns, numerous nonofficial manifestations of Confucianism have re-emerged in contemporary China. Confucian traditions have come to play an increasingly significant role in fields such as religion, spirituality, moral self-cultivation, philosophy, (pseudo-) science, and children's education. While most of these applications belong to a merely private realm, various local initiatives to organize classes and compile new textbooks based on Confucian classics to be used in children's preschool and primary school education border on competences that used to belong to official institutions in the decades since 1949 (Billioud 2007; Billioud and Thoraval 2007, 2008).

The most challenging interpretations of Confucianism, however, can be found in academic discourse. As early as 1984, liberal scholars based at the prestigious Beijing University founded a nongovernmental academic organization called the Chinese Culture College. During frequent open lectures and seminars during the second half of the 1980s, eminent mainland and overseas Chinese scholars were invited to exchange their views about Chinese and Western culture. Only a few of those liberal Confucianists propagated the introduction of Western-style democracy, and their aim in studying Confucianism has been "to initiate a peaceful political transition in order to promote political transparency within China" (Ai 2008; see also Dirlik 1995).

It was at this juncture that the party-state leadership felt the need to react and to recapture lost grounds in academic discourse. In March 1986 the State Education Commission organized a meeting that called for a revival of Confucianism in contemporary China, at least of those elements of "New Confucianism" that were compatible with the project of modernization. Starting that year, and well into the 1990s, the Chinese government funded various academic projects on New Confucianism that produced dozens of books and several hundred academic papers (Ai 2008). In this official interpretation of Confucianism, the aim is to enrich Marxism by drawing on the essence of traditional doctrines. In Fang's words, Confucianism should be studied and modified "under the stances, principles, and methodologies of Marxism, Leninism, and Mao

Zedong Thought" (1991). Traditional elements of Confucianism most appealing to this tailor-made socialist version are the love of social order and stability, acceptance of hierarchy, devotion to the family and the state, and so on. These elements—which apparently are most qualified to support the legitimation of authoritarian rule—resonate with traditional cultural values that are still rooted very deeply in the political cultures and societies of mainland China as well as on Taiwan (Shi 2001).

The battle of discursive hegemony had not been won, however. Starting in 1989, and with increasing vigor over the 1990s and 2000s, a third interpretation of Confucianism was established, spearheaded by prominent scholars such as Jiang Qing and Kang Xiaoguang. These self-proclaimed "Confucians," claiming to represent the true essence of traditional Confucianism (*rujia*), seek to rediscover the Confucian values of benevolence, righteousness, propriety, wisdom, sincerity, harmony, loyalty, and filial piety, as a programmatic alternative to Marxist ideology, which they regard not only as alien to China, but as standing in the way of realizing the great nation's historical mission. They demanded a "political or ideological Confucianism" to replace Marxism as orthodox ideology representing Chinese culture, and more recently even suggested the party might "Confucianize the CCP" and to "peacefully transform the CCP through Confucianism." Chinese people had the right to be ruled properly by a ruling class elected by "Confucians with virtue" in a "Confucian authoritarian regime" (Jiang 1989; Kang 2005, 2007; Fang and Luo 2007; cf. Ai 2008). As this vocabulary reveals, the legitimacy of authoritarian rule by the CCP came under direct assault from another authoritarian utopia formulated by restorative Confucians.

Faced with the ongoing challenge of competing interpretations of Confucianism, it seems the new party leadership under Hu Jintao decided to draw back from this academic battle and to "neutralize" this contested element of tradition by reconfiguring it within the larger context of "traditional Chinese culture." Although official slogans such as the goal to create a "well-off society" or "social harmony" bear some vague connotations of Confucian notions, these notions are reduced to sterile clichés representing an amorphous imaginaire of historical achievements and future greatness that is referred to as Chinese culture. The Opening Ceremony of the 2008 Olympic Games presented an ideal-type manifestation of this reconstructed ensemble of Chinese cultural identity. While the Communist revolution and the subsequent eras of party rule were not covered in the show, the honor of hosting the sports mega-event and sponsoring this firework of symbols clearly bolstered the party-state's claim to represent the cultural identity of the Chinese nation.

Walking the Tightrope of Democracy and Governance

In our analysis of party debate between 2003 and 2007, we found that one cluster of 7 prescriptive variables that we labelled "institutions" could account for 21% of the variations across the 26 prescriptive variables (Gilley and Holbig 2009). Chinese Party analysts and scholars take the institutionalization of the regime seriously as a strategy of legitimation. Four of the factors—bureaucratic efficiency, the empowerment of people's congresses, the rule of law, and inner party democracy—fall within the normal understanding of institutionalization. These reflect the normal concepts of "rational-legal" legitimation as understood by Weber or Huntington. Institutionalization here means the development of more autonomous, specialized, capacity-rich, and noncorrupt institutions for the formulation and implementation of public policy.

But three other factors included in the institutionalist cluster—the incorporation of new social groups, consultative democracy, and electoral democracy—in fact concern popular input. The concept of "democracy" has been appropriated by the party as a strategy of institutionalization— and the propaganda strategy of using the term "Western-style democracy" to distinguish it from normal democracy is aimed at paving the way for this strategy to succeed (Xia, D. 2008). In addition to the well-known and widely established semicompetitive elections at the village level, Zhu Lingjun describes a variety of direct election experiments of people's congresses, leadership committees, and leaders of both government and party at the township and county (or district and city) levels as well those that are expected to uphold legitimacy. In addition to this, the party is experimenting with consultative and deliberative forums where civic leaders, social groups, and commoners are invited to help formulate public policies (Zhu 2006, Ch. 8).

All this is believed by the party to be a key source of legitimacy because it is a way to ensure that the CCP responds to growing social complexity and value shifts. Of course, democracy is not alien to the CCP's traditional claim for legitimacy; on the contrary, the claim for popular sovereignty has always been one of the two pillars of the CCP's justification of its authority, the other pillar being the scientific doctrine of Leninism. Debating democracy in China always means walking the tightrope between socialist and other, competing (liberal, social-democrat, Confucian, deliberative, etc.) claims toward the correct interpretation of the principle of popular sovereignty (Markus 1982; Holbig 2009). The contested nature of direct township elections in China—where bottom-up democratic urges compete with top-down Leninist ones—nicely reflects the tensions inherent in the CCP's embrace of the word "democracy."

Objectively, institutionalization has been increasingly seen by scholars as a source of legitimacy for the CCP (Yang 2004; Nathan 2003). Indeed, China tends to be relatively well-governed for a country of its income level, according to World Bank Institute governance indicators data. In linking democracy to the substantive outcome of popularly perceived good governance, rather than to procedural guarantees, Beijing has reclaimed democracy for its own. As Shi Tianjian notes, "the regime has been able to define democracy in its own terms, drawing on ideas of good government with deep roots in the nation's historical culture and more recent roots in its ideology of socialism" (Shi 2009).

Problems arise, then, when the state suffers a governance-based performance failure. Though its response to the 2008 Sichuan earthquake was generally applauded in China, the death of up to 10,000 school children in the disaster as a result of the collapse of schools and school dormitories has created a genuine social movement, and makings of a minor legitimacy crisis. Corruption is another good example. A scathing report on corruption in China issued by the Organisation for Economic Co-operation and Development (OECD) in 2005 warned that the party's legitimacy was threatened, in particular by widespread absconding with funds whose levels amounted to several percentage points of GDP per year. The report has subsequently disappeared from the OECD's list of publications. In a Hunan Organization Department survey of 200 cadres in 2001, corruption was cited as second only to underdevelopment as a source of legitimation problems (Zhu 2006, 312). This is a reminder that subjective perceptions of corruption matter most of all. Corruption has its own indirect corrosive influences on legitimacy by undermining capacity and effectiveness. But its direct impact on legitimacy occurs only if it becomes known and disliked (Beetham 1991).

As for elections, there is considerable debate concerning the legitimating effects of electoral participation in China. China's scholars and party school researchers express a lot of interest in the potential of "orderly" political participation as an untapped source of legitimacy (Xia, J. 2008). Some outside scholars such as Birney and Kennedy argue that village elections have indeed legitimated the local state in China, but only where the elimination of township interference in the procedures has given them a genuine procedural validity (Kennedy

2009). In other words, where "democracy" actually legitimates, it is not the "orderly" democracy managed by top-down Leninist institutions that seeks to govern according to popular wishes but the "disorderly" bottom-up democracy in which procedural matters are key.

The CCP hopes to depend on institutionalization in the future even as incomes and expectations rise—Singapore is the oft-cited model, but "bureaucratic-authoritarian" Latin America is perhaps a better analogy. Those models show that more efficient, professional, transparent, and consultative institutions can satisfy demands for voice and participation alongside effective governance for a considerable time, consistent with neomodernization theory. Indeed, China's value trajectory in the Inglehart/Welzel studies shows an unusually high emphasis on rational-legal rule and an unusually low emphasis on individual empowerment for a country of its income level (Inglehart and Welzel 2005).

Finally, it is worth mentioning explicit "liberal" strategies of legitimation. These are rare. Notions of human rights, civil society, the separation of party and government functions, and multiparty democracy remain marginal or even inimical to the CCP's overall plans. The party wrote human rights into the state constitution in 2004 and in 2009 issued a National Human Rights Action Plan. But the protection of human rights remains largely rhetorical. Perhaps more importantly, the party has never quite succeeded in wholly eliminating the liberal view from Chinese politics—a view born in the reform era in the 1979 Democracy Wall and 1989 Tiananmen movements, and recently relaunched as a movement of 300-plus intellectuals, among them Nobel Peace Prize winner Liu Xiaobo, calling themselves the Charter 08 Movement in imitation of Czechoslovakia's Charter 77 group. The manifesto demanded democratic constitutional change and declared "political legitimacy must come from the people."

Mass values may be a long way from liberal norms, but the critical views of social activists and liberal intellectuals offer a constant challenge to the party's illiberal strategy. Yet the salience of these emergent liberals remains low. As the sympathetic sister of one of the leaders of the China Democracy Party noted after it was easily crushed in 1998–1999,: "they failed to take the measure of the national mood" (Zha 2007, 54).

Conclusion

Compared to most regimes in the Asian region, macro-indicators of legitimacy in China suggest relatively strong overall legitimacy even if alternative measurement approaches—based on either alternative causal functional forms or on behavioral data—offer reasons for thinking legitimacy is more fragile. Potential challenges of regime legitimacy at the disaggregate level are abounding, as flocks of petitioners remonstrating against corruption, environmental and labor scandals, mass protests against CCP rule in Tibet in 2008 and in Xinjiang in 2009, and the silenced signatories of the *Charter 08* remind us. On the other hand, there is much evidence of an unusually agile, responsive, and creative party effort to maintain its legitimacy through economic performance, nationalism, ideology, culture, governance, and democracy as defined in terms of popular sovereignty under the leadership of the party. While ideology, culture, and governance seem to be relatively durable, other sources of legitimacy are vulnerable in varying ways. Economic performance could fail, nationalist indignations could erupt, or official openings toward incremental steps of democratization could come under pressure from inside the party. During the summer and fall of 2010, Hu Jintao and Prime Minister Wen Jiabao made vague but repeated promises of political liberalization, obviously in an attempt to respond to longtime expectations of political reform before stepping down from power in 2012. Yet, the award of the Nobel Peace Prize in October to Liu Xiaobo was enough to stall this initiative of top-down democratization as it gave hardliners in the CCP a welcome excuse to clamp down on all liberal interpretations of democracy, foreign and domestic alike. The international dimension, which could be only touched upon in this chapter, adds to this complexity. External perceptions of the Chinese party regime oscillate between a self-righteous and systematic infringer of citizen's rights and a role model for developing countries.

Scholars thus approach the question of legitimacy in contemporary China with much trepidation. They want to avoid a teleology of inevitable democratization as well as an inevitable authoritarian durability. Though legitimation challenges and failures exist, the CCP has so far overcome them. The issue for analysts is to develop predictive models that can identify *ex ante* when this is no longer true. In pursuing that goal, we are taken into the dynamics of CCP survival and are forced constantly to ask questions about social change and state adaptation. Using the lens of legitimacy allows us to focus on all the important issues of contemporary Chinese politics.

References

Ai, Jiawen. 2008. "The Refunctioning of Confucianism: The Mainland Chinese Intellectual Response to Confucianism since the 1980s." *Issues and Studies* 44: 29–78.

Barmé, Geremie R. 1995. "To Screw Foreigners Is Patriotic: China's Avant-Garde Nationalists." *The China Journal* 34: 209–234.

Beetham, David. 1991. *The Legitimation of Power*. Houndsmills: Macmillan.

———. 2001. "Political Legitimacy." In *The Blackwell Companion to Political Sociology*, edited by Kate Nash and Alan Scott, 107–116. Malden, MA: Blackwell.

Billioud, Sebastien. 2007. "Confucianism, 'Cultural Tradition' and Official Discourses in China at the Start of the New Century." *China Perspectives* 3: 50–65.

Billioud, Sebastien, and Joel Thoraval. 2007. "Jiaohua: The Confucian Revival in China as an Educative Project." *China Perspectives* 4: 4–21.

———. 2008. "The Contemporary Revival of Confucianism: Anshen liming or the Religious Dimension of Confucianism." *China Perspectives* 3: 88–106.

Brown, Jeremy. 2007. "From Resisting Communists to Resisting America." In *Dilemmas of Victory: The Early Years of the People's Republic of China*, edited by J. Brown and P. Pickowicz, 105–129. Cambridge, MA: Harvard University Press.

Chen, Jie. 2004. *Popular Political Support in Urban China*. Washington, D.C.: Woodrow Wilson Center Press.

Deng, Xiaoping. 1989. "Speech to Cadres and Soldiers of the Beijing Martial Law Corps, Beijing." June 9. http://web.peopledaily.com.cn/deng/.

Dirlik, Arif. 1995. "Confucius in the Borderlands: Global Capitalism and the Reinvention of Confucianism." *Boundary 2* 2: 229–273.

Eastman, Lloyd E. 1984. *Seeds of Destruction: Nationalist China in War and Revolution, 1937–1949*. Stanford: Stanford University Press.

Fang, Keli. 1991. "Makesizhuyi yu Zhongguo chuantong wenhua de guanxi" [Marxism and Its Relations with the Chinese Traditional Culture]. In *Zhongguo Makesizhuyi zhexue qishi nian* [Seventy Years of Chinese Marxist Philosophy], edited by Dezhi Zhao and Wang Benhao, 62–63. Shenyang: Liaoning daxue chubanshe.

Fang, Guogen, and Luo Benqi. 2007. "Rujia sixiang, wenhua jiaoliu yu goujian hexie shehui" [Confucian Thinking, Cultural Exchange, and Constructing a Harmonious Society]. *Shehuikexue zhanxian* [Social Science Front] 2: 328–330.

Friedman, Edward. 2008. "Raising Sheep on Wolf Milk: The Politics and Dangers of Misremembering the Past in China." *Totalitarian Movements and Political Religions* 9: 389–409.

Gilley, Bruce. 2006. "The Meaning and Measure of State Legitimacy: Results for 72 Countries." *European Journal of Political Research* 45: 499–525.

Gilley, Bruce, and Heike Holbig. 2009. "The Debate on Party Legitimacy in China: A Mixed Quantitative/Qualitative Analysis." *Journal of Contemporary China* 18: 339–359.

Gore, Lance L. P. 2003. "Rethinking the Collapse of Communism: The Role of Ideology Then and Now." In *Damage Control. The Chinese Communist Party in the Jiang Zemin Era*, edited by Gungwu Wang and Zheng Yongnian, 27–63. Singapore: Eastern Universities Press.

Gries, Peter Hayes. 2004. *China's New Nationalism: Pride, Politics and Diplomacy*. Berkeley, CA: University of California Press.

Holbig, Heike. 2009. "Ideological Reform and Political Legitimacy in China: Challenges in the Post-Jiang Era." In *Regime Legitimacy in Contemporary China. Institutional Change and Stability*, edited by Schubert Gunter and Thomas Heberer, 13–34. London: Routledge.

Inglehart, Ronald, and Christian Welzel. 2005. *Modernization, Cultural Change, and Democracy: The Human Development Sequence*. Cambridge; New York: Cambridge University Press.

Jia, Qingguo. 2005. "Disrespect and Distrust: The External Origins of Contemporary Chinese Nationalism."*Journal of Contemporary China* 14: 11–21.

Jiang, Qing. 1989. "Zhongguo dalu fuxing Ruxue de xianshi yiyi jiqi mianlin de wenti" (The Practical Implications and Problems of Reviving Confucianism in Mainland China] (2 Parts). *Ehu* [Legein Society] 170: 29–38; 171: 22–37.

Kang, Xiaoguang. 2005. *Ren zheng* [Rule by Morality]. Singapore: Bafang Press.

———. 2007. "Ruan liliang jianshe yu Rujia wenhua fuxing" [The Construction of Soft Power and the Revival of Confucian Culture]. *Tianya* [Frontiers] 1: 32–38.

Kennedy, John James. 2009. "Legitimacy with Chinese Characteristics: 'Two Increases, One Reduction'." *Journal of Contemporary China* 18: 391–395.

Laliberté, André, and Marc Lanteigne, eds. 2008. *The Chinese Party-State in the 21st Century. Adaptation and the Reinvention of legitimacy*. London and New York: Routledge.

Lewis, John W., and Litai Xue. 2003. "Social Change and Political Reform in China: Meeting the Challenge of Success." *China Quarterly* 176: 926–942.

Li, Lianjiang. 2008. "Political Trust and Petitioning in the Chinese Countryside." *Comparative Politics* 40: 209–226.

Link, Perry. 2008. "A Short Anatomy of Chinese Nationalism Today, Testimony before the U.S.-China Economic and Security Review Commission: Access to Information and Media Control in the People's Republic of China." June 18, http://www.uscc.gov/hearings/2008hearings/transcripts/08_06_18trans/link.pdf.

Lu, Ailin. 2005. "Shehui zhuanxing qi Zhongguo Gongchandang zhizheng hefaxing ziyuan de weihu yu chonggao" [The Maintenance and Reconstruction of the Resources of CCP's Ruling Legitimacy during Social Transformation]. *Lilun yu Gaige* [Theory and Reform] 6: 56–60.

———. 2006. "Xin shiqi weihu yu peiyu dang de hefaxing ziyuan de lujing xuanze" [The Strategic Choice to Maintain and Cultivate the Legitimacy Resources of the CCP in the New Era]. *Qiushi* [Seeking Truth] 1: 18–21.

Makeham, John. 2008. *Lost Soul: 'Confucianism' in Contemporary Chinese Academic Discourse.* Cambridge, MA: Harvard University Press.

Markus, Maria. 1982. "Overt and Covert Modes of Legitimation in East European Societies." In *Political Legitimation in Communist States*, edited by T.H. Rigbyand Ferenc Fehér, 82–93. London & Basingstoke: Macmillan.

Nathan, Andrew. 2003. "Authoritarian Resilience." *Journal of Democracy* 14: 6–17.

Nie, Pingping and Hu Qizhu. 2008. "Zhizheng dang hefaxing the yishix-ingtai shiyu fenxi" [Analysis of the Ruling Party's Legitimacy from the Perspective of Ideology]. *Qiushi* [Seeking Truth] 2: 19–22.

OECD. 2005. *Governance in China. Paris: Organization for Economic Cooperation and Development.*

Pan, Philip P. 2008. *Out of Mao's Shadow: The Struggle for the Soul of a New China.* New York: Simon & Schuster.

Peterson, Glen. 2008. "To Be or Not to Be a Refugee: The International Politics of the Hong Kong Refugee Crisis, 1949–55." *Journal of Imperial & Commonwealth History* 36: 171–195.

Renmin Ribao [People's Daily]. 2003. "Zai 'san ge daibiao' zhongyao sixi-ang lilun yantaohui shang de jianghua" [Speech Delivered at the Theory Symposium on the Important Thought of "Three Represents"]. July 2, 1–2.

———. 2004. "Chongfen renshi kexue fazhanguan de zhidao yiyi—Lun shuli he luoshi kexue fazhanguan" [Fully Acknowledging the Guiding Significance of the Scientific Outlook on Development—On the Establishment and Implementation of the Scientific Outlook on Development]. March 22, 1–2.

———. 2005a. "Zhonggong zhongyang guanyu zai quandang kaizhan yi shijian 'san ge daibiao' zhongyao sixiang wei zhuyao neirong de baochi gongchandangyuan xianjinxing jiaoyu huodong de yijian" [Opinions of the CCP Central Committee on Launching the Party-Wide Education Campaign to Preserve the Progressiveness of Communist Party Members by Implementing the Important Thought of the 'Three Represents' as Its Core Content]. January 10, 1–2.

———. 2005c. "Hu Jintao zai shengbuji zhuyao lingdao ganbu tigao gou-jian shehuizhuyi hexie shehui nengli zhuanti yantaoban de jianghua" [Hu Jintao's Speech at the Special Study Course for Leading Cadres at the Ministerial and Provincial Level on Raising the Capacity to Build a Harmonious Socialist Society]. June 27, 1–2.

Roskin, Michael. 2009. *Countries and Concepts: Politics, Geography, Culture.* New York: Pearson/Longman.

Schubert, Gunter. 2008. "One-Party Rule and the Question of Legitimacy in Contemporary China: Preliminary Thoughts on Setting Up a New Research Agenda." *Journal of Contemporary China* 17: 191–204.

Shambaugh, David L. 2008. *China's Communist Party: Atrophy and Adaptation.* Berkeley: University of California Press.

Shi, Tianjian. 2001. "Cultural Values and Political Trust: A Comparison of the People's Republic of China and Taiwan." *Comparative Politics* 33: 401–419.

———. 2008. "China: Democratic Values Supporting an Authoritarian System." In *How East Asians View Democracy*, edited by Yun-han Chu, Larry Diamond, Andrew J. Nathan, and Doh Chull Shin, 209-237. New York: Columbia University Press.

Song, Qiang. 2009. "Interview." *Beijing Review* 52: 23.

Song, Xiaojun, Xiaodong Wang, Jisu Huang, Qiang Song, and Yang Liu. 2009. *Zhongguo bu gaoxing. Da shidai, da mubiao ji women de neiyou waihuan* [Unhappy China. The Great Time, Grand Vision and Our Challenges]. Beijing: Kong Hong Book.

Sun, Xiaowei, and Yan Sun. 2003. "Yishixingtai: Zhongguo Gongchandang zhengzhi quanwei hefaxing rentong de sixiang jichu" [Ideology: The Ideological Fundament of Identification with the Legitimacy of the CCP's Political Authority]. *Daizong Xuekan* [Journal of Daizong] 7: 5–6.

Sun, Yan. 1995. *The Chinese Reassessment of Socialism, 1976–1992*. Princeton: Princeton University Press.

Unger, Jonathan. 1996. *Chinese Nationalism*. New York:East Gate.

Wan, Jun. 2003. "Xin shiji Zhongguo Gongchandang chuantong hefaxing ziyuan mianlin de tiaozhan" [Challenges for the Traditional Resources of Legitimacy of the CCP in the New Century]. *Kexue Shehuizhuyi* [Scientific Socialism] 3: 30–33.

Wang, Gungwu. 2008. *China and the New International Order*. New York: Routledge.

Wang, Zhengxu. 2005. "Political Trust in China: Forms and Causes." In *Legitimacy: Ambiguities of Political Success of Failure in East and Southeast Asia*, edited by L. White, 113–139. Singapore: World Scientific.

Xia, Defeng. 2008. "Zhongguo gongchandang zhizheng hefaxingde lujing fenxi" [An Analysis of the Routes to Governing Legitimacy for the CCP]. *Shiji Qiao* [Century Bridge] 6: 6–9.

Xia, Jinmei. 2008. "Gongming youxu zhengzhi canyu dui dang zhizheng hefaxingde yingxiang" [The Effects of Orderly Political Participation on the Party's Governing Legitimacy]. *Journal of Zhengzhou Institute of Aeronautical Industry Management* [Social Sciences Edition] 27: 203–205.

Xin, Yan. 2005. "Tichu 'zhengzhi hefaxing' de wenti jiujing juyou hezhong zhengzhi hanyi?" [What Are the Political Implications in Raising the Question about 'Political Legitimacy'?]. *Dangshi wenhui* [Abstracts of CCP History Studies] 10: 52–53.

Yang, Dali L. 2004. *Remaking the Chinese Leviathan: Market Transition and the Politics of Governance in China*. Stanford: Stanford University Press.

Zha, Jianying. 2007. "Enemy of the State." *The New Yorker*, April 23.

Zhang, Xuejuan. 2009. "Chongtu dui zhengzhi hefaxingde yingxiang zuoyong shenxi" [The Effects and Role of Conflicts on Political Legitimacy]. *Shandong xingzheng xueyuan shandong sheng jingji guanli ganbu xueyuan xuebao* [Journal of the Shandong Administration Institute and the Shandong Economic Management Cadres Institute] 1: 19–23.

Zhao Suisheng. 2004. *A Nation-State by Construction. Dynamics of Modern Chinese Nationalism.* Stanford: Stanford University Press.

Zhou, Shangwen. 2006. *Hefaxing shiye xia de Sulian zhengzhi* [Soviet Politics from the Perspective of Legitimacy]. Shanghai: Shanghai People's Press.

Zhou, Xincheng. 2008. "Yixie ren guchui de 'pushi jiazhi' shizhi shang jiu shi Xifang de jiazhi" [The 'Universal Values' Advocated by Some People Are Actually Western Values]. *Guangming Ribao*, September 16, http://theory.people.com.cn/GB/49150/49152/8041823.html.

Zhu, Lingjun. 2006. *Yi zhi yu chong tu: zheng dang yu qun zhong guan xi de zai si kao* [*Consensus and Conflict: Thought on Relations between the People and the Ruling Party*]. Beijing, China: People's Press.

CHAPTER 3

Political Legitimacy in Vietnam under Challenge

Carlyle A. Thayer

This chapter examines the challenges to the legitimacy of Vietnam's one-party state and the state's responses to these challenges in the period from 1986 to the present. The chapter is divided into four sections. The first section provides a brief overview of the evolution of the Vietnamese state and the historical basis of regime legitimacy from 1945 to 1976. The second section considers the evolving challenges to the political legitimacy of one-party rule mounted by southern war veterans, communist intelligentsia, nonparty elites, peasants, retired senior generals, and prodemocracy activists with a particular focus on the period after the collapse of socialism in Eastern Europe and the Soviet Union in 1989–1991. Critics challenged the basis of the regime's legitimacy on four fronts: ideology, economic performance, legal-rational, and nationalism. The third section examines the regime's responses to each of these challenges. Finally, the chapter concludes by noting that Vietnam's one-party state rests on multiple sources of legitimacy and party elites have accommodated and adjusted their policies in response to criticisms from their critics.

Vietnam's One-Party State

The Socialist Republic of Vietnam (SRV) was formally established in 1976 following military and political reunification of North and South Vietnam. The genesis of the SRV dates back to September 1945 when a communist-led movement known popularly as the Viet Minh seized power and declared Vietnam's independence under the name Democratic Republic of Vietnam (DRV). National elections were held in January 1946 to provide legitimacy for Southeast Asia's first communist state.

In late 1946, the DRV was driven from power by French military forces and the DRV was forced to reconstitute itself as a resistance government. After an eight-year war, Vietnam was partitioned and the DRV was reconstituted in North Vietnam. Thus, from its very foundation, the political legitimacy of Vietnam's one-party state has rested on the vanguard role of the Vietnam Communist Party in mobilizing national resistance against foreign domination on the basis of appeals to patriotism and nationalism.

In the period from 1954 to 1965, the Vietnam Communist Party (VCP)[1] imposed authoritarian rule through a political system modeled on the Soviet Union and the People's Republic of China. The Vietnamese economy was transformed along socialist lines through land redistribution, collectivization of agriculture, nationalization of industry, and the institution of central economic planning. Vietnam adopted its first Three-Year Plan in 1958 and its first Five-Year Plan in 1960 both of which gave priority to the development of heavy industry. During this period the basis of regime legitimacy was expanded to include Marxist-Leninist ideology and legal-rational authority

Over the next decade, 1965–1975, the struggle to reunify Vietnam by armed force took center stage and quickly escalated. Northern youth were conscripted for military service in the south while North Vietnam became subject to an Air War (1965–1968 and 1972). Communist North Vietnam's army prevailed and Vietnam was unified on April 30, 1975. During the decade-long Vietnam War, the political legitimacy of the DRV regime was based once again on patriotism and nationalism in resisting foreign aggression. A new basis of legitimacy was added—the charismatic leadership of Ho Chi Minh, particularly after his death in 1969.

The formal reunification of North and South Vietnam in 1976 resulted in the imposition of the DRV's political system on the entire country. Four formal structures make up this political system: the Vietnam Communist Party, the people's armed forces, the state bureaucracy (central and local government), and the Vietnam Fatherland Front (an umbrella group for mass organizations). There is a high degree of overlap if not fusion between the VCP, the state apparatus, armed forces, and mass organisations. Most senior party members are dual-role elites who simultaneously hold leadership positions in one of the other three structures of power. The VCP provides the leadership nucleus through party committees in all official political, economic, military, and social organizations comprising the Vietnamese state. This type of political system has been characterized as "mono-organizational socialism" (Thayer 1992b, 110–112).

Throughout the period from 1954 to 1986, the Vietnam Communist Party based its claim to political legitimacy primarily on its success in defeating foreign aggressors (France, Japan, the United States, the Khmer Rouge, and China). This involved appeals to Vietnamese patriotism and nationalism and the charismatic leadership of Ho Chi Minh. At the same time, the VCP also based its legitimacy on socialist ideology that provided the justification for Vietnam's development model of transforming an economically and culturally backward country into a modern one. After 1986, when Vietnam embarked on a major reform program known as *doi moi* (renovation), performance legitimacy became the main basis of regime legitimacy. As Marxism-Leninism lost its salience, Vietnam's leadership increasingly began to stress the importance of "Ho Chi Minh thought" as the ideological basis of regime legitimacy.

Challenges to Political Legitimacy

This section analyzes chronologically seven major challenges to the political legitimacy of Vietnam's one-party state. During the period from 1986 until the present, the basis of regime legitimacy increasingly shifted to performance legitimacy, that is, the successful management of economic development and growth, and the maintenance of political stability against the threat of peaceful evolution. Party critics challenged the basis of regime legitimacy on three fronts. They argued that Marxism-Leninist ideology was outmoded, legal-rational authority had been undermined by authoritarian rule, and national unity had been undermined.

Veterans of the Southern Resistance

In May 1986, in the face of mounting socioeconomic difficulties, members of the communist movement in southern Vietnam came together and formed a Club of Former Resistance Fighters. The club was initially a mutual aid association dedicated to improving the lives of veterans. Its leadership comprised several notable high-ranking southern party and military figures (Thayer 1992a, 14–15).

After the Sixth National Party Congress in late 1986, the activities of the southern veterans quickly moved from self-help and group discussion to the overtly political. In 1988, the veterans held a series of meetings that attracted ever-larger audiences. Speeches by club members were tape recorded and circulated as cassettes. They also published a veterans' magazine and newspaper, *Truyen Thong Khang Chien* (Tradition of Resistance) whose circulation soon extended from Saigon to Hanoi. Articles in the newspaper blamed current socioeconomic ills on the hasty reunification of the country. Southern veterans condemned corruption, incompetence, and party secrecy and called for openness, intraparty democracy, personnel changes, and the serious implementation of *doi moi*.

In 1988, following the death of premier Pham Hung, a southern party veteran, the Club of Former Resistance Fighters mounted their first direct challenge to the party leadership. In April, the Club circulated a petition that questioned the Politburo's prerogative to appoint a replacement without wider consultations. The Club's petition called for the selection of a new premier by a free and fair secret ballot. In June, the Club sent the petition, accompanied by over one hundred signatures, to the party Central Committee and National Assembly for their consideration.

The actions by southern party and military veterans, especially their attempts to link up with counterparts in the north, took place outside of VCP guidance or control. The Club appealed to a large group of party and army veterans whose basic material needs were not being met by the state. Members of the Club, therefore, demanded that it be officially recognized as a legal association thus putting it on a par with regime-approved mass organizations. In other words, the Club was directly challenging the party's system of mono-organizational socialism.

The VCP reacted to these developments by arresting and detaining prominent Club leaders; others were marginalized. The VCP replaced the Club with an alternative organization, the Vietnam War Veterans Association, and co-opted individual members of the Club into its leadership. The new War Veterans Association, while specifically established to address the needs of the large veterans constituency, was also molded along the lines of other regime mass organizations with a party committee embedded in its leadership structure. It was duly enrolled as the newest member of the Vietnam Fatherland Front. The Club was not heard of again but several of its leaders, such as Do Trung Hieu, continued dissenting from the party line.

Vietnam's Communist Intelligentsia and the Collapse of Socialism

Since reunification in 1975, Vietnam's political process has become institutionalized and regularized through the holding of national party congresses at five-yearly intervals (Thayer 1988). National party congresses have the authority to rewrite the party's platform and statutes, adopt long-term socioeconomic policies, and elect a new leadership. Therefore, the lead up to a party congress invariably provoked intense internal party debate among its cliques and factions under the principle of democratic centralism.

Such was the case in 1991, prior to the Seventh National Party Congress, when internal party discussion took place under the shadow of China's suppression of its prodemocracy movement, the collapse of socialism in Eastern Europe, and the disintegration of the Soviet Union. These momentous events provoked one of the most serious challenges to the authority and political legitimacy of the VCP by senior members from within the party who questioned the continued salience of ideology and criticized the party's closed undemocratic decision-making process. Five party members played a particularly prominent role: Tran Xuan Bach, member of the party's Politburo; Lu Phuong, the former deputy minister of culture in the southern Provisional Revolutionary Government (1969–1976); Bui Tin, editor of the Sunday edition of the party's newspaper and a retired army Colonel; Dr. Nguyen Khac Vien, former director of the Foreign Languages Publishing House, Vietnam's external propaganda arm; and Hoang Minh Chinh, a prominent victim of the 1967 "antiparty affair."[2]

During the final months of 1989, Tran Xuan Bach, a member of the party's elite inner circle, emerged as a staunch supporter of political liberalization at a time when the official VCP line was to promote economic reform and political stability. Bach became increasingly outspoken as he addressed audiences at the Economics Club and the Union of Vietnam Scientific and Technological Associations. He argued that Vietnam's rigid central planning process and system of state socialism were being undermined by the development of a commodity economy and "social democratization" and, therefore, required that the reform process be stepped up rather than curtailed.

In January 1990, Bach participated in an exchange of views on party building and leadership sponsored by the standing committee of the Hanoi party organization. This meeting considered the relationship between social democracy and proletarian dictatorship, and economic renovation and the political system. Bach forcibly argued that economic and political reforms must be carried out simultaneously. Increasingly Bach found his views out of step with those of his Politburo colleagues who, drawing lessons from Eastern Europe and the Soviet Union, argued that political liberalization would be destabilizing. They gave priority to economic reforms. Bach refused to alter the tenor or content of his views.

In March 1990, Bach's actions precipitated a showdown with his Politburo colleagues at the eighth plenum of the party Central Committee. This meeting was one of the longest and stormiest plenary sessions in the party's history. Each member of the Politburo and Secretariat was required to conduct a self-criticism of their activities over the past three years. During his self-criticism Bach admitted he had violated party regulations but refused to apologize. As a result he was summarily dismissed from the Politburo. An official communiqué declared that Bach was expelled for "grave violations of party organizational and disciplinary principles, which have caused many bad consequences" (*Hanoi Domestic Service*, March 28, 1990).

Coincidentally, in March 1990, Lu Phuong (1990) authored an essay that argued Marxism-Leninism was never intended as an ideological guide for all time and was introduced into Vietnam by Ho Chi Minh as a tool to fight against France and the United States. According to Phuong, the dogmatic application of Marxist-Leninist ideology had resulted in economic stagnation and political and cultural degeneration. In his view the party should turn over its power to the people and government and become just another legal mass organization. The sting was in the tail of his essay where Phuong asked rhetorically whether the changes he advocated would come about peacefully or through the collapse of the party as in Eastern Europe (quoted in Hiebert 1993, 26). In 1994, Lu Phuong was refused permission to travel overseas and the following year he was expelled from the party because he publicly expressed his dissenting views in an interview with Radio France Internationale (*Reuter*, December 9, 1995). His writings were also banned.

Bui Tin, a retired army veteran and leading journalist, became politically energized in 1986 as the momentum for reform built up within the party. He became frustrated when his written proposals for change failed to gain traction. In November 1990, during a trip to Paris, Bui Tin took the dramatic step of presenting a "Citizen's Petition" to the Vietnamese ambassador to France (Bui Tin 1990). This document was immediately leaked to the BBC and Radio France Internationale. Bui Tin then aired his views in public in an extended series of interviews with the BBC's Vietnamese language service.

Bui Tin's petition was written in response to the internal solicitation of party members' views on draft policy documents prepared for the forthcoming seventh party congress. Bui Tin was extremely critical of the party leadership and its pursuit of an outmoded model of socialism that had undermined national unity and led to a loss of popular support. Bui Tin called for the establishment of "a democratic regime, genuinely popular with a socialist option" (1990, 14). In order to achieve this he suggested that the Vietnam Communist Party and the Socialist Republic of Vietnam be renamed, respectively, the Vietnam Workers' Party and Democratic Republic of Vietnam. Bui Tin also called for the revitalization of the Vietnam Fatherland Front and its mass organizations, and a substantial reduction in the size of the army and security forces. He concluded his petition by calling for democratic elections to establish a Government of National Reconstruction that would unite all the Vietnamese people at home and overseas.

Bui Tin's "Citizen's Petition" represented a serious challenge to the party leadership's political legitimacy because of his status as a war veteran and high-profile commentator in the Vietnamese press. But in airing his views in the foreign media and seeking exile abroad Bui Tin had crossed a red line. He was expelled from the party, and his wartime contributions denigrated in the press. As late as 2009 Bui Tin was still referred to as a reactionary in the Vietnamese state-controlled media.

The fourth prominent member of the communist intelligentsia to challenge the VCP's political legitimacy was Dr. Nguyen Khac Vien. In January 1991, he addressed a letter to the chairman of the Vietnam Fatherland Front in which he argued that the party's leadership was old, frail, and outmoded in thinking, and the party's monopoly of power from central to local level had undermined the authority and efficacy of elected state organs (Nguyen Khac Vien 1991). He called on the party leadership to step aside so a younger generation could take over. In conclusion, Vien urged the seventh party congress to take concrete steps to restore "real democracy" to Vietnam by dismantling its bloated apparatus and turning over staff, property, and executive power "to the organs elected by the people and to the state" (6).

Dr. Vien's petition struck a raw nerve because it came at the precise moment when the VCP Central Committee was deliberating on policy and leadership changes to be considered by the seventh congress. Since Dr. Vien had used authorized channels and was retired from government service he was not subject to any punitive action. He passed away in 1997.

The fifth major communist intellectual to challenge the ideological basis of the party's political legitimacy was Hoang Minh Chinh. In January 1991, he circulated a "Commentary on the Draft Platform" in which he argued that the party had pursued a policy of "infantile dogmatic leftist deviation" from its formation in 1930 to the present

(Hoang Minh Chinh 1991). Because of this, Chinh argued, the party had undermined Ho Chi Minh's successful strategy of uniting all Vietnamese, regardless of race, religion, or political belief, into one great national unity bloc. Further, he argued that the party's monopoly of power was the source of its degeneration. By way of solution, Chinh advocated a democratic political system with checks and balances and the abandonment of socialism in favor of a market economy.

There was a great deal of common ground among these five Communist Party intellectuals, indicating that their views were widely shared among party reformers. In the months leading up to the seventh congress the dissenters' views were vilified in the media by party conservatives.

Challenges to Ideological Orthodoxy

In 1993 it was announced that the VCP would convene its first ever mid-term national conference (i.e., to be held in the interim between two party congresses) to consider major policy documents including the interim Political Report by the party's secretary-general. The circulation of the draft Political Report once again prompted critical responses by elite members of the communist intelligentsia. Establishment intellectuals charged that Marxism-Leninism was an outdated ideology, economic and political reforms did not go far enough, and the party tolerated corruption and abuse of power. They argued for greater freedom of expression. These critiques were photocopied and widely circulated.

In 1991, Dr. Phan Dinh Dieu, a prominent nonparty mathematician, startled the party establishment when, in an address to a seminar organized by the editor of the party's leading journal, he argued that Vietnam would have to study foreign doctrines in order for Vietnam to determine the best way to develop (Thayer 2006, 119). The party reacted to Dieu's criticism by launching an ideological counterattack. The April 1991 issue of the party's ideological journal, *Tap Chi Cong San*, for example, carried an article by the editorial board challenging his views. Other media commentators accused unnamed party critics of intellectual arrogance.

The following year, Dieu argued in an interview with a foreign academic that "Marxism-Leninism had little to offer a country trying to overcome poverty" and should be abandoned altogether (Tønnesson 1993). Party leaders were divided on how to respond. In August 1993, it was reported that Dieu had been dismissed from his post as vice chairman of the National Center for Scientific Research. Yet, a few months later, around the time of renewed press attacks on him, Dieu was invited by the party secretary-general to an informal meeting to discuss his views on reform efforts.

Phan Dinh Dieu was joined in his criticism by two other prominent intellectuals, Nguyen Xuan Tu, a professor of biology who wrote under the *nom de plume* Ha Si Phu ("Hero Professor of Hanoi"), and Nguyen Phong Ho Hieu. Professor Tu was widely known in intellectual circles for his written criticisms of communism that he circulated privately. In 1993, Tu wrote an extended essay in which he argued: "[Marxism-Leninism has been] unable to achieve national reconciliation and the construction of a democratic society and a market economy…It is necessary for us to give up a foreign theory which is not suitable for our country" (Nguyen Xuan Tu 1983). Professor Tu was arrested in December 1995 after giving a series of interviews critical of the government to overseas radio stations.

Nguyen Phong Ho Hieu was a southerner who quit the party in 1990. In August 1993 he was invited to address a meeting of the Youth and Students Club held under the auspices of the Ho Chi Minh City's Social Sciences Committee. In his presentation Hieu dismissed Marxism as irrelevant to the contemporary world and noted that it had contributed to the collapse of socialism in Europe. Vietnam, he argued, should drop the title "socialist republic" and declare the end of the socialist market economy. Once the American embargo had been lifted and Vietnam's economy exposed to the outside world, Vietnam would be "assimilated into the world's democratic trend," and the people would demand political freedom and the end to the party's monopoly of power, he asserted (quoted in Hiebert 1993, 26).

In late October 1993, responding to mounting criticism by prominent intellectuals, the party's Ideology and Culture Committee issued a warning to members that they would be punished if they were caught distributing or possessing materials that opposed socialism. Intellectuals who were sympathetic to the conservative line were approached and asked to prepare a rebuttal to the underground tracts that were in circulation. Press articles began to appear that attacked so-called internal enemies. In October and November, party dailies in Ho Chi Minh City, *Saigon Giai Phong*, and Hanoi, *Nhan Dan*, published a two-part series attacking an unnamed mathematician for his "ideological errors" (Hiebert 1993, 26). This was a clear reference to Phan Dinh Dieu.

Renewed Challenges to Ideological Orthodoxy

In January 1994, the VCP convened its first mid-term national conference in Hanoi. The conference identified "four dangers" facing

Vietnam: the danger of being left behind economically by regional countries, the danger of peaceful evolution against socialism, the danger of corruption, and the danger of the breakdown of social order and security (*Voice of Vietnam*, January 22, 1994). The promulgation of the "four dangers" signaled the rise in influence of ideological conservatives within the VCP. Immediately after the mid-term conference, for example, Tran Dinh Huynh, director of the Institute for Party Building, was dismissed for criticizing party policy at a seminar and Hoang Chi Bao, a staff member at the Institute for Marxism-Leninism and Ho Chi Minh Thought was removed for publishing two books that downplayed the achievements of international communism.

Nonetheless, the VCP was once again engulfed in a continuing intense internal debate over the role of ideology. This surfaced at the eighth plenum of the Central Committee in January 1995. At this meeting a group of disgruntled reformers moved a motion to jettison "dictatorship of the proletariat" and "democratic centralism" from the party lexicon. The motion lost narrowly after an acrimonious debate. Other contentious issues concerned the draft civil code, socioeconomic issues and human rights, and how the party would function in a "law governed state." After the plenum the Secretariat issued a confidential circular that branded party dissidents as "dangerous elements" because of their views. Five individuals were signaled out: Nguyen Trung Thanh, Hoang Minh Chinh, Do Trung Hieu, Le Hong Ha, and Tran Do (Thayer 2006).

In March 1995, Nguyen Trung Thanh, a cadre assigned to the Central Committee's Organization Commission, sent an open letter to high-level party officials asking them to reconsider the antiparty affair of 1967. Thanh argued that the trial had been based on questionable evidence and its findings should be reopened for review. Simultaneously, an unsigned letter written by persons close to the individuals and families of those arrested in the "antiparty affair" was sent to an activist group in Paris that promptly published it. The letter provided details of 47 victims. Nguyen Trung Thanh was dismissed from the party for violating discipline. Thanh was supported by Hoang Minh Chinh, who also raised the question of rehabilitating the victims of the 1967 antiparty affair.

Party dissidents sought to challenge the ideological legitimacy of one-party rule by questioning the party's infallibility by raising the antiparty affair. Critics argued that the so-called revisionists had been correct in their assessment of China, as borne out by China's subsequent alliance with the Khmer Rouge and its attack on Vietnam's northern border in 1979. In sum, party dissidents argued that if the party erred in 1967 it could not claim to be infallible in present circumstances. This assertion implicitly called into question the ideological basis of the political authority of the current leadership.

Angry party conservatives responded by calling for a renewed crackdown on those who raised the antiparty affair. In June 1995, police rearrested Hoang Minh Chinh.[3] Police also detained Do Trung Hieu, a former member of the Club of Former Resistance Fighters, who distributed leaflets in Ho Chi Minh City that criticized the failure of the party's policy on national reconciliation in the South in 1975. Both were charged under Article 205-a of the Criminal Code for "abusing democratic liberties and violating the interests of state and social organizations." In November 1995, Chinh and Hieu were sentenced, respectively, to 12 and 15 months in prison.

Mass Peasant Demonstrations in Thai Binh Province

In mid-1997 and extending well into 1998, a massive peasant protest erupted in Thai Binh province in northern Vietnam over grievances directed at local government officials. As senior party leaders sought to diffuse the situation, they were stung by criticism leveled by Tran Do, the most senior party member after Tran Xuan Bach to question the legitimacy of the party's ideology and monopoly of power (Thayer 2006, 124–129). Tran Do was a native of Thai Binh province with impeccable revolutionary credentials. Do was a retired army general and former head of the Central Committee's Ideology and Culture department.

In late 1997/early 1998, Tran Do wrote a 13-page open letter, "The State of the Nation and the Role of the Communist Party," to Vietnam's top party leaders, National Assembly, and the government (Tran Do 1997–1998). According to General Do the events in Thai Binh province were the first time that tens of thousands of peasants—the backbone of the revolution—confronted local officials over abuse of power and corruption. Do bluntly concluded that the origins of this massive protest arose from the contradiction between socialism and the market economy and were caused by "us" and not "enemies from abroad." "One must devour the other," he argued, and, therefore, the party should abandon its ideology.

Do's open letter also contained a trenchant critique of Vietnam's one-party system. He argued that the party's concentration of power had led to the emergence of a new ruling class of "new capitalists" who amassed private wealth and stood against the interests of the people. Marxism-Leninism had been applied to the entire society with disastrous results and it was now time to consider "other schools of thought." To overcome the failure of state socialism, Do agued for the mobilization of the "intellectual power of the people" to create a democratic system based on political freedom, human rights, and rule of law. The party leadership must relinquish its monopoly of power and permit the National Assembly and Vietnam Fatherland Front to exercise greater authority, he concluded. If Vietnam did not undertake these reforms, it faced "two cruel dangers," the collapse of the party-state due to its inability to overcome socioeconomic malaise, and the disintegration of the Vietnam Communist Party due to prolonged confusion and instability. Tran Do attached an appendix to his open letter that outlined draft regulations covering basic political rights (freedom of speech, press, and publication), an anticorruption monitoring agency, and a lengthy proposal to democratize the nomination procedures for election to the National Assembly.

General Do was eventually expelled from the party and this provoked an outcry. Hoang Huu Nhan, former Haiphong City party secretary, retired Lieutenant General Pham Hong Son, and Nguyen Van Dao, a senior cadre formerly attached to the Central Committee's Economics Commission, all lodged written protests, while Colonel Pham Que Duong, former editor-in-chief of the army's history journal, resigned from the party. In addition, 11 other retired party cadres also signed a letter of protest (Thayer 2006, 129).

Challenging the Regime's System of Surveillance

In 2004, two of Vietnam's most respected retired military generals raised the issue of interference in internal party affairs by General Department II (military intelligence). General Department II (GD II) first attracted attention in 2001 when its role in wire-tapping the telephones of senior party officials was exposed on the eve of the ninth national party congress. As a consequence, the incumbent party secretary-general, Le Kha Phieu, failed in his bid for reelection. The Chief of the General Staff and the head of the General Political Department both received reprimands (Thayer 2008, 304–305).

General Vo Nguyen Giap sent a private letter to the senior party leadership demanding an investigation into the "extra-legal" activities of GD II. He noted that the party Central Committee, Politburo, Secretariat, and Central Control Committee had all considered the matter without taking any corrective action. Giap charged that for many years GD II had tried to manipulate factionalism within the VCP to its advantage and had smeared the political reputations of many leading figures including himself (Vo Nguyen Giap 2004).

General Giap's allegations were supported by retired major general Nguyen Nam Khanh in a letter sent to the senior party leadership (Nguyen Nam Khanh 2004). He accused the GD II of "slandering, intimidation, torture, political assassination," and manipulation of internal party factionalism for its own partisan purposes. Khanh provided excerpts from the GD II's classified *News Bulletin* to back up his accusations. There has been no further public information to indicate what action, if any, has been taken on these complaints.

Societal Challenges to the VCP's Political Legitimacy

Since 2006 there has been a marked change in the nature of challenges to the political legitimacy of the VCP. In the past such challenges arose from the actions of individual party members and members of the intelligentsia acting in small cliques in virtual isolation from each other (Thayer 2006). But in recent years there has been a concerted effort by nonparty activists to form explicitly political associations dedicated to the promotion of democracy, human rights, religious freedom, and workers' rights and to confront the party on these matters (Thayer 2009b, 2010a).

An unprecedented number of so-called political organizations and parties were formed between 2004 and 2006. These groups are considered illegal by the state and, therefore, have no official standing in Vietnam's system of mono-organizational socialism. These "political organizations" represent only a handful of individuals and are little more than the personal cliques of the group's leader. In 2006, Vietnam's prodemocracy activists and political groups coalesced into an identifiable network, marking a new development in Vietnamese politics (Thayer 2009b). On April 6, 116 persons issued an Appeal for Freedom of Political Association that they distributed throughout Vietnam via the Internet. On April 8, 118 persons issued a Manifesto on Freedom and Democracy for Vietnam ("Tuyen Ngon Tu Do Dan Chu Cho Viet-Nam Nam," April 8, 2006).[4] These statements called upon the Vietnamese state to respect basic human rights and religious freedom and to permit citizens to freely associate and form their own political parties. These prodemocracy petitioners became known as Bloc 8406 after the date of their founding manifesto.

Bloc 8406 represents a diverse network of professionals primarily concentrated in urban centers throughout the country, particularly in Hue, Ho Chi Minh City, Hai Phong, Hanoi, Da Nang, and Can Tho. It produced a fortnightly, *Tu Do Ngon Luan* (Free Speech), in both hardcopy and electronic format. In 2006, Vietnam hosted the summit meeting of the Asia Pacific Economic Cooperation (APEC) forum. To avoid unwanted publicity affecting the international prestige this summit would bring to Vietnam, police and security officials were relatively circumspect in their harassment and repression of Bloc 8406. Nonetheless, police actions provoked a public protest by prodemocracy advocates. On April 30, Bloc 8406 issued a letter signed by 178 supporters condemning police actions. By the end of the year, foreign observers reported, the support base for Bloc 8406 had expanded to over 2,000, many under the age of 30 (Steinglass 2006).

In August 2006, Bloc 8406 publicly announced a four-phase proposal for democratization, including the restoration of civil liberties, establishment of political parties, drafting of a new constitution and democratic elections for a representative National Assembly (Mudie 2006). Two months later, members of Bloc 8406 issued an open letter to the leaders of the APEC leadership summit, asking for their help in promoting democracy in Vietnam. Shortly after, Bloc 8406 attempted to enlarge its base by forming a coalition with the banned Unified Buddhist Church of Vietnam and the Vietnam Alliance for Democracy and Human Rights.

After the APEC Summit security forces initiated a two-year campaign of rounding up key leaders and summarily convicting them in court. Seven Bloc 8406 members, including high-profile lawyers Nguyen Van Dai, Le Thi Cong Nhan, and Catholic priest Father Nguyen Van Ly were arrested, tried, and convicted in 2007. By 2008 it appeared that Bloc 8406's leadership had been effectively decapitated and Vietnam's network democracy had been snuffed out. Nonetheless, small networks of activists continued to press for political, civil, and religious rights through the Internet and contact overseas Vietnamese prodemocracy political parties. In May–July 2009, a further seven prodemocracy political activists, including lawyer Le Cong Dinh, were arrested, tried, and imprisoned. Dinh was later charged with attempting to overthrow the socialist state (Thayer 2010b).

In 2009–2010, Vietnamese security authorities turned their attention to the emerging amorphous network of individual bloggers who independently posted social and political commentary on the Web (Thayer 2009a). These blog sites discussed a number of issues including corruption, environmental concerns, economic issues (especially, inflation), and land disputes between the Catholic Church and the State. No issue was more sensitive than Vietnam's relations with China. Bloggers tapped into a vein of growing anti-Chinese nationalist sentiment by raising Chinese involvement in bauxite mining in the Central Highlands and Chinese assertiveness in the East Sea (South China Sea). By the end of 2010 police had arrested an estimated 40 political activists including a number of prominent bloggers.

The events of 2006–2010 demonstrate that political dissent in Vietnam has taken on a greater organizational form with the appearance of nascent "political parties" and trade unions as well as special interest groups representing independent journalists, human rights advocates, and former political prisoners (Thayer 2009b). The stillborn alliance between Bloc 8406 and the Unified Buddhist Church of Vietnam represents evidence that the compartmentalization between dissident groups of the past is now breaking down. There is no discernable evidence, however, that the prodemocracy movement is coalescing into a significant force able to challenge the power of Vietnam's one-party state.

Regime Responses

Between 1986 and the present the political legitimacy of Vietnam's one-party state has come under continual challenge by a small number of senior party officials, party and nonparty intellectuals, prodemocracy dissidents and "citizen bloggers." These challenges were first mounted as Vietnam attempted to overcome the serious socioeconomic crisis of the mid-1980s. Party critics challenged the authority and hence the political legitimacy of the VCP leadership in three main interrelated areas: ideology, economic performance, and legal-rational governance.

Party dissidents severely criticized the party leadership for its dogmatic adherence to outmoded Marxism-Leninism that they argued should be abandoned. Some critics argued that other unspecified doctrines needed to be examined to evaluate their applicability to Vietnam's crisis conditions. Party dissidents also argued that the VCP's attempt to develop a market economy and socialism at the same time was incompatible if not contradictory (in the ideological sense of antagonistic contradictions). They argued that attempts to maintain state socialism and a market economy only made matters worse because it created a "new capitalist" elite. Other critics argued that Vietnam should develop a commodity market economy and abandon any pretense of a "socialist orientation."

Party dissidents also criticized the VCP over the pace and scope of economic and political reforms. They challenged the priority accorded to economic growth over political liberalization. These critics argued that both needed to be carried out in tandem. Political reforms were generally viewed by party conservatives as part of the "plot of peaceful evolution" designed to overthrow Vietnam's socialist regime. They gave priority to maintaining political stability.

But it was political governance that attracted the critics' greatest attention. They argued that the main cause of Vietnam's crisis lay in the nature of the one-party system itself that had been corrupted by power and had begun to degenerate. They advocated a thoroughgoing reform of the party apparatus and leadership structure, gradual political reform leading to increased political pluralism, and the restoration of national unity through the creation of a new united front.

They also challenged the VCP's rationale for maintaining a monopoly of power. In particular, they focused on the lack of internal party democracy and secrecy of the decision-making process that they argued led to corruption and the abuse of power. Many critics pointed out that Vietnam's "great unity bloc" had fallen apart and that a true government of national unity and reconciliation was needed to take its place. In the critics' view, the VCP should be made subject to the rule of law and disentangle itself from interference in the day-to-day running of the government. In their view, the entire party/state apparatus needed to be completely overhauled so it could effectively operate in a system of checks and balances.

Finally, party dissidents argued for genuine democratic reform. They were joined in 2004 and after by a nascent middle-class movement of pro-democracy activists. Both the party dissidents and nonparty prodemocracy activists called for senior officials and state organs to be popularly selected through free and fair democratic elections. In order to achieve these aims, the critics argued for the implementation of the full range of political and civil rights—freedom of speech, freedom of assembly, freedom to publish, freedom to form political associations, and so on.

The discussion above underscores that repression is the default position of Vietnam's one-party state when the basis of its political legitimacy is challenged. There are gradations in how repression is applied. Party members who make their criticisms of one-party rule public are punished more than those who use approved internal channels. Party members who air their views abroad fare less well than those who keep their criticisms at home. Nonparty members are the worst affected because Vietnam's one-party state will not countenance any group that explicitly organizes itself to confront the VCP and its policies.

Nevertheless, the Vietnamese one-party state has responded to mounting challenges to its political legitimacy by instituting a number of significant economic and political changes to accommodate its critics. While the official mantra still stresses that Vietnam is a "market economy with a socialist orientation," in practice Vietnam's integration into the global economy through membership in the World Trade Organization has accelerated the development of a national economy driven by market forces. Vietnam's party-state has made progress in reforming and privatizing state-owned enterprises (though a residue of state subsidies remains) and there has been an explosion in the growth of the private sector. In 2006, party members in state-owned enterprises that had been privatized were permitted to retain their membership in the party, and in 2010 new draft statutes authorized a pilot program permitting private entrepreneurs to join the VCP.

Since 1992, when Vietnam adopted a new state constitution, concerted efforts have been taken to enhance the powers of the National Assembly and to make government more efficient by replacing collective leadership with a system of ministerial responsibility. An electoral law adopted at that time required that every constituency be contested. Provision has been made for the selection of independent and nonparty candidates through nomination by mass organizations or self-nomination. Each election since 1992 has seen a high turnover of deputies, including incumbents standing for reelection. Nonetheless, the number of party members in the National Assembly hovers at the 90% mark and the number of successful self-nominated candidates has never exceeded 3 deputies out of a total of 500.

Over the past decade and a half, the state bureaucracy has been streamlined through a series of administrative reforms. State officials are now required to declare private wealth including property and businesses in the hands of family members. In reaction to events in Thai Binh province, a program of "grassroots democracy" was implemented to improve governance at local level by improving transparency. Plans are currently underway to replace the two-tiered system of local government—people's councils and people's committees—with one directly elected body.

The VCP itself has also taken steps to reform itself. Since 1992 it has instituted a gradual process of disengaging itself, at least at the national level, from the day-to-day operation of the government bureaucracy. The Central Committee reduced the number of its committees and commissions that had direct supervisory oversight of the state apparatus. The party has moved to bring about an orderly generational turnover of its highest elected organ. At each national party congress roughly one-quarter to one-third of Central Committee members are retired. The same holds for the Politburo. The party has brought in age restrictions and limits to incumbency. The VCP has also responded to pressures from within the party by permitting party delegates to the 2006 tenth national congress a greater say in the selection of the party secretary-general.

Conclusion

Vietnam's one-party state has been in the process of transition from a "hard authoritarian" to a "soft authoritarian" state since 1986. During this period VCP leaders have tried to disentangle the overlapping and often chaotic structures of party and state. The VCP has assumed responsibility for laying out the long-term strategic policies for Vietnam. Since 1992, the government (state apparatus and legislature) has been tasked with managing and implementing these priorities. As a result, Vietnam's political structure has been altered but the commanding role of the party remains. Collective leadership over the state apparatus has given way to Cabinet government and ministerial responsibility. The National Assembly gradually has been given increased powers to create a state based on "rule of law," but Vietnam nevertheless remains very much a state of "rule by law."

The advent of *doi moi* in 1986 and Vietnam's open door policy to the international community has led to a new set of political challenges as Vietnam's economy has become increasingly integrated with the global economy. The basic features of Vietnam's mono-organizational political system have come under increasing strain (Thayer 1995). The ability of the party to lead, let alone exert control, in all spheres of society has been undermined by both elite and societal pressures (Thayer 2009b).

The legitimacy of Vietnam's one-party state since 1986 has largely rested on performance legitimacy, that is, success in delivering economic growth, and the maintenance of political stability for society at large. In this respect the regime has been very successful as measured by high GDP growth rates accompanied by a marked decline in the national incidence of poverty. The debate over the compatibility of socialism with a market economy has been largely eclipsed by the integration of Vietnam's economy into the global economy through membership in the World Trade Organization.

The VCP has proven adaptable in various other ways in responding to the challenge of its critics. Marxism-Leninism has all but lost its salience as a source of legitimization. Party officials now stress the pragmatism of "Ho Chi Minh thought" and the somewhat vague formulation of a "socialist orientation" for Vietnam's emerging market economy. Nonetheless, the VCP is adamant about retaining its grip on power. At the tenth party congress in 2006, senior party officials readily admitted that widespread corruption was a major challenge to the legitimacy of the socialist state. The new prime minister, Nguyen Tan Dung, came into office with a firm pledge to root out this scourge. His efforts have been only partly successful and at the end of his first term Vietnam still languished in the bottom tier of Transparency International's index of corruption.

The political legitimacy of the Vietnam Communist Party rests on multiple sources. The VCP still retains some political legitimacy based on its leadership in the various wars of national resistance against foreign intervention, as inheritor of the charismatic legitimacy of Ho Chi Minh and legal-rational legitimacy due to its longevity in office and maintenance of political stability. Since 1986, the political legitimacy of Vietnam's one-party state has rested largely on performance legitimacy. For example, the VCP has been successful in extricating Vietnam from socioeconomic crisis, promoting economic growth, and reducing poverty. Since 1995, Vietnam has gained international legitimacy through diplomatic recognition by the United States, membership in the Association of Southeast Asian Nations (ASEAN), membership in the WTO, and its recent nonpermanent membership on the United Nations Security Council.

Despite all the VCP's efforts at economic, administrative, and political reform, Vietnam's one-party system is still likely to be challenged to make good its goal of creating a "law-governed state." Domestic groups will press the VCP to end its repression of political dissent by applying existing constitutional provisions providing for "freedom of opinion and speech, freedom of the press, the right to be informed, and the right to assemble, form associations and hold demonstrations in accordance with the provisions of the law" (Article 69), as well as provisions of Article 70 that provide for freedom of religion. In sum, the legal-rational basis of regime legitimacy will continue to come under challenge.

Vietnam is clearly liberalizing but not fully democratizing. Party elites appear willing to consider the views of domestic critics and accommodate these views when feasible. For example, the role of the press has fluctuated between comparative openness in investigating corruption followed by heavy-handed repression against journalists who have delved into sensitive issues. The future is likely to witness multiple sites of contestation—in the National Assembly, Vietnam Fatherland

Front, and Vietnam Communist Party itself—as party dissidents and nonparty activists press their reform agendas. Historical evidence from the past two decades suggests that Vietnam's leaders have and are continuing to negotiate among themselves the pace and scope of change. Although Vietnam remains a "soft authoritarian" one-party regime, its political legitimacy rests on multiple sources including responsiveness to challenges from within and below to speed up the pace and scope of political change.

Notes

1. The Vietnam Communist Party was also known as the Indochinese Communist Party (1930–1951) and Vietnam Workers' Party (1960–1986).
2. Hoang Minh Chinh continued to advocate political change after his release from jail in 1967 and was imprisoned again in 1981.
3. Chinh died in February 2008.
4. One signatory to the April 6 appeal withdrew, and three new signatories were added for a total of 118.

References

Bui Tin. 1990. "A Citizen's Petition." *Vietnam Commentary* 18 (November–December): 13–15.

Hiebert, Murray. 1993. "Dissenting Voices." *Far Eastern Economic Review* 2 (December): 26.

Hoang Minh Chinh. 1991. "Commentary on the Draft Platform." *Vietnam Commentary* 20 (March–April): 6–11.

Mudie, Luisetta. 2006. "Vietnam Nervous Over Emerging Pro-Democracy Voices." *Radio Free Asia*, September 29. Accessed February 5, 2010. http://www.rfa.org/english/vietnam/vietnam_8406-20060929.html.

Lu Phuong. 1990. "Chu Nghia Xa Hoi Viet Nam Di San Va Doi Moi" [The Legacy of Vietnamese Socialism and Renovation]." *Doan Ket* (7/8): 24–29.

Nguyen Khac Vien. 1991. "Letter to the Vietnam Fatherland Front." *Vietnam Commentary* 20 (March–April): 4–6.

Nguyen Nam Khanh. 2004. "Thu cua Thuong tuong Nguyen Nam Khanh gui Lanh dao Dang ve su long quyen cua Tong cuc 2" [Letter from Major General Nguyen Nam Khanh to the Party Leadership Regarding the Abuse of Power by General Directorate 2]. *Quê Me: Action for Democracy in Vietnam* (June 17). Accessed February 5, 2010. http://www.queme.net/vie/docs_detail.php?numb=145

Nguyen Xuan Tu. 1993. "Doi Dieu Suy Nghi Cua Mot Cong Dan" [Reflections of a Citizen].

Steinglass, Matt. 2006. "Dissident Numbers Grow in Vietnam." *Voice of America*. October 16.

Thayer, Carlyle A. 1988. "The Regularization of Politics: Continuity and Change in the Party's Central Committee, 1951–1986." In *Postwar Vietnam: Dilemmas in Socialist Development*, edited by David G. Marr and Christine P. White, 177–193. Ithaca, NY: Southeast Asia Program, Cornell University.

_____. 1992a. *Political Developments in Vietnam: From the Sixth to Seventh National Party Congress*. Regime Change and Regime Maintenance in Asia and the Pacific Discussion Paper Series No. 5. Canberra, Australia: Department of Political & Social Change, Research School of Pacific Studies, The Australian National University.

_____. 1992b. "Political Reform in Vietnam: *Doi Moi* and the Emergence of Civil Society." In *The Developments of Civil Society in Communist Systems*, edited by Robert F. Miller, 110–129. Sydney, Australia: Allen & Unwin.

_____. 1995. "Mono-Organizational Socialism and the State." In *Vietnam's Rural Transformation*, edited by Benedict J. Tria Kerkvliet and Doug J. Porter, 39–64. Boulder, CO: Westview Press.

_____. 2006. "Political Dissent and Political Reform in Vietnam, 1997–2002." In *The Power of Ideas: Intellectual Input and Political Change in East and Southeast Asia*, edited by Claudia Derichs and Thomas Heberer, 115–132. Copenhagen S, Denmark: Nordic Institute of Asian Studies Press.

_____. 2008. "Vietnam." In *PSI Handbook of Global Security and Intelligence: National Approaches*, vol. 1—*The Americas and Asia*, edited by Stuart Farson, Peter Gill, Mark Phythian, and Shlomo Shapiro, 300–317. Westport, CT and London: Praeger Security International.

_____. 2009a. "Political Legitimacy of Vietnam's One Party-State: Challenges and Responses." *Journal of Current Southeast Asian Affairs* 28 (4): 47–70.

_____. 2009b. "Vietnam and the Challenge of Political Civil Society." *Contemporary Southeast Asia* 31 (1): 1–27.

_____. 2010a. "Political Legitimacy in Vietnam: Challenge and Response." *Politics & Policy* 38 (3): 423–444.

_____. 2010b. "The Trial of Le Cong Dinh: New Challenges to the Legitimacy of Vietnam's Party-State." *Journal of Vietnamese Studies* 5 (3): 196–207.

Tønnesson, Stein. 1993. "Applying Mathematics and Democracy (Interview with Phan Dinh Dieu)." *NIASnytt* 2: 11–14.

Tran Do. 1997–1998. "Tinh hinh dat nuoc vai tro cua dang Cong San" [The State of the Nation and the Role of the Communist Party]. Faxed copy of General Tran Do's letter sent to the Party, National Assembly, Government and Concerned Friends, received from the BBC Vietnamese Service on February 9, 1998. 13 pp. with 5 page appendix.

Vo Nguyen Giap. 2004. Letter to Central Committee, Comrade Secretary-General, Comrades of the Politburo, Secretariat and Central Control Committee, January 3.

CHAPTER 4

The Struggle for Political Legitimacy in Thailand

Björn Dressel

Introduction

At the start of the twenty-first century, conflicting notions of political legitimacy once again caused political instability in Thailand. The most visible signs of a legitimacy crisis were the military's ouster of popularly elected prime minister Thaksin Shinawatra in 2006, the rewrite of the acclaimed 1997 "People's Constitution" in early 2007, and the fall of two prime ministers within a year of their election. The unprecedented degree of political polarization—exacerbated by an imminent monarchical succession—introduced deep insecurity throughout the country.

From this uncertainty emerged "shirt movements"—political camps. Yellow-shirted supporters of the People's Alliance for Democracy (PAD) cried "Save the Nation" and "We Will Fight for the King." Their mass action first prompted the 2006 coup and then accelerated the downfall of two succeeding governments. In reaction, red-shirted supporters of Shinawatra and his dissolved Thai Rak Thai (TRT) party organized the United Front of Democracy against Dictatorship (UDD). Decrying the "judicial coup" that had dissolved their party and banned its leaders from politics, the red shirts replicated PAD civil disobedience campaigns and directed them against the government of Abhisit Vejjajiva, leading to a violent though unsuccessful attempt in April 2009 to overthrow the government and then to a more peaceful three-month occupation of the city center—the largest protests in Thai history—in early 2010. This was met in May by a government crackdown that left hundreds dead and many more injured. Any hope of reconciliation ended, and the gulf in Thai society widened.

The choice of colors is significant. Yellow, the color of Buddhism, also represents Monday, the day of the king's birth. Revolutionary red has a less obvious Thai connection, and the notable absence of any royal symbolism, together with UDD attacks against the king's Privy Council, suggests at worst outright republican leanings. Smaller, less active groups adopted blue, associated with the queen, or white, which in combination with the Thai flag seems to refer to nation-based unity.

Especially at the red and yellow extremes, today's conflicts repeat a pattern of polarized notions of regime legitimacy that has been apparent throughout modern Thai history (see, e.g., Prudhisan 1992, 22–23; Baker and Pasuk 2005, 263–265). The traditional conception of a stratified paternal-authoritarian state in which power emanates from the king promotes the state ideology of "nation, religion, king" formulated by the modernizing Chakri dynasty in the nineteenth century. PAD yellow shirts see the very existence of the Thai nation as critically linked not to popular sovereignty but to this core trinity. Threats, whether internal ("majoritarian tyranny") or external (globalization), are regularly used to justify paternalist rule.

But an opposing tradition, rooted in the commoner-intellectuals of the nineteenth century and refined in the twentieth, assigns legitimacy to popular sovereignty. It promotes government based on the rule of law and institutions such as the constitution. Rather than attributing to Thailand a mystical unity, this republican vision embraces its diversity. This is clearly the view of red-shirt leaders—though not necessarily of Thaksin himself.

Though contending notions of state legitimacy were vividly illustrated in 1932, 1973, and 1992 (see below), rapid modernization and pressures from globalization have propelled the tensions to the fore. The traditional establishment failed to garner wide public support for the 2006 coup or the 2007 constitution, demonstrating how the traditional trinity is being questioned. Combined with the urgency created by the imminent monarchical succession and the direct challenge posed by Thaksin, the clash of ideologies could be explosive. Reconstructing a common understanding of legitimacy will be crucial if stability is to return.

In what follows, I start by reviewing Thailand's history of ideological contention. I then contrast the traditional objects of legitimization, "nation, religion, king," with the notions captured by terms such as constitutionalism, popular sovereignty, and performance to illustrate how different social forces have interpreted legitimacy over time. Finally, I reflect on what the Thai situation implies both for the study of legitimacy and Thailand's future.

The Historical Context

Thailand, a nation of 60 million, is the only country in mainland Southeast Asia that was never colonized, though it gradually adapted to Western institutions under a modernizing monarchy in the nineteenth century. Though there remains the largely unopposed authority of the monarchy, the Buddhist *sangha* (monastic order), and the dominance of the bureaucracy, both military and civilian, rapid modernization since the mid-1900s has introduced a vigorous middle class and an active civil society. Even the newest constitution describes Thailand as a parliamentary democracy with a constitutional monarchy and unitary administration. Consequently, Thailand's polity must accommodate both the new and the old.

Siam's evolution into Thailand began with King Mongkut (Rama IV, 1804–1873), who introduced cautious reforms that strengthened the monarchy and opened the country gradually to the West. More radically, his son, King Chulalongkorn (Rama V, 1853–1910), observing Western territorial encroachment, undertook far-reaching nation-building reforms that made it possible to administer Siam from the center. The nationalist discourse of King Vajiravudh (Rama VI, 1881–1925) reinforced the new order: it gradually replaced a traditional spatial-political geography based on cosmology and personal ties with a model of territory and borders. Centralizing the administration enhanced royal power—and the preeminence of the monarch (Thongchai 1994).

Early in the twentieth century, spreading ideas about nation, state, and progress brought challenges that culminated in a bloodless 1932 coup by young Western-educated civilian and military reformers against King Prajadhipok (Rama VII, 1892–1941). The coup transformed Thailand into a constitutional monarchy with modern democratic state structures—though not substantial democratic practices.

After the coup, not only did divisions emerge among the coup leaders but royalists, civil servants, and the military also asserted claims for control over state power (Girling 1981: 121–122)—claims complicated by rapid economic growth, modernization, and the deepening integration of Thailand into the world economy. Starting in the late 1960s, mass protests by students and workers against war, corruption, and military rule ushered in a brief period of democratic experimentation (1973–1976). Its brutal termination by the military shaped a whole generation of future leaders, and also prompted the gradual opening of the political system (Prudhisan 1992). By the 1980s candidate- and vote-buying had become widespread, and provincial business interests came to dominate parliament, turning cabinet positions into personal pork barrels and plundering the public revenues (Pasuk and Baker 1998; Hicken 2001; McVey 2000).

The increasing demands in the 1990s of a growing urban middle class deeply concerned about money politics culminated in 1997 in the democratically drafted "People's Constitution," the first such in Thailand's tangled constitutional history (Connors 2002; Harding 2001; McCargo 2002b). Embodying the belief of urban reformers that it was possible to engineer democracy and good governance, the new constitution made far-reaching institutional changes to enhance stability, popular participation, and political accountability (Dressel 2005).

Yet democratic governance in Thailand since these reforms has been tenuous. Under Prime Minister Shinawatra's "business populism," the 1997 constitution, though supporting more stable and effective government, did not prevent the administration from interfering with the new oversight agencies, undermining the rule of law, and engaging in at best opaque practices (McCargo 2003; Pasuk and Baker 2005, 2002; Thitinan 2003; Kuhonta 2008). The continuing influence of Thailand's traditional bureaucratic elites, civilian and military, and the immaturity of Thailand's democratic culture were reflected in the 2006 coup. Confronted with a populist leadership that threatened their interests, the very urban elites that had catalyzed the People's Constitution rushed to support the traditional networks, ousting the elected government and producing a deliberately less democratic constitution. Unfortunately, because the new constitution is less legitimate than its predecessor and fails to provide the inclusive governance the Thai people have come to expect, it proved yet another source of instability.

Thailand is once more at a crossroads. In a rapidly modernizing country with deepening linkages to the global economy, new social actors seek political accommodation. Today the monarchical elites face demands from urban liberal elites; modern bourgeois interests, such as those of Thaksin and his circle; and increasingly from the politically mobilized rural and urban poor—each with its own ideas about what constitutes a legitimate political order.

The Trinity Endures

Thailand's history reveals multiple sources and objects of legitimization. I classify these notions of legitimacy as traditional (enduring) or modern (fragile) before dissecting them individually. This will help us describe how social actors have constructed, redefined, and used these concepts—each time altering Thailand's political landscape.

The "nation, religion, king" (*chart, sasana, phra mahakasat*), emphasized during the reign of King Vajiravudh to inculcate devotion to Thai unity, has been the foundation of Thai identity for close to 200 years. While its power lies in the interrelation of its components (the king as protector of the faith embodies the nation; the durability and independence of the nation depend on the monarchy and the Buddhist religion), each has also been itself a source of legitimacy.

Monarchy

The monarchy is almost unchallenged as a source of legitimacy and object of legitimization. Its revival since the mid-twentieth century derives from moral leadership and its roles as extraconstitutional arbiter and symbol of unity in times of crisis. Though the informal power of the throne remains almost unchallenged, increasingly it is considered a model of governance that is at odds with the liberal democracy and popular sovereignty Thai people have come to expect. A look at how it has been transformed over time provides insights into how legitimacy has been constructed in modern Thailand.

In a careful mix of revivalism and Westernization, the late Chakri rulers initiated reforms designed to transform the monarch into a modern, if absolute, ruler. King Mongkut (1851–1868), for instance, gradually embraced Western science and education at the court. Yet he also revived royal ceremony, skillfully deploying Hindu and Buddhist religious symbols and rituals to unite and purify the Buddhist *sangha* and accentuate religious ideals. For him, the monarchy was both modern and traditional (Baker and Pasuk 2005, 48–52).

When Chulalongkorn created a salaried bureaucracy and established an independent financial base through the Privy Purse Bureau (PPB), citizens were for the first time linked to the king through a functional bureaucracy rather than an "exemplary center." The link was tightened by Vajiravudh's nationalist agenda—exemplified by the new "nation, religion, king" mantra. As the monarchy increasingly came to embody the nation, the identity of the king shifted "away from a sacral bodhisattva toward a Kaiser-like figure" (Handley 2006, 37). The monarchy gained financial security, dynastic continuity, and a dominant role in the new government; its powers were defined as absolute.

The 1932 replacement of absolute with constitutional monarchy transformed that role—but it did not end attempts to reconstruct the political authority of the monarchy. As power struggles intensified between militarist, royalist, and pro-Pridi liberals, for instance, senior royal advisor Prince Dhani Nivat began promoting the Sukothai model of a naturally elected monarch who "justifies himself as the King of the Righteous" (Prince Dhani Nivat 1947, 95) and emphasized the monarch's role as protector of the people and of Buddhism. Arguing against the constitution as "a pure foreign conception," the prince asserted that the king's inherent morality and wisdom were the true sources of law. Others argued that only the king, not elected representatives, could "represent the whole people" (Phraya Siwisanwaja, cited in Somkiat 1986, 326).

These royalist efforts met with stiff resistance from nationalist prime minister Phibun Songkhram (1938–1944, 1948–1957), who not only blocked attempts to reinstate royal power through the constitution but also restricted the king's public duties to a few rituals (Pasuk and Baker 2005, 176). But the fortunes of the royalists rose after the 1957 coup by General Sarit, a member of a military generation that had not been involved in the 1932 coup. After royal endorsement of his coup, Sarit promoted the young monarch, King Bhumipol, for his own purposes, encouraging an expanded royal role (Thak 2007, 204–214).

Meanwhile, the king's growing interest in rural development (matching Sarit's emphasis) brought the monarchy exposure in rural areas, and the extension of royal charities built relationships with senior military and civilian bureaucrats, the Buddhist establishment, and some in the growing business community (Thak 2007, 178). This new alignment was highly beneficial to all, but as Baker and Pasuk (2005, 180) remark, "[t]he lurch to Americanization turned the monarchy into an alternative symbol of nation and tradition; the corruption of the generals and their cronies created an opportunity for the monarchy to assert a revived and modernized form of moral leadership; and the harsh results of rapid development gave the king a role as defender of the weak." The monarchy revived.

With the support of Prime Minister Prem (1980–1988), the king's public role was expanded: He promoted rural development (royal projects of village uplift) and was increasingly portrayed as a "farmer king" or "developer king" by such agencies as the National Identity Office (Baker and Pasuk 2005, 235–236; Handley 2006, 295). His ceremonial role also expanded, as monarchical celebrations since the 1980s vividly illustrate.[1] And eventually the king became more closely associated with orthodox Buddhism through royal ritual and growing interest in royal patronage for certain monastic lineages.

By the 1990s the monarch was increasingly celebrated as "a modern *thammaracha* and a moral counterweight to the excess of military and business," especially since because of his image of "devotion to the peasantry, constant ceremonial presence, promotion as the centrepiece of national identity, and increasing longevity, the king's *barami* (charisma, innate authority) steadily increased" (Baker and Pasuk 2005, 237). Recast as the righteous ruler guaranteeing stability, unity, and moral leadership against the political forces of greed, the monarch emerged legitimized in the eyes of the public, especially the urban middle class.

By now the king's political authority seems almost unchallenged. Paradoxically, though, the new prestige is accompanied by uncertainties. Recent debates on the application of the *lèse majesté* law reveal deepening rifts over the role of the monarchy.[2] With the king ill, the concern over succession is raising questions about the extent to which the monarchy is institutionalized beyond King Bhumipol himself; the heir apparent, Prince Vajiralongkorn, is deeply unpopular (Handley 2006, 440–446).[3]

Religion

As a value system emphasizing meritorious action and individual responsibility, Buddhism has been the integrative core of Thailand's traditional culture for centuries (Keyes 1987, 32–39; Girling 1981, 153–154); it also has formal organizational and ideological links with the state. Throughout history Buddhism has not only regulated religious activity, but also has been used to mobilize popular support for royal rulership as well as for political ideologies and activities, such as nationhood, development, and stability.

Theravada Buddhism spread in Siam in the sixth century, and it was made a state religion when the Thai kingdom of Sukothai was established in the thirteenth century. It offered benefits for both rulers and ruled: Urban society was drawn by its openness and inherent egalitarianism (Baker and Pasuk 2005, 19). Premodern rulers could appropriate the ideas of supernatural powers in Buddhist thought to reinforce their reigns, and cooperation with the *sangha* promised not only moral legitimization but also a means of social control (Somboon 1977). In negotiations over division of leadership roles, royal protection and patronage were exchanged for administrative power over the *sangha* and monastic approval of their rule (Skilling 2007). Over time this transformed the king into the *dhammaraja*, the righteous ruler, and the potential *bodhisatva* who helps others to ascend the spiritual ladder to nirvana (Somboon 1993a).

The Chakri rulers recognized the benefits of tying the structures of the *sangha* to the absolute state (Keyes 1987, 56–61). Under King Mongkut, who spent almost three decades as a monk before ascending the throne, the *sangha* was purified and united. He gave the Thammayut sect, which has a more rigorous code of conduct, the prominent position it still retains.

Chulalongkorn's Sangha Reform Act of 1902 added momentum; it rendered the king de facto head of the church by asserting the royal government's responsibility for the priesthood, with sole right to confer clerical rank, and the ecclesiastical administration was formalized and centralized under Thammayut control (Handley 2006, 34). To help preserve moral order, his successor, Vajiravudh, introduced daily prayers in schools, police stations, and government departments (Thompson 1941, 368–369). Thus Buddhism became an instrument of royal political legitimacy.

Others also used Buddhism for political ends. For instance, Phibun's ultranationalist leadership challenged royal control with the Sangha Act of 1942, which sought to democratize the *sangha* (at the expense of the Thammayut sect) and give the government, not the monarch, a direct say in clerical appointments (Handley 2006, 60). Under Phibun, who was careful to portray himself as a champion of Buddhism, the government gave direct financial assistance to a growing number of temples (Thak 2007, 66).

Even more dramatically, Sarit, taking king and Buddhism as absolute values, deliberately employed both to support his goals and protect Thailand against communism and regional separatism (Somboon 1977, 128–138). With another Sangha Act in 1962, as in 1902 the Thammayut sect was reinstated; dissenting voices within the *sangha* were weeded out for having communist leanings, and the pattern was set for decades (see Somboon 1993b, 128–136).

This helps to clarify the struggle between the Thaksin government and the PAD over nomination of a new Supreme Patriarch after power struggles within the *sangha* in 2005.[4] PAD leader Sondhi Limthongkul accused Thaksin of ignoring royal prerogatives and interfering with the indivisible unity of religion and monarchy. The use of religious disputes in political conflict escalated after the 2006 coup, prompting an unsuccessful attempt at a new Sangha Law. Control of religious structures is still central to the legitimization of political authority in Thailand.

Nation

"Nation," the third pillar, is an abstract concept, a mystical unit of solidarity (*samakhitham*), the sense of an "imagined community" (Anderson 1983).[5] Yet the concept and its political expression "nationalism" have been central to numerous efforts to consolidate political legitimacy in Thailand. Thaksin employed this highly durable discourse skillfully after the 1997 financial crisis. Recently PAD has employed a nationalist discourse, though very different, to mobilize against Thaksin and lend credibility to its antidemocratic "New Politics."

The concept has deep roots in the "official nationalism" of the later Chakri rulers, though it really emerged only a decade after they were overthrown. *Chat,* the idea of the nation, was first articulated by the educated elite during the reign of King Chulalongkorn but not fully popularized until King Vajiravudh's sixth reign (Barmé 1993, 15–17). Recognizing the challenges emanating from an emerging middle class, a mobilized Chinese community, and tensions within the royal elite, Vajiravudh "began moving all the policy levers of official nationalism: compulsory state-controlled primary education, state-organized propaganda, official rewriting of history, [an ersatz] militarism . . . and endless affirmation of the identity of dynasty and nation" (Anderson 1983, 95). His efforts combined two ideas: (1) Thai independence based on the monarchy and Buddhism; and (2) the monarchy was the people's representative. Portraying the monarch as "lord great warrior" of Thai-ness and independence, Vajiravudh attempted to direct popular loyalty to the king rather than the cultural geopolitical state (see Vella 1978). Official state nationalism, rather than mass nationalism, became central.

Efforts to create a notion of Thai identity on a mass scale emerged shortly after the absolute monarchy fell. Because the new bureaucratic elites felt a need to reconstruct legitimacy after a constitutional order was adopted, the new discourse sought to raise the nation itself over the throne. It stated that the "the good of the people [*ratsadon*] is more important than that of the government, but the good of the nation [*chat*] is . . . more important than that of individuals" (Barmé 1993, 88). Thus whoever could control the concept of "the good of the nation" would rule legitimately.

This logic was carried into subsequent nationalist narratives. While Pridi had hoped to make the public loyal to nation *and* constitution, his successor, the ultranationalist Phibun Songkhram, made concepts like *phunam* (leader) and *chatniyom* and *rathaniyom* (nationalism and state-ism) explicit state ideology. Perhaps responding to the rise of fascism in Europe and Japan, which emphasized national identity, the government changed the country's name from Siam to Thailand, adopted a national anthem, and proposed measures of economic nationalism. Phibun also convened state conventions that resulted in the "Thai-ification" of language, culture, and daily life (Barmé 1993, 174).

The paternalistic Sarit again emphasized on the nation by promoting Thai tradition and culture and expressing his fatherly (*phokun*) concern for the nation (Thak 2007, 130–137). Thus he set a pattern for reinterpreting the nation as symbolizing the unity of the leader (and bureaucracy) and the people.

"Nation" continues to be a source of legitimacy. For instance, after the Asian financial crisis and the resentment it built against outside forces (globalization, the IMF), Thaksin, to consolidate power, resorted to nationalist rhetoric and a generous display of nationalist symbols, such as the Thai flag, celebration of "independence day" as part of Thailand's early IMF loan repayment, and government action against critical foreign journalists on grounds of national security (McCargo and Pathmanand 2005, 84; Pasuk and Baker 2004, 140–142). More subtly, a new economic discourse cast nationalism as a driving force behind development and even globalization, advocated for Asian regionalism, and ultimately portrayed Thaksin as champion and guardian of the country (Kasian 2002; Glassman 2004). This somewhat risky storyline put him at odds with both radical populist elements in his own party and with the monarchy, which had begun to advocate localism and self-sufficiency (Handley 2006, 417–420).

The PAD also promoted nationalist narratives. In their outcry over the sale of Thaksin's Shin Corp empire, Thailand's biggest telecommunications and satellite network, to Singapore's state-owned Temasek Holding, its leaders accused the prime minister not just of tax evasion but of "selling the nation" (*khai chart*) and jeopardizing "national security"—a claim that helped the military justify the coup as reestablishing "national unity" (Kasian 2006). PAD leaders then stirred nationalist sentiments against the decision of the Samak government to support Cambodia's unilateral application for listing the disputed Preah Vihear Temple as a World Heritage site, arguing that Thailand's territorial sovereignty was at stake (the coup-appointed Constitution Court in 2009 affirmed the questionable legal reasoning). Suggesting that war was the only suitable response, the PAD became ultranationalist. Thus the national narrative remains relevant for constructing political legitimacy today.

Alternative Sources of Legitimacy Emerge

In response to sociopolitical changes, over time all three pillars of the traditional trinity—nation, religion, king—have undergone considerable reinterpretation. Because Thailand's traditional political establishment views the trinity as nonnegotiable, it continues to support paternalist elite rule and see citizens as subjects rather than political participants. With the trinity elevated to a national ideology actively promoted by the government through all state organizations, there would seem to be little room for alternative sources of legitimacy. Yet alternative notions of legitimacy seem to be arising in the ideas of popular sovereignty and constitutional governance that Thais have experienced recently. Though very fragile, these offer a very different conception of state-society relations.

Constitutionalism

Constitutionalism as source or referent of legitimization may seem problematic. Consider that Thailand has had 18 constitutions since 1932, yet power has changed hands more often through coups d'état than through constitutional means. Nor have new constitutions been able to check executive power—their primary purpose was to consolidate and facilitate the rule of whichever group acquired power (Harding 2001; Chai Anan Samudavanija 2002). New powerholders were careful to draft a new constitution each time, suggesting they saw the constitution as a legitimizing instrument.[6] Moreover, if too much attention is given to Thailand's constitutional volatility, there is a risk of underestimating the constitutional impulses that have arisen throughout Thai history, first under Pridi and Phibun but also briefly in the 1970s or more durably in the 1990s. In fact, the substantially different discourse that emerged in the 1990s reinforced constitutionalism as critical to political legitimacy.

The 1932 coup against the absolute monarchy in many respects launched these developments. Despite previous discussions in royal circles about moving to a constitutional monarchy and efforts in official historiography to portray King Prajadiphok (Rama VII) as having "granted" Thailand's first constitution, it was the original coup promoters, organized as the People's Party, who promoted the constitution as a source of public loyalty. To create political legitimacy, in the mid-1930s Pridi and Phibun intensified state efforts, which would popularize the constitution.

The public discourse was designed to link the constitution to aspects of national unity and progress and make it an object of national importance (*sing saksit khong chat*). To give it equal footing with the tra-ditional trinity, a new Constitution Association led by Wichit undertook to also link the constitution to religion. Monks were recruited to pro-mote it in the countryside, and miniature constitutions were distributed to local shrines, to be surrounded by images of the king and Buddha. Gradually Constitution Day was elevated into the premier public holi-day, and in 1939 there was installed a new Constitution Monument that would for decades remain the largest monument in Bangkok. In short, the constitution became a means to legitimize the new elite politics, rather than a compact defining relations between citizen and state, as liberals like Pridi might have wanted.

In the following decades there was a gradual decline from "con-stitutional idealism to formalistic constitutionalism" that supported dominant elite groups (Yano 1978, 127). Under Phibun (1933–1938; 1948–1957) the constitution remained near the center, and gradually there was a move to emphasize on other sources of legitimacy, such as charismatic leadership (*than phu nam*) and the nation. As a conse-quence, Pridi's 1946 constitution—one of the most progressive in Thai history—was replaced within three years, and under Sarit constitu-tional practice was effectively abandoned by 1967 in favor of his pater-nal "Thai Buddhist democracy." And while subsequent governments returned to formal constitutional practice, continually rewritten consti-tutions (six between 1968 and 1978) constitutions could hardly claim public loyalty.

Yet from time to time struggles for a more substantive liberal con-stitutional order also emerged, most notably in 1973 when students mobilized over half a million people in support of a new constitution (Morell and Chai-Anan 1981). That marked the beginning of a cautious return to a rule-based constitutional system and gradual political lib-eralization, a trend advanced under the caretaker government of Prime Minister Prem Tinsulanonda (1980–1988) and then by the return to a liberal democratic order in 1992 after the popular uprising against the regime of General Suchinda (Hewison 1997; Ockey 1994).

In the 1990s, with dissatisfaction mounting among urban elites over how poorly Thai democracy functioned (cabinet instability, rise of money-based politics, etc.), reforming the constitution again became the center of efforts for political reform (see Amon 1994; Prawes 1995). Creation and promulgation of the 1997 People's Constitution has often been described as a turning point in Thai constitutional history (Pasuk and Baker 2002; Connors 2002; McCargo 1998; Harding 2001). Not only was it the first constitution drafted with wide public participation but the dynamics of the drafting process produced far-reaching, and often surprisingly progressive arrangements (Klein 1998; Borwornsak and Burns 1998; Dressel 2005, 2009). True, the 1997 reforms were still essentially an urban elite project to mitigate the "vagaries" of majoritarian politics (McCargo 2002b, 3; Hewison 2004), but they might also be seen as a sign of a qualitatively different constitutional discourse—one arising from the aspirations of liberal elites and the middle classes to establish ground rules for an increasingly plural and participatory society.

It has become clear, however, how fragile that achievement was. Under Thaksin (2001–2006) the government interfered with, perhaps actively undermined, many of the new constitutional arrangements (Kuhonta 2008; McCargo 2008). Moreover, middle-class support for the 2006 coup and the 2007 constitution illustrates the ambivalence of many liberal elites about honoring constitutional parameters if their interests are threatened (Hewison 2007; Dressel 2009). Combined with continuous interventions by extraconstitutional power centers like military and monarchy and the 2006 antiliberal discourse of conservative academics about a "Thai kind of constitution," constitutionalism is far from being a sturdy source of legitimization in contemporary Thailand (Dressel 2009; Connors 2008).

Still, there may be grounds for cautious optimism. Major social actors increasingly focus their arguments on the constitution itself. PAD has pledged to defend the 2007 constitution; the red shirts argue for a return to that of 1997. Both thus seem to view constitutionalism as the only acceptable basis for the exercise of political authority and thus as a lasting basis for legitimization. This is particularly intriguing considering the impending monarchical succession.

Popular Sovereignty

Popular sovereignty is closely, though not always comfortably, intertwined with liberal aspects of the 1997 constitution. With the expansion of the franchise and the mobilization of extrabureaucratic forces in Thai society, it has steadily gained importance as a basis for legitimization, though its value is depleted because representative institutions (e.g., parties, parliament) are inadequate. And the elite discourse on Thai-style democracy, despite differences among the participants, argues that an uneducated citizenry cannot make proper use of the democratic process and advances notions of sovereignty "shared" between the monarchy and the people (Hewison and Kengkij 2010; Connors 2008). However, the populist leadership of Thaksin and his claim that the mandate he received gave him authority to rule demonstrates the contemporary relevance of popular sovereignty for political legitimization.

Popular sovereignty first gained importance as a source of legitimization after the 1932 coup. Having come to power to establish democracy, the new leaders used the constitution to gradually open political participation beyond the ranks of nobles and aristocrats to the masses. While actual practice later fell shy of stated ambitions—about half the members of the assembly were appointed and parties other than the People's Party were severely constrained—it did use elections as a channel for public involvement.

In 1955 the change in political dynamics became clear when Phibun's government rapidly lost legitimacy because of rigged elections, setting the stage for Sarit's coup in 1957. The coup itself, built on growing public discontent, illustrated not just the increasing role of the military but even more the growing importance of the masses. In fact, Sarit's insistence that his actions reflected the public will marked in many respects "a new era in Thai politics, with consequences for the substance of the legitimizing principles" (Saitip 1995, 201).

But Sarit's authoritarian rule, which effectively abrogated the constitution and ended parliamentary elections, also provoked efforts to reinterpret notions of popular sovereignty. Leadership was recast in paternalistic terms as representing the popular will, and Western institutions were portrayed as "alien" and "unstable" if they were not reconciled with indigenous principles (*lakkanmuang Thai*). This reasoning gave rise to a discourse on "Thai democracy" as a "system suitable to the special conditions of Thailand," in which sovereignty was not exercised by the people directly but "realized" through the modernized state. The theme proved influential for decades, even after a return to elections and formal constitutional order. In fact, it was because of popular demands in the 1970s for more political participation that long-time Democrat Party leader and Prime Minister Kukrit Pramoj (1975–1976) gave renewed intellectual impetus to notions of a Thai-style democracy (*prachatthippatai baep thai*) in which mass demands for participation would be counterbalanced by a strong executive; an implicit social contract of shared sovereignty between monarchy and people; and moral leadership by political elites (Hewison and Kengkij 2009). Such discourse helped legitimize the caretaker governments of Prem Tinsulanond (1980–1988) and Anand Panyarachun (1991; 1992).

Paradoxically, though, the return to a full-fledged liberal democratic order after the 1992 prodemocracy protests reinforced only partially popular sovereignty as a basis for political legitimization. While the protests illustrated the growing importance of the masses, rampant corruption in subsequent democratic governments for many urban elites discredited the majoritarian-electoral process itself (Pasuk and Baker 2002, 425–428; Anek 1996). The 1997 constitution reflects these ambiguities. Though confirming a commitment to popular sovereignty and participation (elected senate, decentralization, public referenda, etc.), it effectively reduced the importance of parliament as the center of politics by strengthening the executive, providing constitutional policy parameters and royal prerogatives, and establishing powerful new oversight agencies (Ginsburg 2009; McCargo 2003). As part of an intellectual agenda of "parliamentary rationalization" a new bachelor's degree requirement for parliamentarians effectively barred 95% of Thais from serving (Amon 1994).

The 2007 constitution, which embodies the anti-Thaksin agenda, has gone further, returning to a partially appointed Senate; increasing the powers of judicial and quasi-judicial agencies; and adopting past electoral rules to minimize the influence of the rural electorate. Reflecting conservative debates on Thai-style democracy, the 2007 version is a clear statement that Thailand's traditional elites are using constitutional mechanisms to deflect popular demands (Dressel 2009). It seems to mark a return to past shallow democratic practice as an "exercise of process over principle, form over substance" (Kobkua 2003, 8).

Are these attempts to reshape notions of popular sovereignty sustainable? The rapid decline in the junta's popularity even among early urban supporters; growing political awareness and mobilization of the marginalized; and above all the continuous populist appeal of Thaksin all seem to suggest that "the masses" have consolidated a role in Thai politics. Another sign is the inability of Prime Minister Abhisit (2007–present) to reverse course on earlier populist policies. Given international pressures to adhere to democratic practice, Thailand's political elites are finding it difficult to question popular sovereignty as a basis for legitimacy (though some within the PAD are certainly trying) as battles rage between social forces about the depth and extent of popular representation. Not without irony, given Thaksin's own disrespect for the democratic process, it is clear that his populist leadership provided critical impetus for such struggles. The outcome will to a large extent depend on another alternative source of legitimacy: performance.

Performance

Performance encompasses a variety of dimensions, from economy to security, welfare, and justice. It is also highly contingent: expectations alter; events are often outside government control; performance dilemmas arise—all of which can make performance ultimately unreliable as a basis for political authority (Alagappa 1995, 41–43). Yet while such general considerations help explain its fragility, performance claims have mattered to Thai political legitimization either by supporting governments or (especially) justifying military interventions. In Thailand performance questions have not been limited to the form of governments but have often animated public preferences for the type of political regime generally. Moreover, Thailand's rapid modernization has produced clashing views about what constitutes good performance and about such aspects of performance as growth versus equity.

The shift from absolute monarchy to bureaucratic polity proved critical for legitimization on the basis of performance. Unable to claim or emulate the religioritualistic performance legitimacy of the Buddhist *dhammic* kingship, civilian and military actors searching for legitimacy had to shift public attention to aspects of economic performance and political order, as Pridi did with his proposals to enhance public welfare, and Phibun in promoting economic nationalism. Building on these foundations, both national development (*phattana*) and security became a Sarit hallmark. As U.S. involvement in the region deepened, growth was established as the primary goal of government, economic policy was put in the hands of technocrats at new agencies, and the policy basis for development was reinforced by five-year plans (Muscat 1994: 88). These structures, considered critical to thwarting communism by maintaining political order, supported Thailand's later rapid economic development (Warr and Bhanupong 1996).

But economic diversification and the visible negative effects of a heavily centralized, top-down development process also prompted resistance and questioning of the government's performance. By the mid-1970s new rural and environmental NGOs were challenging the technocratic development agenda as environmental degradation grew, natural resources were depleted, and rural and indigenous livelihoods destroyed (Gohlert 1991). Similarly, urban civil society and business groups began to seek more involvement in political and economic decision making—demands that gradually spawned a renewed focus on equity issues under Prem and Anand (Saitip 1995, 215–216).

With the return to full-fledged democratic practice in the 1990s, the public again began to scrutinize performance. Claiming legitimacy based on democratic principles alone proved increasingly unsustainable when governments failed to meet the good governance standards of the urban middle class. With the Asian financial crisis proving a clear example of failed economic and political performance, performance legitimization returned to center stage.

Playing to the postcrisis mood, Thaksin made policy performance a critical part of his electoral appeal and his right to rule. Drawing legitimacy from his success in business, he initiated a "CEO style" of governance, emphasizing a high-risk, high-reward strategy. This meant a policy package his critics dubbed "Thaksinomics" (Pasuk and Baker 2004, 99–133): a commitment to high growth, competitiveness, deepening regionalism, and social spending. In politics Thaksin advocated a "quiet" approach (*kanmueang ning*) in which the government is primarily concerned with "problem-solving" for citizens, leaving little room for protest and dissent (64).[7] Democracy itself was declared "just a tool, not our goal"; the goal was "a good lifestyle, happiness, and national progress" (*Nation*, December 11, 2003).

To deliver Thaksin eventually pushed for performance-based reforms within national and provincial administrations, tightening government oversight of the bureaucracy in the process. While challenges soon emerged—the royalist discourse on "self-sufficiency," urban protests against government abuse, and separatist challenges in the South due to government heavy-handedness—Thaksin set benchmarks for performance under democratic rule, as the inability of the Democrat Party to diverge from some Thaksin policies demonstrates. Constraints exerted by the 2007 constitution are also likely to make performance claims harder to achieve.

Thailand at the Crossroads

Constitutionalism, popular sovereignty, and performance constitute alternative sources of legitimacy in Thailand. All are rooted in the search of bureaucratic actors for broad-based legitimization since the 1932 coup against the absolute monarchy. Global processes of democratization, liberalization, and performance-based governance have meanwhile increased their relevance. There is, however, a lack of consensus about the content, appropriate mix, and actual influence these sources should claim in Thailand. The problem is exacerbated by the challenge to modern sources from the traditional trinity of nation, religion, king, which as currently interpreted is generally irreconcilable with them. Yet as continuing political turmoil and debates about Thai-style democracy illustrate, because these modern sources of legitimacy have become central to political power struggles in Thailand, they have the potential for ultimately transforming political authority.

The return of the military to politics, continuing constitutional instability, and a deeply polarized society are all signs that political legitimacy is being questioned in Thailand. With a rapidly modernizing and increasingly pluralistic polity, the competing values of multiple power centers are fuelling continuing power struggles. That is why formal institutional arrangements in support of an enduring political order are persistently fragile.

The tension between traditional and modern sources of legitimization first emerged in the 1932 coup. The coup based its challenge to the old order on the alternate legitimizing principles of popular sovereignty and constitutionalism, but it failed to establish these principles because of factional infighting and limited popular support. As a result, the traditional trinity has not only endured but has even been elevated to a state ideology. Meanwhile, although liberal-democratic values have taken root elsewhere in the world, it has not been possible to resolve the tension in Thailand, which lacks a broad-based commitment to them.

Thus the paradox: state officials in Thailand continue to use the traditional trinity to legitimize their operations even though their own position depends on the constitution, popular sovereignty, and (increasingly) performance. Thaksin's populist rule, which challenged the ideology of traditional power centers, brought this tension to the fore. That is why the political crisis has turned gradually into a wider crisis over the legitimacy of the political order.

Much is at stake. The clashes between yellow and red shirts, and the harsh government crackdown on the latter, are the latest example of clashing concepts of political authority and state-society relations. At one pole is the traditional trinitarian vision of a paternal state, with monarchy and traditional elites heading a hierarchical social order. At the other is a younger, weaker, yet sturdy liberal-egalitarian tradition anchoring state authority in constitutional principles, democratic ideals of popular sovereignty, and pluralist discourse among equal citizens. In principle, these are mutually exclusive: the monarchical networks advocate for a traditional, limited "Thai-style democracy"; the urban middle class support a "royal liberalism"; Thaksin's supporters own his vision of a strong state based on a populist-managerial leadership. What will emerge depends on numerous unresolved power struggles, many related to monarchical succession and the growing mobilization of the formerly disenfranchised.

Whatever emerges, Thailand offers insights for theoretical debate on political legitimacy. Often in any political context there are multiple sources of legitimacy, and governments are hardly ever purely legitimate or illegitimate. Often, a partial legitimacy depends on how well political actors can muster support from a variety of sources. Modern and traditional sources of legitimization may coexist despite considerable tension. Such coexistence is quite typical of transitional societies. The question is to what extent there is, as the literature hints but is far from proving, a uniform transformative path toward a universal set of modern legitimizing principles.

The Thai case also underscores the critical role of social actors in the construction of legitimacy. As the role of the "masses" in the political process has increased in Thailand, the relation between rulers and ruled is increasingly dynamic. The role of social actors in value formation, for instance, when global ideas are adapted to the local context, is not well understood. Thailand is also a vivid reminder that a legitimate political order depends on not only shared values but also accommodation of different social actors. It thus draws attention to the role of agency in legitimacy, an aspect that—apart from the traditional focus on leadership types—has rarely been considered.

Finally, a focus on social actors clarifies the critical relationship between legitimacy and struggles over political power. Moving beyond cultural values, the Thai case makes a compelling argument for anchoring the analysis of legitimacy within social struggles over access to power. It urges us to go beyond descriptions of contemporary crisis to look for historical patterns.

The Thai case is rich in ideas for theoretical and empirical investigation. With the monarchical succession looming and little indication that political calm will soon return, daunting political legitimacy issues will remain central to an understanding of contemporary Thai politics. How Thailand emerges from its current crisis will be of importance well beyond its borders.

Notes

Björn Dressel is a Senior Lecturer at the Crawford School of Economics & Government at the Australian National University (ANU). Research for this chapter was supported by the Australian Research Council (ARC) Centre of Excellence in Policing and Security (CEPS).

1. Examples include celebrations of the Bangkok bicentenary (1982); the Sukothai kings' legendary invention of the alphabet (1983); longest reign of any living monarch (1992); the Diamond jubilee of his accession to the throne (2006); and the year-long celebration of the eightieth birthday (2007).
2. See, for instance, Borwornsak Uwanno's three-part series in defense of lèse majesté in the *Bangkok Post* (April 7–9, 2009)
3. Art. 23 (II) in the 2007 constitution was recently changed to allow a female royal to ascend to the throne.
4. See, for a good summary of events, Ukrist Pathmanand "Nation, Religion and Monarchy in the Fight against Thaksin," *Prachathai*, August 13, 2008.
5. The Thai concept of the "nation" is so semantically challenging that this section is probably not doing justice to it. Thongchai Winichakul (1994) gives a good overview.
6. The only exception is 1958–1967 under Sarit, which saw the effective abrogation of the constitution and rule by a barebones "interim constitution" (B.E. 2502).
7. See Thaksin's comment: "I am confident that politics are quiet nowadays because people are happy with the work of the Thai Rak Thai Party. I check the feeling of the people all the time" (Speech, 28 December 2003), quoted in Pasuk and Baker (2005, 170).

References

Alagappa, Muthiah. 1995. "The Bases of Legitimacy" In Political Legitimacy in Southeast Asia, *East-West Center Series on Contemporary Issues in Asia and the Pacific*, edited by Muthiah Alagappa, 31–53. Stanford: Stanford University Press.

Amon Chantharasombun. 1994. *Khonstitichanaelism thang ok khong prathet thai* [Constitutionalism: Way out for Thailand]. Bangkok: Public Policy Institute.

Anderson, Bendict. 1983. *Imagined Communities: Reflections on the Origin and Spread of Nationalism*. London: Verso.

Anek Laothamatas. 1996. "A Tale of Two Democracies: Conflicting Perceptions of Elections and Democracy in Thailand." In *The Politics of Election in Southeast Asia*, edited by R. H. Taylor, 201–223. New York: Cambridge University Press.

Baker, Christopher John, and Phongpaichit Pasuk. 2005. *A History of Thailand*. New York: Cambridge University Press.

Barker, Rodney. 1990. *Political Legitimacy and the State*. Oxford: Clarendon Press.

Barmé, Scot. 1993. *Luang Wichit Wathakan and the Creation of a Thai Identity*. Singapore: Institute of Southeast Asian Studies.

Borwornsak Uwanno, and Wayne D. Burns. 1998. "The Thai Constitution of 1997: Sources and Process." *University of British Columbia Law Review* 32: 227–247.

Chai-Anan Samudavanija. 2002. *State Building, Democracy and Globalization*. Bangkok:Institute for Public Studies (IPPS)

Brown, A. J. 1983. "Awakening the Wild Tigers (An Annotated Translation with Introduction)." B.A. Honours Thesis., Canberra.

Coedes, George. 1968. *The Indianized States of Southeast Asia*. Translated by S. B. Cowing. Honolulu: East West Center Press.

Connors, Michael Kelly. 2002. "Framing the 'People's Constitution.'" In *Reforming Thai Politics*, edited by D. McCargo, 37–55. Copenhagen: NIAS.

———. 2008. "Article of Faith: The Failure of Royal Liberalism in Thailand." *Journal of Contemporary Asia* 38 (1): 143–165.

Dressel, Björn. 2005. "Strengthening Governance Through Constitutional Reform." *ADB Governance Brief* 13: 1–4.

———. 2009. "Thailand's Elusive Quest for a Constitutional Equilibrium, *1997–2007*." *Contemporary Southeast Asia* 31: 296–325.

Englehart, Neil A. 2003. "Democracy and the Thai Middle Class." *Asian Survey* 43: 253–279.

Gawin Chutima. 1990. "The Rise and Fall of the Communist Party of Thailand (1973–1987)." *Occasional Paper 12*, University of Kent at Kenterbury, Centre of South-East Asian Studies.

Ginsburg, Tom. 2009. "Constitutional Afterlife: The Continuing Impact of Thailand's Postpolitical Constitution." *International Journal of Constitutional Law* 7: 83–105.

Girling, John L. 1981. *Thailand: Society and Politics*. Ithaca: Cornell University Press.

Glassman, Jim. 2004. "Economic 'Nationalism' in a Post-Nationalist Era: The Political Economy of Economic Policy in Post-Crisis Thailand." *Critical Asian Studies* 36: 37–64.

Gohlert, Ernst W. 1991. *Power and Culture: The Struggle against Poverty in Thailand*. Bangkok: White Lotus.

Handley, Paul. 2006. *The King Never Smiles: A Biography of Thailand's Bhumipol Adulyadej*. New Haven: Yale University Press.

Harding, Andrew. 2001. "May There Be Virtue. New Asian Constitutionalism in Thailand." *Australian Journal of Asian Law* 3: 236–260.

Heine-Geldern, Robert G. 1956. *Conceptions of State and Kingship in Southeast Asia, Southeast Asia Data Paper, No. 18*. Ithaca: Cornell University.

Hewison, Kevin, ed. 1997. *Political Change in Thailand. Democracy and Participation*. London and New York: Routledge.

———. 2004. "Crafting Thailand's New Social Contract." *The Pacific Review* 17: 503–522.

———. 2007. "Constitutions, Regimes and Power in Thailand." *Democratization* 14: 928–945.

Hewison, Kevin, and Kengkij Kitirianglarp. 2010. "'Thai-Style Democracy':
The Royalist Struggle for Thailand's Politics." In *Saying the Unsayable:
Monarchy and Democracy in Thailand*, edited by Soren Ivarsson and Lotte
Isager, 179–202. Copenhagen: NIAS.

Hicken, Allen. 2001. "Parties, Policy and Patronage: Governance and Growth
in Thailand." In *Corruption: The Boom and Bust of East Asia*, edited by J. E.
L. Campos, 163–182. Quezon City: Ateneo de Manila Press.

Jackson, Peter A. 1999. "The Enchanting Spirit of Thai Capitalism: The
Cult of Luang Por Khoon and the Postmodernisation of Thai Buddhism."
Southeast Asian Research 7 (1): 5–60.

Kasian, Tejapira. 2002. "Post-Crisis Economic Impasse and Political Recovery
in Thailand: The Resurgence of Economic Nationalism." *Critical Asian
Studies* 34: 323–356.

———. 2006. "Toppling Thaksin." *New Left Review* 39: 5–37.

Keyes, Charles F. 1987. *Thailand. Buddhist Kingdom as Modern Nation-State*.
Boulder and London: Westview Press.

Klein, James R. 1998. "The Constitution of the Kingdom of Thailand, 1997:
A Blueprint for Participatory Democracy." *Working Papers Series*. Bangkok:
Asia Foundation.

Kobkua Suwannathat-Pian. 2003. *Kings, Country and Constitutions: Thailand's
Political Development 1932–2000*. Richmond: RoutledgeCurzon.

Kuhonta, Alex Martinez. 2008. "The Paradox of Thailand's 1997 'People's
Constitution': Be Careful What You Wish For." *Asian Survey* 48:
373–392.

McCargo, Duncan. 1998. "Alternative Meanings of Political Reform in
Contemporary Thailand." *The Copenhagen Journal of Asian Studies* 13:
5–30.

———. 2002a. "Democracy under Stress in Thaksin's Thailand." *Journal of
Democracy* 13: 112–126.

———. 2002b. "Introduction: Understanding Political Reform in Thailand." In
Reforming Thai Politics, edited by D. McCargo, 1-18. Copenhagen: NIAS.

———, ed. 2002c. *Reforming Thai Politics*. Copenhagen: NIAS.

———. 2003. "Balancing the Checks: Thailand's Paralysed Politics Post
1997." *Journal of East Asian Studies* 3: 129–152.

———. 2005. "Network Monarchy and Legitimacy Crisis in Thailand."
The Pacific Review 18: 499–518.

———. 2008. "Thailand. State of Anxiety." In *Southeast Asian Affairs 2008*,
edited by D. Singh and L. C. Salazar, 332–356. Singapore: Institute of
South East Asian Studies.

McCargo, Duncan, and Ukrist Pathmanand. 2005. *The Thaksinization of
Thailand*. Copenhagen: NIAS.

McVey, Ruth, ed. 2000. *Money and Power in Provincial Thailand*. Chiang Mai:
Silkworm Books.

Morell, David, and Chai-Anan Samudavaija. 1981. *Political Conflict in Thailand:
Reform, Reaction, Revolution*. Cambridge, MA: Oelgeschlager, Gunn, Hain.

Muscat, Robert J. 1994. *The Fifth Tiger: A Study of Thai Development Policy.* Armonk, NY: United Nations University Press; M.E. Sharpe.

Ockey, James. 1994. "Political Parties, Factions and Corruption in Thailand." *Modern Asian Studies* 28: 251–277.

Pasuk, Phongpaichit, and Chris Baker. 1998. *Thailand's Boom and Bust.* Chiang Mai: Silkworm Books.

———. 2002. *Thailand: Economy and Politics,* 2nd ed. Kuala Lumpur: Oxford University Press.

———. 2004. *Thaksin. The Business of Politics in Thailand.* Bangkok: Silkworm Books.

———. 2005. "'Business Populism' in Thailand." *Journal of Democracy* 16: 58–72.

———. 2008. "Thaksin's Populism." *Journal of Contemporary Asia* 38: 62–83.

Pasuk, Phongpaichit, and Sungsidh Piriyarangsan. 1996. *Corruption and Democracy in Thailand.* Chiang Mai: Silkworm Books.

Prawes, Wasi. 1995. *Political Reform: The Way out for Thailand.* Bangkok: Mo Chao Ban.

Pridi Banomyong. 2000. *Pridi by Pridi: Selected Writings on Life, Politics, and Economy.* Translated by Chris Baker and Pasuk Phongpaichit. Chiang Mai: Silkworm Books.

Prince Dhani Nivat. 1947. "The Old Siamese Conception of the Monarchy." *Journal of the Siam Society* 36 (2): 91–106.

Prudhisan Jumbala. 1992. *Nation-Building and Democratization in Thailand: A Political History.* Bangkok: Chulalongkorn University Social Research Institute.

Riggs, F. 1966. *Thailand: The Modernization of a Bureaucratic Policy.* Honolulu: East-West Center.

Saitip Sukatipan. 1995. "Thailand: The Evolution of Legitimacy." In *Political Legitimacy in Southeast Asia. The Quest for Moral Authority,* edited by M. Alagappa, 193–223. Stanford: Stanford University Press.

Skilling, Peter. 2007. "King, Sangha and Brahmans: Ideology, Ritual, and Power in Pre-modern Siam." In *Buddhism, Power and Political Order,* edited by I. Harris, 182–215. London: Routledge.

Somboon Suksamran. 1977. *Political Buddhism in Southeast Asia: The Role of the Sangha in the Modernization of Thailand.* London: Palgrave Macmillan

———. 1993a. *Buddhism and Political Legitimacy.* Bangkok: Research Dissemination Project, Research Affairs, Chulalongkorn University.

———. 1993b. "Buddhism, Political Authority, and Legitimacy in Thailand and Cambodia." In *Buddhist Trends in Southeast Asia,* edited by T. Ling, 101–144. Singapore: Institute of South East Asian Studies.

Somkiat Wanthana. 1986. "The Politics of Modern Thai Historiography." PhD diss., Monash University.

Tambiah, Stanley Jejaraya. 1976. *World Conqueror and World Renouncer: A Study of Buddhism and Polity in Thailand against a Historical Background.* Cambridge: Cambridge University Press.

Thak, Chaloemtiarana. 2007. *Thailand. The Politics of Despotic Paternalism*. Chiang Mai: Silkworm Books.

Thamsook, Numnonda. 1978. "Pibulsongkram's Thai Nation-Building Programme during the Japanese Military Presence, 1941–1945." *Journal of Southeast Asian Studies* 9: 233–252.

Thitinan, Pongsudhirak. 2003. "Thailand. Democratic Authoritarianism." *Southeast Asian Affairs*: 275–290.

Thompson, Mark R. 2007. "The Dialectic of "Good Governance" and Democracy in Southeast Asia: Globalized Discourses and Local Responses." *Globalities Studies Journal* 10: 1–19.

Thompson, V. 1941. *Thailand: The New Siam*. New York: Macmillan.

Thongchai, Winichakul. 1994. *Siam Mapped: A History of the Geo-body of a Nation*. Honolulu: University of Hawaii Press.

Vella, Walter F. 1978. *Chaiyo: King Vajiravudh and the Development of Thai Nationalism*. Honolulu: University Press of Hawaii.

Warr, Peter G., and Bhanupong Nidhiprabha. 1996. *Thailand's Macroeconomic Miracle. Stable Adjustment and Sustained Growth*. Washington, DC; Kuala Lumpur: World Bank; Oxford University Press.

Yano, Toru. 1978. "Political Structures of a 'Rice-Growing State'." In *Thailand: A Rice-Growing Society*, edited by Y. Ishii, 115–158. Kyoto: Centre for Southwest Asian Studies.

CHAPTER 5

Political Legitimacy in Indonesia: Islam, Democracy, and Good Governance

Greg Barton

The success of Indonesia's democratic transition has implications that go well beyond Southeast Asia. President
Suharto's abrupt resignation in May 1998 opened the way
not only for democracy but also for Islamist politics, after four decades of
authoritarian suppression of political Islam. The elections of 1999, 2004,
and 2009 have allowed voters in the world's largest Muslim nation to
respond to Islamist claims that political legitimacy can only be found in
religious politics and an Islamic state. Consequently, the push for democratic reform in the Middle East has observers looking to Indonesia for
evidence that Islam and secular democracy are compatible.

A striking feature of the reformist protests that swept the Middle
East and Northern Africa in early 2011 was their secular nature. The
calls for political transformation in the heartland of the Muslim world
were couched in the universally familiar language of freedom of expression, freedom from oppression, social justice, and democracy. Even in
Egypt, where for decades the only movement of dissent organized on
a massive scale has been that of the Muslim Brotherhood, the protests
that toppled Mubarak's 30-year-strong authoritarian regime had little
to say about religion.

The Islamic exceptionalism of Brotherhood-style Islamism, with its
distinctive theocratic rhetoric of Islamic law (*sharia*) and Islamic state
was conspicuous by its absence in every country where protests took
place. There was no evidence of a "clash of civilizations" (Huntington
1993, 1996). The justification of authoritarianism by Mubarak and his
fellow tyrants as being a necessary bulwark against illiberal religious

fundamentalism look contrived and implausible in the face of the same sort of secular calls for democratic reform that had been seen earlier in Eastern Europe and Asia.

But the question remains, especially in Egypt, about what sort of democracy the hard-won free and fair elections will deliver. Middle-class-led protest movements are one thing but open democracy is another thing entirely. Secular democracy and Islam are widely believed to be antithetical. By themselves, it is argued, either secularism or democracy might be accommodated in Muslim majority states, but not both together. In as much as democracy exposes the limits of legitimacy for regimes, ideologies, and political movements it is assumed that secularism lacks sufficient popular support to survive without the protection of authoritarian rule. In the short-term the Brotherhood is likely to do well in a democratic Egypt. It will take years before the nature of Egyptian democracy becomes clear but some insight can be found in the experience of another large Muslim nation that threw off three decades of military-backed authoritarian rule.

Post-Suharto Indonesia now stands alongside modern Turkey as a leading example of successful secular democracy in a Muslim majority state. Given the long-contested place of Islam in the Indonesian republic, the failure of the Islamist parties to effectively challenge the legitimacy of the popular secular parties suggests that for the vast majority of Indonesian Muslims secular democracy and Islam are absolutely compatible.

Democratic Transition

Not that many years ago, conversations about Indonesia's future were marked by anxiety and uncertainty. It seemed unlikely that the generals would retreat from power, the economy looked as if it might never return to the levels of growth that up until the Asian Financial Crisis had been lifting the burgeoning population of the world's fourth largest nation out of poverty, and Indonesia's modest middle class and limited civil society suggested there was little chance of achieving a full transition to liberal democracy. Only a decade ago, the Indonesia of today would have represented a best-case scenario that would take decades, if ever, to achieve. Certainly, no one could have predicted that in 2009 Southeast Asia would have one successful democratic nation marked by political openness, social stability, and steady economic growth—and that that nation would be Indonesia. Beginning with a peaceful transition from Suharto to Habibie and a surprisingly reformist interim presidency, together with a surprisingly quick and clean withdrawal of the military from politics, the last dozen years have delivered outcomes that we would not have dared to expect in May 1998. Remarkably peaceful and successful free and fair elections in 1999 were followed by the election of Abdurrahman Wahid. The transition from the reformist but beleaguered Wahid presidency to the Megawati presidency was peaceful and unproblematic. Another successful legislative election and the direct election of President Susilo Bambang Yudhoyono in 2004, followed by successful regional elections, a surprisingly rapid resolution to the crisis in Aceh, and years of solid economic growth saw Indonesia finally become a stable democracy. The uneventful elections of 2009 endorsed Yudhoyono's style of secular nationalism, disappointed his Islamist rivals and generally confirmed secular democracy, along with economic development and good governance, as source of political legitimacy (Barton 2008).

Indonesia's successful transition to democracy calls into question earlier assessments of the capacity of civil society in Indonesia and draws attention to the generally positive and substantial contribution of Islamic leaders and Islamic civil society movements to reform and democratization. One of the reasons that observers were fearful about what would follow the inevitable conclusion of the authoritarian Suharto regime was that Indonesia was thought to have a middle class too small, and a civil society too limited, to successfully underwrite transition to democracy. It was widely felt that social upheaval and widespread violence would follow the end of the Suharto regime and that true democracy would not be established on an enduring basis. The reasons why these expectations proved wrong are complex and varied, and as such are highly debatable. But one thing that does seem clear is that Indonesian civil society achieved much more than what was expected partly because the involvement of religious leaders and religious mass organizations such as *Muhammadiyah* and *Nahdlatul Ulama* (NU) effectively acted to give Indonesia a stronger and more extensive civil society than its limited middle class could otherwise have produced (Hefner 1997, 2000, 2005). Certainly, when it comes to reckoning with the individual contributions of religious leaders such as former NU leader Abdurrahman Wahid and former *Muhammadiyah* leader Amien Rais it is the Islamic leaders in particular who stand out as the champions of reform. It was Wahid and like-minded civil society colleagues who for more than a decade had challenged the authoritarian excesses of the Suharto regime and in its final years had channeled broad social coalitions to push for reform (Barton 2002). None of this would likely have resulted in substantial change were it not, of course, for the financial crisis of 1997. But without this leadership and the burgeoning groundswell of social support for reform it is just as likely that Suharto would have weathered the storm and not resigned. It is of more than just symbolic consequence that the leaders who went into the palace to speak to the president in his final days in office represented Indonesia's foremost Islamic leaders, led by Nurcholish Madjid, acting not in the name of Islam per se but rather in the name of democracy and reform.

It is not possible to make a quantitative assessment of the contribution made by Islam, Islamic leaders, Islamic movements, and Islamic ideas to the peaceful transition that followed Suharto's resignation and to the positive channeling of communal (and potentially sectarian) energies through the formation of political parties and the support of those parties in a remarkably peaceful fashion in the July 1999 elections. Nevertheless, there is considerable evidence for arguing that Islamic leaders, movements, and ideas played an important role in ensuring that Indonesia's transition to democracy was as peaceful and as consequential as it turned out to be. The world's largest Muslim country, despite misinformed views to the contrary, is as "Islamic" as any other country in the Middle East or Asia (Hassan 2008). The leaders who succeeded Suharto—Habibie and Wahid—who might best be seen as transitional presidents were well-known for their earlier leadership of Islamic organizations. Although eccentric and unconventional they pushed through important reforms and raised expectations of what democratic government should look like in Indonesia, upholding secular principles while allowing competing religious claims to be marketed to voters.

One of the great question marks hanging over Indonesia's transition to democracy was whether it would be able to channel religious sentiment into the political process in an orderly fashion or whether it would become victim to rampant expectations and youthful idealism expressed in an excessively radical and nonconstructive fashion. After all, in recent decades it has become clear across the Muslim world that radical Islamism represents one of the most effective, therefore, attractive, avenues for channeling dissent.

As was discussed above, it is widely expected that the Muslim Brotherhood will be a powerful political force in post-Mubarak Egypt, at least in the short-run. The situation in Suharto Indonesia was always very different and from the beginning there was never any doubt that a plethora of different political interests and parties could expect to do well. And, indeed, the results of the elections of 1999, 2004, and 2009 showed the capacity of Indonesia's nascent democracy to effectively channel competing interests in an orderly and balanced fashion.

Each of the three parliamentary elections held in 1999, 2004, and 2009 were remarkably peaceful and orderly, despite the challenges of reaching 170 million voters spread across an archipelagic developing nation as wide as continental United States. All of the large parties made reference to Islam in their campaigns, some Islamic parties appealed primarily to observant Muslims but campaigned on secular principles and some other Islamist parties campaigned for application of *sharia* and the (eventual) achieving of an Islamic state. The Islamist parties, all of which are modeled on the Egyptian Muslim Brotherhood, enjoyed their newfound freedoms but ultimately failed to live up to their own aspirations of achieving broad support as it became clear that 9 out of 10 voters do not find radical Islamism attractive enough to vote for.

This is a very significant outcome because the secular character of the state remained the central unresolved issue regarding political legitimacy in the nationalist movement and during the period of parliamentary democracy in the 1950s. This issue reemerged in the wake of the collapse of the Suharto regime in 1998. It was unclear whether secular democracy had sufficiently broad support in the world's largest Muslim majority country to ensure the legitimacy of both the secular state and the elected government or whether Western-style secular democracy needed to evolve into a more uniquely Islamic form of democracy to achieve enduring legitimacy. Engaging with this issue requires examining the development of Islamism in Indonesia and then analyzing the nature of secularism and the level of support that it finds amongst political parties and voters in Indonesia today. The results of the post-Suharto elections in 1999, 2004, and 2009 are central to this discussion but they need to be read in the context of the past 80 years.

Indonesia has successfully contained a major terrorist threat through impressive police actions and open judicial processes, achieved sustained economic growth rates in excess of 6%, and steadily advanced a series of reforms supporting health and education and, with the exception of Papua, largely resolved separatist tensions in its Western and Eastern extremities. It seems reasonable to argue that Indonesia has now reached a point where it can be said to have successfully completed a democratic transition and demonstrated that large Muslim societies can reconcile Islam and secular democracy.

Before going any further, however, it is necessary to define the concept of the secular state. One of the most significant recent works by an

Islamic intellectual on this topic is *Islam and the Secular State: Negotiating the Future of Sharia* by Abdullahi Ahmed An-Na'im, a Sudanese trained scholar of classical Islamic jurisprudence and professor of law at Emory University (2008). An-Na'im's confidence in the deep compatibility of Islam and democracy is increasingly shared by scholars of Islam within and without the Muslim community.

An-Na'im begins his book with an elegantly simple definition of a secular state, and it is the one that will be used in this chapter.

> In order to be a Muslim by conviction and free choice, which is the only way one can be a Muslim, I need a secular state. By a secular state I mean one that is neutral regarding religious doctrine, one that does not claim or pretend to enforce sharia—the religious law of Islam—simply because compliance with *sharia* cannot be coerced by fear of state institutions or faked to please their officials. This is what I mean by secularism in this book, namely, a secular state that facilitates the possibility of religious piety out of honest conviction. (2008, 1)

In other words, An-Na'im defines a secular state as one in which the state is involved with neither the interpretation nor enforcement of belief and piety, leaving these matters to individual conviction. In principle this seems clear but in practice the boundaries between piety and legality will inevitably be contested in areas such as family law. Nevertheless, the principle of the state not entering into the policing of morals (beyond enforcing the law and thereby protecting the rights of others) and the interpretation and enforcement of religious practice is clear and, in general, political parties in Muslim majority nations fall into two camps: those that accept and support the principle of secularity and those that contest and reject it. By this measure, French or Turkish laïcité goes well beyond what is required (and perhaps desired) in a secular state, as does even the U.S. practice of not recognizing religious holidays. And the existence of a state church, such as occurs in England, Germany, and Scandinavia, does not, in itself, jeopardize the secular character of the state. But prohibiting or penalizing proselytism and conversion, or enforcing fasting, such as occurs in many Muslim majority nations, including nations as modern and cosmopolitan as Malaysia, does diminish the secular character of the state.

A year after the publication of An-Naim's *Islam and the Secular State*, another seminal work on the topic by a Muslim writer was published by a leading academic press. Nader Hashemi's *Islam, Secularism, and Liberal Democracy* (2009) is informed by a deep understanding of the historical development of secular democracy in Europe. Hashemi takes a long-term historical perspective on the development of secularism and liberal democracy. He begins by exploring the experience of the English Puritans in the sixteenth and seventeenth centuries to understand the circumstances that shaped John Locke's bold writing on secularism.

Hashemi sets out clear grounds for confidence that Muslim societies will find their own ways to reconcile religion and secular democracy. He argues that "in societies where religion is a marker of identity, the road to liberal democracy, whatever other twists and turns it makes, cannot avoid passing through the gates of religious politics." He explains that "in order for secularism to survive over the long term as a key political principle and value of liberal democratic politics, it must develop strong intellectual roots from within society in order to survive." In other words, he believes that exact forms of democracy and secularism need to be developed from within individual Muslim societies and that Islamic intellectuals need to develop Islamic arguments to support both if they are to find legitimacy. Significantly, he concludes his book by examining the evidence that this is possible in the recent experiences of Turkey and Indonesia.

Pancasila and the Struggle to Create a Nonsectarian State

In the days before the declaration of Independence in August 1945 there had been considerable dissent regarding whether Indonesia should be declared to be an Islamic state or not. In their rush to be ready with their declaration of independence and make preparations to resist the returning Dutch forces, the nationalists quickly put together a draft constitution intended to be a stopgap measure until there was time to draft a more complete constitution. (It would take more than four years of militia resistance before the Dutch succumbed to both nationalist pressure and international condemnation to allow their former colony to become free at the end of 1949.) In the end the argument came down to a single sentence that formed the preamble to the 1945 constitution.

The basic political philosophy of the new nation had already been drafted in the form of five precepts—*pancasila* in Sanskrit, echoing the five precepts of Buddhism—intended to provide a basic political philosophy for the new nation. Sukarno had introduced a preliminary draft on June 1, 1945, in a speech to the Independence Preparatory Committee entitled "The Birth of Pancasila." Sukarno and his coauthors intended *Pancasila* to be understood as a nonsectarian affirmation of religious values in a secular framework (An-Na'im 2008, 258–266; Baso 2005).

The final form of *Pancasila* was developed by a committee of nine nationalist leaders and presented in the preamble to the 1945 constitution in a text known as the Jakarta Charter (*Piagam Jakarta*, Hosen 2007, 60–80). The first precept spoke of belief in the one true God and, in the eyes of its drafters, established the basis for theistic secularism. The remaining precepts, which spoke of "just and civilized humanity," "the unity of Indonesia," "consultative democracy," and "social justice for the entirety of Indonesian society" were seen to couch the concerns of both religious and secular nationalists in a common language. In the face of strong criticism from largely modernist Islamist leaders it was agreed that the first *sila* would read: "belief in God with the obligation of adherents of Islam to live according to Islamic law" (*Ketuhanan dengan kewajiban menjalankan syariah Islam bagi pemeluk-pemeluknya*) (Boland 1971, 25–26).

This statement, which became known as the "seven words" of the Jakarta Charter, was deliberately ambiguous. It was by no means clear what authority it would endow the state with to intervene in private religious practice. Even so, some of the senior nationalists, including NU's Wahid Hasyim who was one of the nine codrafters, became anxious that including these words would suggest moving in the direction of becoming an Islamic state. On August 18, the wording of the first *sila* was changed to "belief in the One true God" and the reference to *syariah* dropped. Masyumi leader Isa Anshary loudly protested that the dropping of these seven words in the Jakarta Charter represented "a 'magic trick'…an embezzlement against the Muslims" (Nasution 1992, 106).

In December 1949, after four years of skirmishing with nationalist militia and facing international condemnation, the Dutch finally gave up their colonial claims on the East Indies. In 1950 the nationalists adopted a new constitution based on parliamentary democracy and established a series of parliamentary governments in preparation for the time when national elections could be held. Initially, the traditionalists and the modernists cooperated together within Masyumi and it appeared as if this single Islamic party had the potential to achieve a majority in a future elected parliament. It did not take long, though, for cultural and social tensions between the urban and sophisticated modernists and the largely rural and rusticated traditionalists to rupture the relationship. The traditionalists, most of whom were associated with NU, felt that the modernists, the majority of whom were linked to *Muhammadiyah*, were not giving them a fair and equal access to key cabinet positions and other offices. As a result in 1952, NU withdrew from Masyumi and went on to contest the 1955 elections as an independent party.

Muhammadiyah was founded in Yogyakarta in 1912 and quickly established itself within the circles of Java's burgeoning petite-bourgeois (Boland 1971; Eliraz 2004; Latif 2008; Nakamura 1983; Woodward 1989). The traditionalist *ulama*—those who by definition had not joined *Muhammadiyah*, and relatively few *ulama* did—admired many aspects of *Muhammadiyah* and could see that its modern system of organization and association gave it the potential to continue growing unimpeded. They were particularly worried, however, by one aspect of the new culture being produced by *Muhammadiyah* and that was the rejection of Sufism and with it a rejection of traditional scholarship. Their fear was that in time traditionalist *madrasah* would diminish in numbers and would be replaced by *Muhammadiyah madrasah*, that, although admirable in many respects for their modern secular education, would fail to train up future generations of Indonesians to become Islamic scholars and at the same time would turn students away from the *Sufi* teachings and practices at the heart of traditionalist Islam. It was for this reason that senior *ulama* came together in January 1926 and formed a group that they called *Nahdlatul Ulama*: the Awakening of the Ulama.

The 1955 elections saw the vast majority of votes, around 80%, split almost evenly among four large parties that neatly drew on contrasting lines of communal affiliation. The largest bloc of votes, 22%, went to PNI (Partai Nasional Indonesia), the Indonesian Nationalist Party; the next largest bloc of votes, 21%, was secured by Masyumi, followed not too far behind by *Nahdlatul Ulama* with 18% and PKI (Partai Komunis Indonesia), the Indonesian Communist Party, with 16% of the votes.

In the wake of these parliamentary elections separate elections were held in December 1955 to elect a 514-member *Konstituante*, or Constitutional Assembly, to hammer out the details of a new permanent constitution. Under the authority of the 1950 Parliamentary Constitution the office of president, held by Sukarno, had limited authority (Legge 2003, 268–308). The Parliamentary committee convened in November 1956 and met throughout the remainder of that year through most of 1957 and 1958, and the first half of 1959, making reasonable progress but still being unable to agree on the final form of constitution. The major stumbling block to agreement had to do with the nature of the Indonesian state and the role of Islam. Voting was held on May 30 and June 1 and 2 to approve the inclusion of the Jakarta Charter in the preamble to the new constitution. NU voted against the proposal and the vote achieved only 56% support, well short of the two-thirds majority required. The *Konstituante* went into recess and never met again. On July 9, 1959, Sukarno issued a presidential decree permanently dissolving the *Konstituante* and declaring a return to the 1945 constitution. The tensions that erupted at the time of the declaration of independence in August 1945 continued to bedevil the new nation a dozen years later.

In 1958, when Sukarno was out of the country, some of the Masyumi leaders, including the locally born Natsir, gathered in the West Sumatran capital of Padang, where *Muhammadiyah* and Islamist ideas had a strong following, in what was seen to be a show of support for the West Sumatran PRRI (Pemerintah Revolusioner Republik Indonesia) separatist movement. The PRRI rebellion, one of a series of small rebellions initiated by mid-ranking military officers in the late 1950s, commenced on February 15, 1958, when Lieutenant Colonel Ahmad Hussein announced the formation of the Revolutionary Government of the Republic of Indonesia in Padang. Despite covert assistance from the CIA the PRRI rebellion quickly faltered and by August forces under the direct control of Army Chief of Staff General Nasution had regained control over all of the rebel areas. The Masyumi leaders seen to be associated with the PRRI rebellion were regarded as traitors by Sukarno and the incident contributed to his growing impatience with Islamist brinksmanship in the *Konstituante*.

Part of the reason that Sukarno and other leaders were so concerned about the PRRI movement was that it came at a time when the new nation was locked in a bitter struggle with radical Islamist separatists in West Java and Southern Sulawesi. These rebellions had begun as reactionary protests by disgruntled militia leaders active in the revolutionary struggle against the Dutch who were upset with the fact that their militias were not offered a place in the new national army. Seizing on disaffection with the dropping of the Jakarta Charter the charismatic Kartosuwiryo, a former rival of Sukarno in the protonationalist Sarekat Islam, in 1948 declared West Java to be *Darul Islam*—the domain of Islam—and claimed to be fighting for the establishment of an Islamic State of Indonesia (Negara Islam Indonesia [NII]). When Kartosuwiryo was apprehended in 1962 and executed it was assumed that the *Darul Islam*/NII was finished. In fact, the movement's resilient social networks have remained intact until the present time and in the late 1980s and early 1990s the movement gave birth to the terrorist group Jemaah Islamiyah (Barton 2004).

Muhammad Natsir and his colleagues did not see themselves as treasonous rebels but rather as loyal nationalists and democrats. They feared rising communist influence in Indonesia both in the PKI and in the president himself. In October 1956 Sukarno had made a state visit to the People's Republic of China where he praised the communists for their achievements in developing China. Inspired by the strong leadership of Chairman Mao and his apparent success in transforming his impoverished nation Sukarno returned home speaking of the need for a new form of strong executive government in Indonesia replacing the chaos of multiparty parliamentary rule. Most parliamentarians were alarmed by this talk but the PKI, and later the PNI, came out in support of the president while Masyumi declared their opposition to the proposal of a weakened legislature and a "mutual cooperation" cabinet under the control of an un-elected National Council.

In March 1957, with Nasution's blessing, Sukarno declared martial law. In April he established a nonparty-political Working Cabinet and in May he pressed ahead with his plan to set up a National Council. In December 1957, in the wake of Dutch intransigence over their remaining colony of West Irian, Sukarno began nationalizing Dutch businesses and handing them over to the control of the Indonesian military.

When Lieutenant Colonel Hussein declared PRRI control of West Sumatra in February 1958, one year after the Permesta rebellion had broken out in Manado, in the predominately Protestant Christian province of North Sulawesi, he had the support of not just the Masyumi leaders but also a considerable array of domestic and international sympathizers. The rebellions were relatively easily put down, especially after the shooting down and capture of CIA agent and pilot Allen Pope in May 1958, and the subsequent exposure of the scale of CIA backing for the rebels forced the United States to withdraw its support (Brichoux and Gerner 2002).

With the *Konstituante* disbanded in July 1959, and the 1945 constitution decreed to replace the 1950 constitution, Sukarno used his heightened executive powers to formally ban Masyumi in January 1960. Sukarno worked to ensure that the Islamists, who had come to dominate Masyumi, played no further role in formal politics throughout the remainder of his presidency.

Sukarno and his Guided Democracy regime triumphed over their critics on the religious and political right but it was a hollow and ultimately unsustainable victory. Tensions between the left and right wings of an increasingly polarized society, the collapse of the economy, and Sukarno's inflammatory rhetoric, together with reckless political gambles such as the Konfrontasi campaign against Malaysian Borneo starting in 1962, left the nation sliding toward disaster.

Islam and Politics under Suharto

The bloody transition from the Sukarno (Old Order) regime to the Suharto (New Order) regime that began in October 1965 with the involvement of the CIA saw a pogrom against members of the Indonesian Communist Party in which hundreds of thousands were killed—many at the hands of *Muhammadiyah* and *Nahdlatul Ulama* communities who justified their action on the grounds that if they did not eliminate the Communists the Communists would eliminate them (Cribb 2001).

Natsir and his fellow Masyumi leaders were hopeful of being politically rehabilitated and playing a role of significance in the new regime. They were to be sorely disappointed. Having rid himself of an enemy on the left, in the form of Communism and the PKI, Suharto was not about to cede ground to an enemy on the right, in the form of radical Islamism and a resurrected Masyumi.

In the 1950s Natsir was regarded as a relatively moderate and sophisticated thinker. At the time of the 1955 election, Islamist political ideology was only just beginning to reach its modern form. Natsir and the others within Masyumi who were in clear support of the Jakarta charter and Indonesia being formed as an Islamic state were influenced both by the ideas of Maududi in South Asia and more directly by the Muslim brotherhood in Egypt, which itself had taken on many of Maududi's ideas.

It was not clear in the 1950s what proportion of Masyumi leaders and followers supported the idea of an Islamic state but it was clear that the idea had stronger support within Masyumi than within NU. In the 1971 election, despite the thwarting of an attempt to resurrect Masyumi in the form of a new party named Parmusi, it was clear that political Islam was still a major force within Indonesia. The 1971 election, the first since 1955, was neither free nor fair but it was sufficiently open that the Suharto regime was able to gain a clear sense of public sentiment. Suharto's new party, Golkar, achieved a solid 62.8% of the vote, assisted considerably by the fact that all public servants and military personnel were required to support Golkar and knew that their choice was being monitored. This ate heavily into support for PNI whose vote dropped from 22.3% in 1955 to 6.9% in 1971. And Parmusi, whose leadership Suharto had stacked with compliant, low-profile figures unconnected with Natsir and other Masyumi leaders gained a mere 5.4% of the 1971 vote, barely more than one-quarter of the 20.9% achieved by Masyumi in 1955. Nevertheless, NU received 18.7% of the 1971 vote, neatly matching the 18.4% it obtained in 1955, helping bring the total support for Islamic parties in the 1971 election to 27.1%.

In 1973 the regime moved to consolidate the nine existing opposition parties into just two parties: the Democratic Party of Indonesia (Partai Demokrasi Indonesia [PDI]) and the United Development Party (Partai Persatuan Pembanguan [PPP]). The former was clearly intended to capture the secular nationalist vote, while the latter was meant to serve as a sop to Islamic interests. Neither party, however, was allowed to develop a strong ideological character beyond these general communal distinctions. Consequently, the United Development Party (PPP) was forbidden from adopting an Islamist platform of the kind that was associated with the Muslim brotherhood. Even so, support for the "Islamic vote" remained strong and in the next election in 1977 PPP achieved 29.3% of the vote, representing a slight increase compared with the 27.1% total achieved by the four Islamic parties contesting the 1971 elections. Support for Golkar remaining largely unchanged at 62.1%, leaving 8.6% for the Democratic Party of Indonesia (PDI).

Four further elections were held at five-yearly intervals by the Suharto regime. These elections were tightly controlled and were intended to produce a tame Legislature that would legitimize but not interfere with the regime. The 500 elected members of the Legislature were augmented by a further 500 appointed members to form a super parliament called the People's Consultant Assembly that met once every five years for the purpose of electing the president. As this assembly was only ever faced with a single candidate for the executive there was little sense of Indonesia functioning as a regular democracy. Suharto's legitimacy came not from this procedural mechanism but from the performance of his regime in delivering significant advances in development, particularly in the area of education and health during the first decades of his regime. Despite the clearly nondemocratic nature of the regime and its reliance upon the military to remain in power, the Suharto regime was, for the most part, a soft authoritarian regime. Although it was capable of significant malevolence toward dissenters, this never reached the level of more hard-line authoritarian regimes elsewhere in the developing world, save for the significant exceptions of periodic crackdowns on radical Islamists and left-leaning students, suppressing separatist movements at either end of the archipelago in Aceh and Papua, and the invasion of East Timor in 1975.

The more benign and positive aspects of the regime came in large measure through its engagement of technocratic expertise and five-year central planning. This was facilitated by the oil boom of the 1970s and revenue from this industry together with revenue from mining, forestry, and agriculture throughout the 1970s, 1980s, and 1990s. This, together with a low-wage manufacturing sector, attracted considerable foreign direct investment. Development remained highly centralized with Java, and in particular the national capital Jakarta, being much more intensively developed than the rest of the archipelago. By the 1990s demands for greater political freedom and freedom from human rights abuses grew steadily stronger. As the regime approached the end of its third decade the question of political transition and of what would replace the Suharto regime became a dominant theme within civil society discourse. There was no question that the vast majority of people aspired to the achievement of free and fair elections and the development of genuine democracy. This was true of Islamist elements as much as it was secular nationalist groups.

The second half of the Suharto era saw Indonesia come under much the same cultural influences that had swept across other parts of the Muslim world, leading to a revival of public interest in Islam and the development of a strong political critique of authoritarianism centered around the Islamist ideas of the Muslim Brotherhood. At the same time, however, many within NU and *Muhammadiyah* were drawn to a more progressive understanding of Islam that was in sharp tension with the Islamism of both the Arab Middle East and of South Asia. The *madrasah/pesantren* system associated with NU had undergone a steady process of reform that had seen most of the *madrasah* develop modern secular curricula that ran alongside classical Islamic studies curricula. At the same time the Department of Religious Affairs had developed increasingly credible state Islamic institutions (IAIN) designed to give *madrasah* graduates an opportunity for tertiary education that combined classical Islamic scholarship with modern social science disciplines. The best of these institutions (with those in Jakarta and Yogyakarta leading the way) produced a stream of bold and original young thinkers. This in turn helped produce a vibrant civil society sector around NU and *Muhammadiyah* and manifested itself in dozens of NGOs concerned with development, social justice, respect for human rights, and modern progressive understandings of Islam. This contributed to what became known as the Renewal of Islamic Thought (*Pembaruan Pemikiran Islam*) movement most closely associated with Nurcholish Madjid in urban modernist circles in the national capital and with Abdurrahman Wahid in traditionalist circles (Barton 1994, 1997a, 1997b; Madjid 1987).

In 1984 Abdurrahman and a group of like-minded reformers were elected to the leadership of NU and immediately withdrew NU office-holders from PPP, severing the formal NU-PPP alliance (Ramage 1995). These progressive Islamic thinkers contributed to the develop-ment of a well-articulated alternative to Islamism.

Post-Suharto Democracy and an Open Contestation of Ideas

When Suharto resigned suddenly in May 1998, and his deputy Habibie replaced him as interim president, it soon became clear that elections would be held the following year and that the restrictions on political par-ties that had prevailed for the last quarter of a century were tossed aside. By July 1998 a plethora of new parties had emerged. Despite his long articulated objection to the linking of politics and religion, Abdurrahman yielded to the desire of many within NU for the formation of the non-Islamist party that would represent more progressive interests. Similarly, within *Muhammadiyah* progressive elements worked to form a new party that would harness interest within *Muhammadiyah's* Islamic mass base for an Islamic but non-Islamist party representing urban Muslims. At the same time PPP was finally free to adopt an explicitly Islamist ideological platform, which it did. Significantly, however, PPP came to represent more a vehicle for socially conservative Muslims than for radical Islamist interests. In other words, PPP stood for the use of religious imagery and phraseology in its political discourse but not for a program that aspired to radically change the nature of the Indonesian state.

The three elections held so far during the post-Suharto period have been generally acknowledged to be free and fair, even if some of the mechanisms and procedures have been imperfect. Political parties have been free to campaign on whatever ideological basis they choose, Communism aside, and consequently it is much easier to discern the level of support for radical Islamist and moderate Islamist ideas along-side secular Islamic platforms and platforms that make only passing mention of Islam. Aside from small Christian and other minority par-ties all of the parties make some mention of Islam in their discourse but a clear distinction can be made between Islamist and non-Islamist par-ties appealing for the votes of observant Muslims and of other parties that can be broadly described as secular nationalist.

In these post-Suharto elections it is clear that only half of the obser-vant Muslim vote—if we can assume that this is what the total vote for Islamic parties represents—went to Islamist parties and that this support was further bifurcated between moderate and radical Islamist parties. Consequently, in 2009, radical Islamism can claim support from no more than 10% of Indonesian voters. This total is virtually the same as that achieved in 2004. At the same time support for moderate Islamism has declined significantly of the past decade. In 1999 PPP achieved 10.7% of the national vote. Support for PPP and its breakaway faction, PBR, fell slightly to 9.4% in 2004 and then slumped to 6.5% in 2009.

There is no question that Islam remains an important element in Indonesian politics. It also seems clear that radical Islamism continues to be a significant element. But its appeal is limited and unlikely to grow much beyond its current level. At the same time, attempts to pass a bill through the Legislature reflecting Islamist interests have met with very mixed results. The controversial so-called antipornography bill eventually passed but only after being substantially watered down. At the local level, a number of local governments passed *sharia* legislation in the earlier part of the decade, causing considerable concern at the time. But this phenomenon appears to have come to a natural end. It is significant that the local government areas in which these initiatives were being tried were on the whole not particularly religious. In other words, local application of *sharia* appears to have been driven largely by a desperate attempt to be seen to consolidate law and order in rough neighborhoods (Bush 2008; Salim and Azra 2003).

Indonesia: A Secular Democracy?

The results of the 10 national legislative assembly elections over the past 55 years, and in particular the 3 national elections held since the restoration of democracy following Suharto's resignation, are evidence of clear support for secular democracy in Indonesia. Not only have Indonesians consistently turned out to vote and otherwise given support to the idea that democratic elections are a primary element of political legitimacy they have also shown relatively little support for Islamism in general and radical Islamism in particular. This is significant because the most comprehensive and substantial critique of secular democracy in Indonesia comes from radical Islamist thought. Some of the radical Islamists associated with groups such as Jemaah Islamiyah, Hizb ut-Tahrir, and many of the other component parts of the Mujahidin Council of Indonesia (Majelis Mujahidin Indonesia [MMI]) declare themselves opposed in principle to both the secular nation-state and democracy. But these groups represent only a tiny fraction of Indonesian society. They can organize impressive mass rallies and other shows of force such as the 100,000-strong rally organized by Hizb ut-Tahrir in 2008 in Jakarta, but their absolute numbers remain small (Osman 2010)

A much larger group of radical Islamists are prepared to participate in the democratic process. There is some doubt as to whether the hard-core within PKS would continue to honor the principles of secular democracy if they were free to abuse them once in government but it is also clear that there is little support in Indonesian society for their position. The fact that they exist at all should not be interpreted as some grave flaw in Indonesian society that threatens democracy. After all, every democracy has an outlier group of voters prepared to support popularist parties with radical agenda.

Social polling suggest that many Indonesians feel some sympathy for the claims of radical Islamists but when it comes to casting their vote in regional and national elections they have overwhelmingly chosen secular parties over radical Islamist parties (Barton 2008). Nevertheless, although radical Islamists do not have sufficient public support to dominate Indonesian politics they do have considerable capacity to act in a spoiling role (Barton 2010). Islamist militia, like the notorious Islamic Defenders Front (Front Pembela Islam [FPI]) have exploited the freedoms of the post-Suharto period to violently harass less conservative Muslims and minority communities such as the small Ahmadiyah and Shia communities as well as Indonesia's larger Christian communities. A worrying synergistic resonance appears to be occurring between semiofficial bodies such as the Ulama Council of Indonesia (Majelis Ulama Indonesia [MUI]), PKS parliamentarians and members of cabinet, such as Minister for Religious Affairs Suryadharma Ali and militia such as FPI. In 2005 MUI issued a *fatwa*, or religious opinion, calling for the banning of Ahmadiyah along the lines of president Zia ul Haq's notorious Ordinance XX issued in Pakistan in 1984. Government officials such as Suryadharma have endorsed this call and in 2008 the government issued a decree banning Ahmadiyah. Sensing a degree of license protests against Ahmadiyah communities have become increasingly violent, cumulating in the beating to death of three community members in a raid in February 2011. Mob attacks on Christian churches have also increased. By 2011 Yudhoyono was facing increasing criticism for failing to take a firm hand in dealing with violent extremism.

More generally, post-transition Indonesia continues to suffer from problems of political stability and rule of law and generally continues to struggle on the lower tier of the league table on global surveys of good governance. It needs to be remembered that Indonesia remains a large and relatively poor nation in which 30% of the population does not have access to electricity and a staggering 60% does not have access to reliable supplies of piped water. It has made a remarkably swift and successful democratic transition but it has decades of catching up to do in development, institution building, and governance. When seen in this broader context, perhaps we should not be surprised that so many Indonesians look to religion, religious law, and religious leaders and institutions to provide the good governance and rule of law that they so deeply desire. Seen from this perspective it is all the more remarkable that so few are willing to vote for radical Islamist parties and that so many express support for *Pancasila*, the 1945 constitution, and democracy. Clearly, however, the ongoing legitimacy of secular democracy will depend on what levels of good governance and rule of law, combined with levels of economic growth, and equitable distribution, Indonesia achieves. The same, no doubt, will prove true in Egypt and the rest of the Middle East. Secular democracy without good governance will quickly be discredited. The evidence so far from Indonesia, however, suggests that prospects for secular democracy in the Muslim world are much better than many had thought.

References

An-Na'im, Abdullahi Ahmed. 2008. *Islam and the Secular State: Negotiating the Future of Shari'a*. Cambridge, MA: Harvard University Press.

Barton, Greg. 1994. "The Impact of Islamic Neo-modernism on Indonesian Islamic Thought: The Emergence of a New Pluralism." In *Indonesian Democracy: 1950s and 1990s*, edited by David Bourchier and John Legge, 143–159. Clayton, Australia: Centre of Southeast Asian Studies, Monash University.

_____. 1997a. "Indonesia's Nurcholish Madjid and Abdurrahman Wahid as Intellectual *Ulama*: The Meeting of Islamic Traditionalism and Modernism in Neo-modernist Thought." *Islam and Christian-Muslim Relations* 8: 323–350.

_____. 1997b. "The Origins of Islamic Liberalism in Indonesia and Its Contribution to Democratisation." In *Democracy in Asia*, edited by Michele Schmiegelow, 427–451. New York: St. Martins Press.

_____. 2002. *Abdurrahman Wahid. Muslim Democrat, Indonesian President: A View from the Inside.* Sydney and Honolulu: UNSW Press and University of Hawaii Press.

_____. 2004. *Indonesia's Struggle: Jemaah Islamiyah and radical Islamism.*Sydney: UNSW Press. [Also published as Barton, Greg. 2005. *Jemaah Islamiyah: Radical Islamism in Indonesia.* Singapore: Singapore University Press.]

_____. 2008. "Indonesia's Year of Living Normally: Taking the Long View on Indonesia's Progress." In *Southeast Asia Affairs 2008*, edited by Daljit Singh and Tin Maung Maung Than, 128–145. Singapore: ISEAS.

_____. 2010. "Indonesia." In *Guide to Islamist Movements*, edited by Barry Rubin. New York: M.E. Sharpe.

Baso, Ahmad. 2005. *Islam Pasca-Kolonial: Perselingkuan Agama, Kolonialism, dan Liberalisme* [Post-Colonial Islam: the Intersection of Religion, Colonialism and Liberalism]. Bandung, Indonesia: Mizan.

Boland, B. J. 1971. *The Struggle of Islam in Modern Indonesia.* The Hague, The Netherlands: Martinus Nijhoff.

Brichoux, David, and Deborah J. Gerner. 2002. *The United States and the 1958 Rebellion in Indonesia.* Washington, DC: Pew Case Studies in International Affairs, Institute for the Study of Diplomacy, School of Foreign Service, Georgetown University.

Bush, Robin. 2008. "Regional Sharia Regulations in Indonesia: Anomaly or Symptom?" In *Expressing Islam: Religious Life and Politics in Indonesia*, edited by Greg Fealy and Sally White, 174–191. Singapore: Institute of Southeast Asian Studies.

Cribb, Robert. 2001. "How Many Deaths? Problems in the Statistics of Massacre in Indonesia (1965–1966) and East Timor (1975–1980)." In *Violence in Indonesia*, edited by Ingrid Wessel and Georgia Wimhöfer. Hamburg: Abera.

Eliraz, Giora. 2004. *Islam in Indonesia: Modernism, Radicalism, and the Middle East Dimension.* Brighton, UK: Sussex Academic Press.

Hashemi, Nader. 2009. *Islam, Secularism and Democracy: Toward a Democratic Theory for Muslim Societies.* New York: Oxford University Press.

Hassan, Riaz. 2008. *Inside Muslim Minds.* Melbourne, Australia: Melbourne University Press.

Hefner, Robert W. 1997. "Islamization and Democratization in Indonesia." In *Islam in an Era of Nation States: Politics and Religious Revival in Muslim Southeast Asia*, edited by Robert W. Hefner and Patricia Horvatich, 75–127. Honolulu, HI: University of Hawaii Press.

_____. 2000. *Civil Islam: Muslims and Democratization in Indonesia.* Princeton, NJ: Princeton University Press.

_____. 2005. *Remaking Muslim Politics: Pluralism, Contestation, Democratization.* Princeton, NJ: Princeton University Press.

Hosen, Nadirsyah. 2007. *Shari'a and Constitutional Reform in Indonesia.* Singapore: ISEAS.

Huntington, Samuel P. (Summer 1993). "The Clash of Civilizations?" *Foreign Affairs* 72: 22–49.

_____. 1996. *The Clash of Civilizations and the Remaking of World Order.* New York: Simon & Schuster.

Jackson, Karl D. 1980. *Traditional Authority, Islam, and Rebellion: A Study of Indonesian Political Behaviour.* Berkeley, CA: University of California Press.

Kaufmann, Daniel, Aart Kraay, and Massimo Mastruzzi. 2007. *Governance Matters 2007: Worldwide Governance Indicators, 1996 to 2006.* Washington, DC: World Bank.

Latif, Yudi. 2008. *Indonesian Muslim Intelligentsia and Power.* Singapore: ISEAS.

Legge, John D. 2003. *Sukarno: A Political Biography.* Singapore: Archipelago Press.

Madjid, Nurcholish. 1987. *Islam, Kemodernan dan Keindonesiaan* [Islam, Modernity and Indonesianness]. Bandung, Indonesia: Mizan.

Nakamura, Mitsuo. 1983. *The Crescent Arises over the Banyan Tree: A Study of the Muhammadiyah Movement in a Central Javanese Town.* Yogyakarta, Indonesia: Gadjah Mada University Press.

Nasution, Buyung. 1992. *The Aspiration for Constitutional Government in Indonesia.* Jakarta: Pustaka Sinar Harapan.

Osman, Mohamed Nawab. 2010. "The transnational network of Hizbut Tahrir Indonesia." *South East Asia Research* 18: 735–755.

Ramage, Douglas E. 1995. *Politics in Indonesia: Democracy, Islam, and the Ideology of Tolerance.* London: Routledge.

Salim, Arskal, and Azymardi Azra, eds. 2003. *Shari'a and Politics in Modern Indonesia.* Singapore: ISEAS.

Wahid, Abdurrahman. 2001. *Pergulatan Negara, Agama, dan Kebudayaan* [The Struggle of State, Religion and Culture]. Jakarta, Indonesia: Desantara.

_____. 2006. *Islamku, Islam Anda, Islam Kita: Agama Masyarakat Negara Demokrasi* [My Islam, Your Islam: The Religion of a Democratic Society]. Jakarta, Indonesia: Wahid.

_____. 2007. *Islam Kosmopolitan: Nilai-nilai Indonesia dan Transformasi Kebudayaan* [Cosmpolitan Islam: Indonesian Values and the Transformation of Culture]. Jakarta, Indonesia: Wahid.

Woodward, Mark. 1989. *Islam in Java: Normative Piety and Mysticism in the Sultanate of Yogyakarta.* New York: Association for Asian Studies.

CHAPTER 6

Legitimacy in Malaysia: Dilemmas and Deficits

William Case

The notion of political legitimacy is imprecise, subjective, and often tautological. Even so, in applying it to Malaysia, we discover some unique utility. Among the countries considered in this volume, Malaysia is the only nation starkly divided along ethnic lines, scored nearly in half between the Malays and non-Malays, the latter a residual, negatively designated category that mainly includes local Chinese, Indians, and social minorities in Sabah and Sarawak. And though this dyad has been muddied somewhat by evolving intraethnic identities, societal perceptions of the government's legitimacy—or lack of it—have historically possessed clear focus.

In its distributions of public resources, the government has heavily favored the Malays. And it has confirmed its material allocations with appeals to nationalist identity and cultural solidarity, helping bind together a communal Malay profile that might otherwise fragment locally. But these same allocations and appeals have also alienated the non-Malays, belittling them with "second-class" citizenship. Under these conditions, democracy's significance as a supplementary source of legitimating appeal has mostly remained weak. Many Malays have sooner appreciated the country's single-party dominance through which their community's privileges have been enforced. And though the non-Malays may seek rule of law and meritocratic advancement, their minority status has limited the attractiveness of electoral competitiveness.

However, though generally clear, perceptions of legitimacy have occasionally been clouded. We will see that the Malay community has itself been divided, drawn to the material distributions issued by the government and to the more intense Islamic religiosity that emanates in opposition. Meanwhile, many non-Malays, though repelled by the government's skewed distributions and cultural appeals, fear that alternatives might be far less accommodative. They recognize too that despite the social mission with which the government has intervened in the economy, its record of economic management has, by regional terms, been sound. After Singapore, Malaysia has attained the highest level of development in Southeast Asia. Further, after Singapore and Japan, it has displayed the lengthiest record of political stability in all of East Asia. Thus, while perceiving the government to possess little legitimacy, many non-Malays have given it conditional support.

In Malaysia, then, a configuration has long persisted in which most Malays have considered the government to be legitimate. And many non-Malays, both on the peninsula and in East Malaysia, have calculated that the government has been at least worthy of support. But after a half-century of independence, these assessments have grown more critical. In the country's most recent general election, held in March 2008, the government was supported by only 58% of Malay voters and 35% of the Chinese (Ong 2008). Many Malays had been alienated by the extent to which top politicians in government, under the cover of distributive policies benefiting the Malays, have disproportionately benefited themselves. Further, in amplifying nationalist and cultural appeals in order to reenergize Malay loyalties, the government deepened the alienation of many non-Malays. There was evidence too that members of both communities had grown more vexed over corrupt practices. Notwithstanding, then, the political controls that characterize single-party dominant systems, the government suffered a severe electoral setback. Top politicians in government fell uncharacteristically into deep introspection. And in canvassing significant political reforms, they began to exchange the nationalist and cultural appeals that they had long emitted for more democratic ones, seeking to revive perceptions of legitimacy through greater checks on government's behavior.

This chapter begins by outlining several dimensions by which citizens in Malaysia evaluate the government's legitimacy or calculate its worthiness of support. It then provides a short account of legitimacy's historical origins and social bases. Next, in developing its core argument, this chapter turns to the deficits in legitimacy that have set in and the ways in which the government has managed the dilemmas that result. Throughout, it argues that variations in legitimacy provide a better explanation for the fluctuations of single-party dominance in Malaysia than do the material and institutional theories that have recently been introduced.

Dimensions of Legitimacy

Let us first revisit the notion of legitimacy, a concept in political science that, while once cherished, has now faded. One reason that legitimacy has fallen from favor is that most analysts reduce it to pedestrian support, inquiring merely how base instrumentalism is elevated, indeed ennobled, by citizens to become beliefs in political rightness. Another reason is that analysts tend casually to treat legitimacy as a systemic all-or-nothing matter, therein failing to distinguish between the many political institutions and policies whose rightness citizens may evaluate quite differently (Weatherford 1992).

This chapter suggests that by conducting study in an ethnically divided society where societal outlooks, even if diversified by class, grow concretized through the valorization of kinship and the vilification of rival communities, we can more readily discover the origins and cognitive processes by which citizens make evaluations of legitimacy. Put simply, in divided societies, citizens mainly gauge the legitimacy of their government by the degree to which, in gaining state power and making public policy, it meets their ethnically framed expectations about political rightness.

We are next confronted by challenges in disaggregating political institutions and procedures, necessary for detecting the multiple sites and varying intensities of legitimacy. Especially in advanced industrial democracies, where myriad executive agencies, legislative and judicial arenas, party vehicles, and procedural conduits can be recorded, the differentiation and weighting of their discrete quotients of legitimacy remains problematic. And countless policy outputs, often uncertain or even contrary in their effects, further obscure assessment. However, by focusing on a case of single-party dominance, where a dominant party and state apparatus fuse in a simpler amalgam yet turn on more than the raw cronyism and brute coercion that prevail at lesser levels of political development, we can more readily make general, yet plausible estimations about vectors of legitimacy. Thus, a relative simplicity in institutions and policies, characteristic of single-party dominant systems, amounts to an analytical virtue, streamlining the entities whose legitimacy is evaluated by citizens.

In structuring analysis, this chapter enumerates two dimensions (see Weatherford 1992, 150) along which evaluations of legitimacy are made (table 6.1). The first dimension involves the institutions and procedures by which a government acquires and exercises state power, the legitimacy of which depends on conformity to established rules (Beetham 1991, 16). The legitimacy of institutional functioning is measurable, then, by the extent to which a government avoids corrupt practices and electoral manipulations. The second dimension involves a government's policy outputs, with legitimacy turning on perceptions of distributive fairness and developmental competence.

In addition, this analysis assumes that in advanced industrial democracies, where institutional functioning is mostly evaluated by citizens as legitimate, perceptions concerning policy outputs matter less. Thus, a government, after accumulating and exercising power in ways regarded as rightful, does not abruptly lose its legitimacy through policy failures. Rather, its respect for institutions and procedures ensures that it can rightfully persist in office and commit errors in policy until it is replaced through an election or vote of no confidence.

Conversely, in single-party dominant systems, where the legitimacy with which institutions and procedures are evaluated by citizens remains shaky, perceptions concerning public policy matter more. Thus, a government whose policy outputs are regarded as fair and competent can deter citizens from closely scrutinizing institutions. But if policy failures mount, citizens may look back to reevaluate institutional functioning more critically, focusing on electoral manipulations, executive abuses, and corrupt practices. And it is now, as judgments begin to shift, that the electoral flywheel reverses, perhaps so overstating deficits in legitimacy that "stunning" elections take place.

Further, in charting this two-step descent in the evaluations made by citizens, we distinguish more clearly between ennobling legitimacy and pedestrian support. Legitimacy is rooted in widely shared beliefs over the normatively rightful acquisition and usage of state power (Beetham 1991). As citizens make their evaluations, then, they do so in heartfelt and collective ways across multiple dimensions, giving legitimacy resilience. And hence, where positive assessments have been made, though a government's performance might slip, legitimacy dissolves only slowly. Lapses in developmental competence, for example,

Table 6.1   Dimensions of Legitimacy

I. Institutions/ Procedures	avoidance of corrupt practices	avoidance of electoral manipulations
II. Policy Outputs	distributive fairness	developmental competence

may be eased by ongoing distributive rightness, therein delaying any shift in public scrutiny from the policy axis to the institutional plane.

Mere support, by contrast, stems from narrow instrumentalist calculations. And in making their estimations, citizens focus closely on a government's continuous provision of particularistic and substantive benefits. Thus, once performance slips in any policy domain, support rapidly fragments across multiple fronts. In a simple approximation, then, of Bruce Gilley's (2005, 32) logic, where a government fails to manage the economy and generate welfare in ways that uplift a defined community, it loses legitimacy. By contrast, where it fails to deliver substantive benefits to individuals, it merely leaks support. Further, we have seen that even where a government retains some legitimacy, it may be stunned by the autonomous impact of elections. But where a government never gained more than support, there is scant surprise over its defeat. Indeed, it is unlikely that such a government can firmly institute, let alone long operate a single-party dominant system, having regularly instead to shore up brittle support with coercion.

Legitimacy's Historical Origins and Social Bases in Malaysia

On first glimmer, Malaysia might hardly have been expected to have displayed long continuities in its political record, whether through single-party dominance or any other regime type. With the country's social structure divided, a bipolar faceoff has set in between the Malays and non-Malays, identified by Donald Horowitz (1993, 20) as the most volatile pattern of ethnic affiliations and rivalries. What is more, rising Islamism in Malaysia has not only sharpened these rivalries, rigidifying identities into a Muslim/non-Muslim dyad, but also deepened fractiousness within even the Malay community over varying religiosity (Liow 2004). The country is also spatially fragmented, with resentments over the ascendancy of Peninsular Malaysia simmering among indigenous non-Malay segments in the resource-rich but less developed states of Sabah and Sarawak.

Further, though Malaysia's economy has grown rapidly industrialized over the past several decades, it has sometimes been punctured by shocks, most epically during the mid-1980s and the late 1990s. This trajectory has created complex sets of middle-class outlooks that, when ignited by crisis, can finally activate the societal pressures for change that were once articulated, albeit in too lineal a way, by modernization theorists. We note too the deepening grievances among urban workers and village cultivators, with gross income disparities in Malaysia perpetuating one of the most lop-sided Gini coefficients in East Asia (Lim 2005).

Yet notwithstanding these sources of structural and spatial tensions, Malaysia has for more than three decades perpetuated political stability through what in a simple typology of authoritarian regimes can best be coded as a single-party dominant system. There have been no executive or military coups during this period. Nor have any transformative social upheavals taken place. Rather, through the dominant party, UMNO (United Malays National Organization), and the multiethnic coalition *Barisan Nasional* (National Front) that it centers, structural tensions have long been managed, firmly instilling among citizens highly ethnicized criteria by which to construct social identity and to evaluate political legitimacy.

A Divided Society and Dominant Party

As the British began to decolonize Malaya after World War II, they yielded to political pressures emanating from a divided society. Indeed, through their overseas recruitment of labor for extractive industries, the British had themselves constructed this society, therein grounding the communally based parties that would later take root. UMNO was formed in 1946 by Malay civil servants and notables. And in resisting the terms on which independence was to be granted, in particular that of equal citizenship rights for the non-Malays, UMNO declared the territory to be *Tanah Melayu* (Malay land), therein deepening its social bases through sentiments of indigenousness and ethnic entitlement.

In these unsettled circumstances, galvanized Malay followings responded with more than support, finding political legitimacy in UMNO's ethnically framed appeals. And in gaining fervor, they mounted sharp protests against the British. Colonial officials relented, acquiescing in new terms for independence through which Malay "special rights" were concretized, mostly involving preferential state hiring and privileging in cultural symbols. Thus, in generating a powerful sense of redress, UMNO appealed to the Malay community through a strongly ethnicized notion of distributive fairness, securing its standing as "protector" (Muzaffar 1979).

Some Chinese took up arms, mounting an insurgency during the late 1940s–1950s labeled the Emergency. With British encouragement, top Chinese businessmen responded by forming the Malayan (later Malaysia) Chinese Association (MCA), while ethnic Indians gathered in the Malay(si)an Indian Congress (MIC). Further, in contesting elections that were introduced in phases during this period, UMNO drew the MCA and the MIC into a coalition that was christened the Alliance. And in competing effectively, the Alliance defeated more genuinely multiethnic vehicles that gathered tenuously on one flank, as well as the more enduring Islamic Party of Malay(si)a (PAS) on the other. UMNO thus perpetuated an ethnic distinctiveness that invigorated Malay followings while coalescing with the MCA and the MIC in order to forge support among non-Malay constituencies. It led the Alliance to victory under the country's electoral democracy that persisted from the mid-1950s through the late 1960s.

But as Kenneth Greene (2007, 10) observes, "founding projects have limited staying power." Though UMNO continued to anchor the Alliance during the decade after independence, it slackened in its use of state patronage to uplift the Malay community. During the 1960s, many Malays gravitated from the rice fields and fishing villages to the country's urban fringes, gazing upon the relative prosperity of Chinese town dwellers. Their expectations about distributive fairness and developmental competence remained unrealized, with the government showing but vapid commitments to bureaucratic expansion and import substitution (Alavi 1996, 35). To be sure, because Malaysia remained an electoral democracy, the legitimacy of the institutions by which UMNO had gained power was not reevaluated more critically by most citizens. But when an election was held in 1969, many Malays, disillusioned by the government's policy outputs, sought to use this avenue to strengthen the standing of PAS.

At the same time, many ordinary Chinese chafed under their "second-class" citizenship. They also felt little emotive solidarity with coethnic tycoons in the MCA. And hence, having given the MCA transient support, they swung in the 1969 election to new, predominantly Chinese parties that had sprouted in opposition, the Democratic Action Party (DAP) and the Malaysian People's Movement (*Gerakan*). Accordingly, with so many Malay and non-Malay voters plumping for these opposition parties, the UMNO-led Alliance was gravely weakened, finally dismaying the Malays while exhilarating many Chinese. Ethnic rioting known locally as the May 13 incident then erupted in Kuala Lumpur, ushering in two years of emergency rule.

In seeking afterward to ease their government's legitimacy deficits, top politicians in UMNO pondered new policy outputs through which to reenergize their Malay followings. Turning first to distributive fairness, they acted on their "contextual" understanding that the Malays found little that was rightful in the norm of "policy neutrality," which Gilley (2005, 15) treats as universally legitimating. Indeed, they resorted now to "reverse discrimination," instituting programs that were branded as the New Economic Policy (NEP). Under this appellation, the state apparatus was elaborated with new public enterprises that vastly increased the benefits that UMNO could disburse to the Malays. What is more, quotas were extended to the private sector, requiring that 30% of equity ownership and corporate hiring be reserved for the Malays in both Chinese- and foreign-owned firms. And during the 1980s, as Mahathir Mohamad commenced his long tenure as prime minister, UMNO began to privatize state assets in order to breed more exclusive cohorts of "Malay millionaires" (Gomez and Jomo 1999, Ch. 4).

UMNO also claimed new developmental competence. Invoking shibboleths like "Look East," multidimensional strategies involving state-led industrialization, foreign-invested manufacturing, and commodities production were put in place (Alavi 1996, 37–57). But just as in its approach to distributive fairness, the government articulated too its developmental competence along ethnic lines, favoring foreign investors over local Chinese entrepreneurs (Jesudason 1987). It also exalted the industrializing achievements of Japan and Korea over those of Taiwan and Singapore (Alavi 1996, 43), while crafting "Asian values" and a national work ethic from congregational notions of the Islamic *ummah*.

Thus, in recalibrating its policy outputs, UMNO earned greater evaluations of legitimacy among the Malays. But by perpetuating "accommodationist elements" (Zakaria 1989), it avoided sacrificing all support among the non-Malays. For example, while imposing new licensing arrangements and ownership quotas through the NEP, it acquiesced in "Ali-Baba" deals—arrangements wherein Malays who had been favored with state contracts or discounted equity were able, while operating respectively as sleeping partners or furtive vendors, to issue stakes to Chinese buyers (Milne and Mauzy 1999, 53). In this way, deep legitimacy deficits among non-Malays were partly offset with new, if transient, measures of support, especially among elites (Means 1991, 313). And even if at the mass level most non-Malays still viewed the NEP as a "blatant form of racial discrimination" (313), their resentments were tempered by their sharing in the country's general prosperity, especially during the early-to-mid-1990s. They also found that UMNO under-enforced its new Malay-centered National Culture Policy, as well as its increasingly Islamist codes. Primary schooling in Chinese and Tamil vernacular remained publicly funded, while Chinese and Hindu places of worship and modes of holiday celebration were still tolerated.

With its policy axis strengthened, UMNO secured enough buffering to be able to restructure the institutional plane too, asserting a new paramountcy that dampened democracy's prospects. UMNO began by co-opting into the Alliance, now rebadged as the *Barisan Nasional,* most of the communally ordered parties that had emerged in opposition, including PAS. It also absorbed many of the parties that had formed after the "merger" of the peninsula with East Malaysia a decade earlier. But UMNO politicians then greatly enhanced their vehicle within this coalition, raising it from its previous standing as *primus inter pares* to utter preeminence. Henceforth, UMNO politicians would lay claim to all top-line ministries within the rapidly expanding state, effectively fusing the party and state apparatuses.

Thus, while parliament was reopened in 1972, political life has remained stunted (see Crouch 1996, Chs. 4–6). Communication has been stifled by sedition laws, licensing restrictions, and media ownership patterns. And assembly has been hindered through registration statutes, permit requirements, and "preventive detention" under the dreaded Internal Security Act (ISA). In contrast, elections have been regularly held within timeframes specified by the constitution. Further, opposition parties have been able to gain a toehold in parliament and even to win state assemblies outright. However, the competitiveness of elections, while significant, has been dampened by the limits on civil liberties, then capped with manipulations that have included an intricate gerrymandering and malapportioning of constituencies, a heavily partisan use of public resources during campaigning, and a plurality system set in a single-member district system that greatly exaggerates the government's majorities (Gomez 1998). Accordingly, for three-and-a-half decades, the UMNO-led *Barisan* has won every general election except for the most recent with the two-thirds majority in parliament that is formally necessary for amending the constitution and emotively crucial for avowing Malay supremacy.

In sum, through policy outputs that accented distributive fairness and developmental competence, the government encouraged more robust evaluations of legitimacy among the Malays, though without exhausting support among the non-Malays. And with legitimacy fixed on this axis, it gained cover enough that it could reconfigure the institutional plane too. In asserting its dominance through UMNO, the government constructed a paradigmatic single-party dominant system that has displayed uncommon durability.

But under a dominant party system, a government typically does much more than manipulate elections. It also routinely engages in grosser executive abuses and corrupt practices. In the Malaysian case, politicians in UMNO, while widely distributing programmatic benefits across the Malay community, laid more intense claim to state patronage for themselves. They also channeled largesse to the new Malay millionaires, as well as Chinese tycoons with whom they came feverishly to collude, triggering a succession of breathtaking financial and corporate collapses throughout the 1980s–1990s. In this context, Malaysia's record of rising prosperity grew flecked with bail-outs and cover-ups (Milne and Mauzy 1999, 68–72).

That the government was able to weather the scandals that resulted indicates that most citizens were looking the other way, with the rightness of policy outputs obscuring the tawdriness of institutions and procedures. And thus, to the extent that citizens addressed institutional functioning, many Malays found legitimacy here too, with elections, though manipulated, helping justly to renew UMNO's dominance. And where the government resorted tactically to coercion to tamp down residual challenges over corrupt practices, most citizens seemed to evaluate even this as legitimate (Jesudason 1996, 32), buying the argument that after May 13 such action was necessary to avoid "confusing the people" and disturbing "racial harmony."

But as argued above, when evaluations of legitimacy are not so driven by strong policy outputs, citizens begin gradually to probe the prior institutions and procedures by which a government gains and exercises state power. As scrutiny shifts from the policy axis to the institutional plane, the corrupt practices and electoral manipulations that had earlier been overlooked now fuel discontents. Thus, as deficits in legitimacy set in, citizens revisit the competitiveness that elections still allow, registering such protest that they advance democratic change. To see how, let us turn to Malaysia's more recent political record.

Legitimacy Deficits and Electoral Competitiveness

Governments that operate single-party dominant systems are sometimes stunned by the results of the contests that they wage. Thus, Levitzky and Way (2002) record cases in Eastern Europe, Africa, and Central America where governments have manipulated multiparty elections, yet met with defeat, leading to their ouster and democratic change. New research agendas have thus emerged over when, under conditions of single-party dominance, elections might be regime-sustaining or regime-subverting (Schedler 2002, 49).

Casting doubt on this agenda, however, Jason Brownlee (2007, 30–32) has used a four-country study to argue that elections do little either to sustain or to subvert single-party dominance. In his "institutional" theory, electoral outcomes are merely a "symptom," registering passively the extent to which governments have maintained their dominant party apparatuses and prevented elite-level defections beforehand. Kenneth Greene (2007, 14, 63, 306), in an influential analysis of contemporary Mexico, suggests similarly that contests are won or lost long before election day. In his "resource" theory of "hyperincumbency" advantage, elections show only the extent to which dominant parties have kept control over public sector resources and state patronage, forcing the opposition parties that it confronts to the ideological fringes.

But recent events in Malaysia show that dominant parties and defectors, as well as state patronage and opposition parties, remain less crucial to the fates of single-party dominant systems than do the sentiments of citizens, the varying tenor of which is best understood in terms of legitimacy. Thus, in Malaysia's most recent general election, held in March 2008, the UMNO-led *Barisan* was dealt a startling setback, seemingly precipitating a democratic transition. Yet, despite this momentous change, we will see that there had been no prior weakening of the dominant party's apparatus or any significant elite-level defections. Nor had the dominant party lost control over public resources and state patronage. Rather, it was precisely the ways in which this party perpetuated its dominance that so eroded perceptions of legitimacy among citizens.

During the last decade of Mahathir's tenure, many of the benefits that had been dispensed to the Malay community were now diverted as patronage to Malay millionaires and collaborating Chinese tycoons. Indeed, during the financial crisis of 1997–1998, the government proposed bailouts for stumbling conglomerates, including a logistics firm headed by Mahathir's eldest son, Mirzan (Haggard 2000, 170). Meanwhile, ordinary Malays were left to cope with hardship unaided. In these circumstances, when Mahathir was challenged in his role as leader of UMNO by his popular deputy, Anwar Ibrahim, he used the party and state apparatuses, fused tightly through single-party dominance, to expel Anwar from UMNO and the cabinet. He then leveled charges of sexual misconduct against his adversary, which resulted in a lengthy trial and prison sentence. Many Malays, their evaluations of policy outputs having already been weakened by distributions they regarded as unfair and a developmental record whose competence they now questioned, discovered yet more grievances through a cultural optic, with Mahathir's treatment of Anwar parsed as violating traditional proscriptions upon humiliating a fellow Malay (Abbot 2000).

Further, many Malays began to scrutinize institutional functioning more closely. Thus, in an election held in 1999, large numbers of rural Malay villagers, dislocated by Mahathir's breakneck industrial policies, found common cause with new urban middle-class Malays alienated by the purging of Anwar and rising corruption. Galvanized by a new social reform movement, these sectors turned from UMNO to PAS. Accordingly, PAS increased its seats in parliament fourfold. However, as an emboldened PAS began to pursue its Islamizing agendas more vigorously, the Chinese community quickened its swing from opposition back to the UMNO-led *Barisan*. Thus, in the wake of the Asian financial crisis, as their paths began to cross, frictions again set in between the Malays and non-Malays.

In October 2003, Mahathir resigned, ceding the prime ministership and UMNO presidency to Abdullah Badawi. Abdullah then promptly raised expectations among the Malays about public policy, giving greater attention to distributive fairness and developmental competence. In brief, he began to refocus attention from the "megaprojects" that had so advantaged the Malay millionaires and their Chinese partners to village-level programs and agricultural schemes. In addition, though the economy never regained the high rates of growth that had prevailed prior to the crisis, it recovered some of its export competitiveness. In this way, in demonstrating fairness and competence while pledging to be a "leader of all Malaysians" (Lee 2008, 187), Abdullah sought to regenerate legitimacy among the Malays while avoiding sacrificing support among non-Malays.

But aware that citizens had begun also to scrutinize institutional functioning intently, Abdullah declared he would curb corrupt practices. He ordered spot checks on the frontline government departments most associated with corruption (Lopez 2003–2004). A royal commission was set up to create an independent government agency to investigate complaints against the police. And corruption charges were brought against a former deputy cabinet minister, a few top bureaucrats, and a prominent Chinese tycoon (Lopez 2004).

The result was that, in an election held in March 2004 only a few months after coming to power, Abdullah led the *Barisan* to its greatest victory ever, winning 65% of the popular vote, which, when heightened through the plurality system, earned it 90% of the seats in parliament

(Moten 2006). Abdullah was thus encouraged to undertake more reforms, requiring next that *Barisan* MPs declare their assets. But more remarkably, in August 2004, the judiciary displayed renewed independence, overturning Anwar's conviction on sexual misconduct charges. And with Anwar having already completed a six-year sentence for corruption, he was immediately freed.

Failing Policy Outputs and Institutional Functioning

At the start of his prime ministership, Abdullah drew positive evaluations of his government's legitimacy. This section shows, however, that assessments of his policy outputs soon soured, with the promise of distributive fairness amounting to little while developmental competence lost luster. In particular, as world energy prices rose sharply during 2007–2008, the government reduced the subsidies that it had long issued to citizens. At the same time, it renewed subsidies for "hugely lucrative" independent power producers (IPPs), many of them owned by Malaysia's "politically connected and wealthiest big business families" (Netto 2008). Thus, survey data reveals that long-standing resentments over the distribution of state contracts, licenses, and credit intensified (Merdeka Center 2008). Protest activity began to mount too. In late 2007, Malay demonstrators were readily convened by PAS leaders in front of Kuala Lumpur's eponymous and "iconic" Petronas twin towers, named for the owner, the national petroleum company.

But if Abdullah did little to dazzle the Malays with new initiatives in distributive fairness or developmental competence, he allowed politicians in UMNO to reenergize their own followings through piercing communal appeals during the party's general assemblies. Indeed, at the meetings in 2006 and 2007, the leader of the party's youth wing drew a ceremonial Malay dagger, the *keris*, in a rousing display of cultural ascendancy (Zahid 2008). Taking the cue, other speakers declared the inviolability of what had come to be labeled the "Malay Agenda" (Lee 2008). The degree to which these appeals may have restored evaluations of legitimacy among the Malays is unclear. But the extent to which they eroded support among the non-Malays grew plain.

Amid weakening evaluations of distributive fairness by the Malays and increasingly searing judgments among non-Malays, as well as disillusion among both communities over developmental competence, both political legitimacy and ordinary support slipped on the policy axis. And as citizens scrutinized institutions and procedures, they took to reevaluating legitimacy more critically on the institutional plane. Abdullah sought to make good on his pledges to curb corrupt practices. But in a single-party dominant system, with UMNO so tightly geared to state patronage, he soon met with resistance from UMNO politicians. Thus, at the party's assembly election in 2004, held barely eight months after the *Barisan Nasional*'s triumph in that year's general election, Abdullah backed away from a ban on lobbying by candidates that he had earlier imposed through which to stem debilitating "money politics." As one party aspirant queried, "[w]hat's the fuss about.... Whatever money given helped us recoup some cost. I do not think that the leadership should be too worried" (quoted in Pereira 2004a). And Abdullah seemed now to concur, lamenting, "[w]hat can I do?" (Pereira 2004b).

In addition, top police officials declared on an internal Web posting their contempt for Abdullah's proposal to set up the complaints commission (Kuek 2006). Indeed, while the police had once dutifully assisted Mahathir in suppressing social reform movements that had grown active over the financial crisis and Anwar's arrest, they threatened now to switch their allegiance from UMNO to PAS. Abdullah thus scaled back drastically the complaints commission that had been canvassed. At the same time, government officials and corporate figures who had been charged with corruption, an action that had fascinated citizens, were acquitted. And Abdullah's own family members were revealed to have entered into deals over government contracts and the privatization of assets, allegedly enriching Abdullah's son and son-in-law (Gatsiounis 2007). Accordingly, as citizens in Malaysia focused on institutional functioning, they rapidly perceived diminishing rightness.

Legitimacy Deficits

As doubts about the rightness of policy outputs spill over to institutional functioning, Gilley (2005, 61) contends that "low legitimacy will tend to create pressures for changes to the state itself." However, Jason Brownlee (2007) counters that sturdy dominant parties effectively mediate patronage across elites, rendering their single-party dominant systems resistant to exogenous pressures. Accordingly, if democratic change is to take place, it must begin in the party itself, with its shortfalls in patronage driving top politicians into the arms of the opposition. Kenneth Greene (2007) similarly attributes the fortunes of dominant parties to the availability of patronage. Thus, in this view, it is only when patronage flows falter, usually through contractions in public resources, that the dominant party weakens, ceding scope for an opposition party to advance democratic change.

But these accounts ignore the extent to which a dominant party, in conducting business as usual—mediating patronage in ways that perpetuate elite loyalties while wrong-footing opposition parties—can deeply alienate citizens. And it is by invoking the notion of legitimacy deficits, first on the policy axis, then on the institutional plane, that we discover the intensity with which grievances may set in, finally driving citizens to mount the pressures that Gilley foretells.

In Malaysia, Abdullah was unable to sustain popular perceptions of rightness. Thus, a proxy for the legitimacy deficits that set in can be found in the unlawful and hence antisystem behaviors to which citizens resorted. During late 2007–early 2008, large-scale protests, proscribed under any well-structured system of single-party dominance, were staged in the capital. Some of these focused specifically on the lack of distributive fairness, with "low-income Malays" decrying the patronage that "a conspicuously consuming elite" extracted through the NEP (Baradan 2007). Ethnic Indian groups, organized through the new Hindu Rights Action Force (HINDRAF), also protested over their community's relative immiseration under the NEP. At the same time, citizens from each of the major ethnic communities amplified their grievances beyond distributive fairness to developmental competence. Numerous protests were mounted as the country's economic recovery began to fray with price inflation and unemployment (Welsh 2007, 1).

In this context, as doubts among citizens about rightness cropped up on the policy axis, they spilled over onto the institutional plane. In particular, a broad umbrella organization known as *Bersih* (Coalition for Clean and Fair Elections) focused on corrupt practices and the manipulations that were likely to quicken as the next election drew near. In doing this, *Bersih* was distinguished by its methods and leadership. Though denied a police permit to hold a public demonstration in late 2007 in Kuala Lumpur, the movement's leaders pressed ahead, revealing through antisystem actions their critical reevaluation of the government's legitimacy. At the same time, they tried to portray themselves as working within the "system," implying their greater rightness. Specifically, after declaring their demands for electoral reforms, *Bersih* led some 60,000 demonstrators to petition the country's king, high symbol of constitutional restraint and the arbiter of Malay culture.

While *Bersih* was led by PAS, it was also joined by the People's Justice Party (PKR), a vehicle formed at the time of Anwar's arrest and "advised" by him after his release. Further, as Anwar traveled round the country, appealing to popular grievances, ordinary citizens began to gain much greater causal force than Brownlee's institutional theory allows. And rather than making an "end run" around the party's uncompromising "early joiners" and "policy radicals," then shunting aside PAS and the DAP, Anwar took more to mediating and conciliating than Greene's resource model would predict (see Ch. 5).

The 2008 General Election

We have seen that under single-party dominance, regular elections are used by governments to help paper over any deficits in legitimacy. With these elections displaying meaningful amounts of competitiveness, governments assert the democratic rightfulness of the institutions by which they gain state power. This competitiveness remains bounded, however, by the limits on civil liberties and sundry manipulations. When citizens grow disillusioned over policy failings, they revisit the medley of institutional dynamics by which they had earlier been lulled, reevaluating power abuses and corrupt practices more critically, but focusing on electoral manipulations with particular scrutiny. As elections approach, manipulations that had helped earlier to disperse societal discontents begin now to inflame them. And in accreting with other grievances, they deepen rather than alleviate deficits in legitimacy. The results are observable in the antisystem behaviors to which citizens then resort, made manifest in their exercising civil liberties with a fervor that single-party dominance proscribes.

Many scholarly analyses of Malaysia's twelfth general election have become available (e.g., Pepinsky 2009; Weiss 2009; Chin and Wong 2009; Case 2010), hence requiring only a short account here. Though the government won this election, it was dealt so startling a setback that it was famously characterized by the DAP's national chairman, Lim Kit Siang (2008) as a "political tsunami." The government's share of the popular vote fell from the approximately 55–65% of the total that it has usually commanded to a bare majority. Notwithstanding the multiplier effects of the plurality system, the *Barisan* won only 140 of parliament's 222 seats, leaving it shy for the first time ever of a two-thirds majority.

It had been expected that the government would lose some support among the non-Malays, their perennial discontents having peaked in recent protests. But the extent to which their worsening perceptions of rightness in the government's policies and institutions would drive them toward opposition, and further, would come to be shared by some Malays too, had not been foreseen. Indeed, Malay voters, in swinging by an estimated 5% against the government, now fanned out across the

PKR, the PAS, and in some districts, even the DAP (Ong 2008). In the election, then, the PKR made stunning gains, the DAP significant ones, and PAS at least held steady. Further, these parties collectively won control over five state assemblies, including those of Malaysia's most developed states, Selangor and Penang.

As we have seen, when the government was dealt a similar blow in the 1969 election, it regained its footing by absorbing most opposition parties into its new *Barisan* coalition, then deeply subordinating them. But in 2008, the opposition was so uplifted by the election that it sought now to gain power in its own right. Thus, even as leaders of the opposition parties bargained over the formation of the state governments that they now controlled, Anwar tried to entice parliamentarians from the *Barisan* to defect. The government looked on anxiously, aware that its traditional legitimating appeals had lost steam.

New Strategies of Legitimation

Though a democratic transition appeared underway in Malaysia, its dynamics departed significantly from the sequencing of factors that has typically been specified in theories about single-party dominance. In institutional and resource theories, the elections that reflect the revised preferences of citizens count for little. It is instead elites who, in confronting shortfalls in patronage, defect from their dominant party thereby initiating democratic change. As Brownlee (2008, 112) states succinctly, "elections do not destabilize regimes; [dominant parties] destabilize their own elections."

But, as the 2008 election approached in Malaysia, no economic crisis or elite-level defections took place. Far more striking at this juncture than the ceaseless factional scheming that reverberates through any political party was the habituated cohesiveness with which politicians in UMNO prepared for the election. Thus, it was only after the contest that the government's resources and patronage declined, with control over five state bureaucracies having fallen to the opposition. And it was only now too, with UMNO gravely weakened, that elite-level fractiousness set in, increasing the risk of cascading defections. UMNO's former chief minister of Selangor, Khir Toyo, replaced now by a PKR assemblymen, initially refused Abdullah Badawi's call to serve as opposition leader in the state assembly. Mahathir then demanded that Abdullah resign, a call that resonated among division leaders. Abdullah resisted, vowing to defend his position at the party's next general assembly. Mahathir then resigned from UMNO, urging others to do the same, then called for them to return to the fold after Abdullah had been forced out.

It had not, then, been any economic crisis, dominant party weaknesses, declining resources and patronage or elite-level defections that fomented democratic change. Shortfalls in patronage and elite-level defections set in only *after* the election. The transition was driven instead by citizens, profoundly reordering their preferences amid deficits in legitimacy and support. And the opposition parties, astonished by their windfall gains, drew closer together as the *Pakatan Rakyat* (People's Alliance) then angled to replace the *Barisan* by encouraging the defections.

With the government quite stunned, its top politicians took to uncharacteristic introspection. Indeed, we see plainly here the ways in which elites, when they confront the low levels of legitimacy that their traditional nationalist and cultural appeals now generate, may take to pledging greater democratic procedures. Historically, single-party dominance suited many Malays while not unduly antagonizing many non-Malays, given the latter's fears of unfiltered majoritarianism. But now the Malays had grown increasingly suspicious of the skewed distributions that UMNO mediated, while the non-Malays lost faith in the UMNO-led *Barisan*'s accommodative posture. In this context, Mohd Khir Toyo, the former chief minister, conceded that the "election results [were] a reflection of UMNO having lost touch with reality. This leaves the party with no option but to tread the path of reform" (Zahiid and Omar 2008). At this juncture, then, with the opposition forging ahead while the government proposed reformist concessions, speculation mounted that Malaysia's twelfth general election heralded a peaceful transition, however slow moving, from a dominant party system to two-party competitiveness and democratic politics (see Baradan 2008).

Under the weight of sociopolitical contradictions, Abdullah finally yielded the prime ministership to his deputy, Tun Najib Razak, in April 2009. And Najib, in then seeking to rekindle support among the non-Malays, only reawakened doubts about legitimacy among UMNO's Malay constituencies. Specifically, Najib fashioned a new shibboleth of *1Malaysia* through which to pledge ethnic harmony. Distributive policy would thus tilt from the NEP's pro-Malay quotas toward a New Economic Model (NEM) under which needy citizens would be aided irrespective of ethnic affiliation. Further, the corrupt practices associated with the NEP would be moderated through new bureaucratic controls and economic liberalization under the Government Transformation Program (GTP). The NEM and the GTP would together undergird an Economic Transformation Program (ETP) that stressed greater private entrepreneurship, while reducing state investment and public subsidies.

However, the course adopted by Najib soon recalled the dilemma that had earlier bedeviled Abdullah. Malay activists, gathering as the Bumiputera Economic Congress in September 2010, warned Najib to preserve their community's special rights and preferential quotas. Najib quickly retreated, reverting to UMNO's more traditional setting. Hence, when the government announced its new five-year Malaysia Plan and the 2011 budget, it was studded with social programs that benefited the Malays and state expenditures on grand projects.

In this context, perceptions of UMNO's legitimacy among the Malays were seemingly reinvigorated. At the same time, support among the non-Malays for the opposition coalition softened, with suspicions deepening between the DAP and PAS, while PKR grew weakened by internal rivalries. And in deepening the opposition's troubles, its leader, Anwar Ibrahim, was again placed on trial for sexual misconduct, paving the way for his jailing. In this way, Malaysia's democratic transition stopped cold. Legitimacy for UMNO's single-party dominance was refreshed, while much support for the PKR-led opposition dissolved in indifference, leaving much of it to gravitate back to the government.

Conclusions

In measuring the transformative impact that citizens can deliver, legitimacy offers a useful tool. Single-party dominance, in tightly amalgamating power hierarchies, gives clarity to the very object whose legitimacy or worthiness of support citizens assess. Second, the perceptions made by citizens are sharpened by a prism of ethnic affiliation and rivalry. What such a framework can reveal is the extent to which even a favored community can reevaluate legitimacy, which is far more worrying for the government than an excluded community's recalculation of support. With loyalties rooted in legitimacy much stickier than those associated with support—and hence, once compromised, more difficult to restore—their slippage suggests to the government that its single-party dominance is particularly at risk.

In addition, Malaysia's intermediate level of political development, inhering in single-party dominance, enables us to examine a thesis that under this form of authoritarian rule, much more than in advanced industrial democracy, any frailty of legitimacy on the institutional plane must be offset by performance on the policy axis.

But many Malays came to doubt the fairness by which benefits were distributed within their community under the NEP, while support from non-Malays grew strained by the behaviors of UMNO politicians. And citizens in both communities grew doubtful too about the government's developmental competence, encouraging them finally to scrutinize institutional functioning more closely. Thus, as elections approached in 2008, they focused not only on electoral manipulations, but also on the power abuses and corrupt practices that earlier had mostly been overlooked.

And yet, single-party dominance appears to have reequilibrated in Malaysia. UMNO's renewed overtures to the non-Malay community again deepened the alienation of its core Malay constituency. But in confronting this timeless sociopolitical dilemma, the UMNO-led government quickly revised its policy outputs in order to reinvigorate legitimacy among the Malays. And the opposition, in lapsing into historical patterns of fractiousness, shed much of the support that it had so recently attracted. At the time of writing, the government seemed poised to call an early election, while the Barisan was projected to regain its two-thirds majority in parliament.

References

Abbott, Jason P. 2000. "Bittersweet Victory: The 1999 Malaysian General Election and the Anwar Ibrahim Affair." *The Roundtable* 893: 245–258.

Alavi, Rokiah. 1996. *Industrialization in Malaysia: Import Substitution and Infant Industry Performance*. New York: Routledge.

Baradan Kuppusamy. 2007. "Leaders Urge Return to Moderation After Protests in Malaysia." *South China Morning Post*, November 27.

———. 2008. "Two-Party System Takes Shape in Malaysia." *Asia Times Online*, April 10, http://www.atimes.com/atimes/Southeast_Asia/JD10Ae01.html.

Beetham, David. 1991. *The Legitimation of Power*. London: Macmillan.

Brownlee, Jason. 2007. *Authoritarianism in an Age of Democratization*. Cambridge: Cambridge University Press.

———. 2008. "Bound to Rule: Party Institutions and Regime Trajectories in Malaysia and the Philippines." *Journal of East Asian Studies* 81: 89–118.

Case, William. 2010. "Transition from Single-Party Dominance? New Data from Malaysia." *Journal of East Asian Studies* 101: 91–126.

Chin, James, and Wong Chin Huat. 2009. "Malaysia's Electoral Upheaval." *Journal of Democracy* 203: 71–85.

Crouch, Harold. 1996. *Government and Society in Malaysia*. Ithaca: Cornell University Press.

Gatsiounis, Ioannis. 2007. "Anti-graft War Backfires in Malaysia." *AsiaTimes.com*, March 21, http://www.atimes.com.

Gilley, Bruce. 2005. "Political Legitimacy in Malaysia: Regime Performance in the Asian Context." In *Legitimacy: Ambiguities of Success and Failure*, edited by Lynn White, 29–66. New Jersey: World Scientific.

Gomez, Edmund Terence. 1998. "Malaysia." In *Political Party Systems and Democratic Development in East and Southeast Asia*, vol. 1, edited by Wolfgang Sachsenroder and Ulrike E. Frings, 226–288. Aldershot: Ashgate.

Gomez, Edmund Terence, and K. S. Jomo. 1999. *Malaysia's Political Economy: Politics, Patronage and Profits*. Cambridge: Cambridge University Press.

Greene, Kenneth F. 2007. *Why Dominant Parties Lose: Mexico's Democratization in Comparative Perspective*. Cambridge: Cambridge University Press.

Haggard, Stephen. 2000. *The Political Economy of the Asian Financial Crisis*. Washington DC: Institute for International Economics.

Horowitz, Donald. 1993. "Democracy in Divided Societies." *Journal of Democracy* 44: 18–38.

Jesudason, James V. 1987. *Ethnicity and the Economy: The State, Chinese Business and Multinationals in Malaysia*. Singapore: Oxford University Press.

———. 1996. "The Syncretic State and the Structuring of Oppositional Politics in Malaysia." In *Political Oppositions in Industrializing Asia*, edited by Garry Rodan, 128–160. London: Routledge.

Kuek Ser Kuang Keng. 2006. "Police 'Attack' IPCMC in Internal Bulletin." *Malaysiakini.com*, May 27, http://www.malaysiakini.com/news/51654.

Lee Hock Guan. 2008. "Malaysia in 2007: Abdullah Administration under Siege." In *Southeast Asian Affairs, Volume 2008*, edited by Daljit Singh and Tin Maung Maung Than, 187–208. Singapore: Institute of Southeast Asian Studies.

Levitsky, Steven, and Lucan A. Way. 2002. "The Rise of Competitive Authoritarianism." *Journal of Democracy* 132: 51–65.

Lim, G. 2005. "Debating an Equitable Malaysia: Towards an Alternative New National Agenda." *Aliran Monthly* 258, http://www.aliran.com/archives/monthly/2005b/8h.html

Lim Kit Siang. 2008. "Political Tsunami in General Election." *Lim Kit Siang for Malaysia*, May 8, http://blog.limkitsiang.com/2008/03/08/political-tsunami-in-general-election/

Liow, Joseph Chinyong 2004. "Political Islam in Malaysia: Problematising Discourse and Practice in the UMNO-PAS 'Islamisation Race.'" *Commonwealth and Comparative Politics* 422: 184–205.

Lopez, Leslie. 2003–2004. "He's No Mahathir, and that's OK." *Far Eastern Economic Review*, December 25–January 1.

———. 2004. "Abdullah Gains in Corruption Fight." *Far Eastern Economic Review*, March 4.

Means, Gordon P. 1991. *Malaysian Politics: The Second Generation*. Singapore: Oxford University Press.

Merdeka Center. 2008 [incorrectly dated 2007]. *12th General Elections—Observations on Issues, Voting Directions and Implications*. http://www.merdeka.org/v2/download/Post%20Election%20Overview%20-%20Presentation.pdf.

Milne, R. S., and Diane K. Mauzy. 1999. *Malaysian Politics under Mahathir.* London: Routledge.

Moten, Abdul Rashid. 2006. "The 2004 General Elections in Malaysia: A Mandate to Rule." *Asian Survey* 462: 319–340.

Muzaffar, Chandra. 1979. *Protector? An Analysis of the Concept and Practice of Loyalty in Leader-Led Relationships within Malay Society.* Penang: Aliran.

Netto, Anil. 2008. "Fuel on Malaysia's Political Fire." *Asia Times Online,* June 11, http://www.atimes.com/atimes/Southeast_Asia/JF11Ae02.html.

Ong Kian Miang. 2008. "Making Sense of the Political Tsunami." *Malaysiakini.com,* March 11, http://www.malaysiakini.com/news/79604.

Pepinsky, Thomas B. 2009. "The 2008 Malaysian Elections: An End to Ethnic Politics?" *Journal of East Asian Studies* 91: 87–120.

Pereira, Brendon. 2004a. "Battling Money Politics Entails Tougher Crackdown." *New Sunday Times,* September 26.

———. 2004b. "Show Us Proof, Says Abdullah." *New Straits Times,* September 25.

Schedler, Andreas. 2002. "The Menu of Manipulation." *Journal of Democracy* 132: 36–50.

Weatherford, M. Stephen. 1992. "Measuring Political Legitimacy." *American Political Science Review* 861: 149–166.

Weiss, Meredith L. 2009. "Edging toward a New Politics in Malaysia: Civil Society at the Gate?" *Asian Survey* 495: 741–758.

Welsh, Bridget. 2007. "Malaysia's November 2007 Protests: Challenge to Legitimacy." *Asia Pacfic Bulletin* 6: 1–2.

Zahiid, Syed Jaymal, and Fathi Aris Omar. 2008. "Khir Toyo: UMNO Has Lost Touch with Reality." *Malaysiakini.com,* April 28, http://www.malaysiakini.com/news/82047.

Zakaria Haji Ahmad. 1989. "Malaysia: Quasi Democracy in a Divided Society." In *Democracy in Developing Countries,* vol. 3: *Asia,* edited by Larry Diamond, Juan Linz, and Seymour Martin Lipset, 347–381. Boulder CO: Lynne Rienner.

CHAPTER 7

The Political Legitimacy of the PAP Government in Singapore

Benjamin Wong and Xunming Huang

I make no apologies that the PAP is the government, and the government is the PAP. (Lee Kuan Yew)[1]

Introduction

The question of political legitimacy continues to be controversial in the case of Singapore given the extreme opinions regarding the tiny island state. To its critics, Singapore is "one of the most outstandingly stubborn cases of authoritarianism" (Sim 2006, 143). Australia's Green leader Bob Brown recently described the PAP government as one that "tramples all over freedom of speech, democracy, the rights of opposition, the ability for public discourse" (Low 2010, A7). Critics seem unable to comprehend why, with its remarkable economic and social progress, Singapore continues to be ruled in an authoritarian fashion. To its admirers, on the other hand, Singapore is a model to be envied, if not emulated. The dean of the prestigious Lee Kuan Yew School of Public Policy regards Singapore as "quite simply the most successful society in the history of humanity" (Kampfner 2009, 15). Tom Plate, an American journalist and distinguished scholar of Asian and Pacific Studies at the Loyola Marymount University in Los Angeles, sees Singapore as "this era's Neo-Utopia, a living example of getting into as utopian a shape as is humanely possible" (2010, 211).

If we were to take the view of its admirers seriously, it would seem that PAP government provides the best model of good governance, and hence of political legitimacy. Moreover, since legitimacy is "always partial rather than total" (White 2005, 3; Narine 2004, 428), the admirers of the PAP government need not claim that Singapore is free from occasional injustices; only that all things considered, there is no better practical alternative to how it can be ordered and governed.

Indeed the PAP government has enjoyed and continues to enjoy broad-based support. But as several scholars have remarked, the level of its legitimacy appears to be rather shallow (Barr and Skrbiš 2008; Narine 2004; Khong 1995). Barr and Skrbiš (2008, 258) interviewed several grassroots leaders from 2003 to 2004, and observed that they displayed "a surprising lack of enthusiasm for the government and a consistent sense of remoteness and disappointment about aspects of the Singapore system." It has also been pointed out that the government has had to engage in "artful manipulations of institutions and procedures" to influence public opinion, discourage opposition, and neutralize critics throughout the course of its long and unbroken rule (Case 2005, 227–228). In other words, the government behaves as if it were "still unsure of its own internal legitimacy" (Narine 2004, 434). And while the government claims to have a strong mandate to rule through regular democratic elections, scholars have often noted that the relation between the government and the people seems to be based on forms of "pragmatic" or "instrumental acquiescence" (George 2007, 129, 133; E. Tan 2010, 82). For a government that believes that it enjoys the trust of the people and that it governs in their best interests, this view of the relation between the people and its government appears rather puzzling.

Following an account of the evolution of the dominance of the PAP government in Singapore politics, this chapter relates the fundamental role that economic development plays in justifying its claim to rule. It then examines the key principles the government appeals to and the practices it engages in to reinforce and sustain its claim to rule. Tensions inherent in each of these sources of legitimacy constantly challenge or qualify the government's ability to manage the diverse and complex social and political interests that have developed alongside the economic progress of the country. Among the most serious challenges to the government's legitimacy is the public's discomfort with the attempt to institutionalize market-based compensation for ministers and senior civil servants, ostensibly based upon the principle of meritocracy. This practice exemplifies the instrumental rationality and elitism that dominates the PAP government, and which shape the nature of the relation between the government and the people. Government and people are bound together in a relationship based on mutual interests rather than the common good. Such a relationship can be stable but requires constant attention to socioeconomic issues and problems that if left unaddressed would weaken or undermine the legitimacy of the PAP government.

Background to PAP Dominance

Singapore is a multiracial society with the Chinese comprising the largest ethnic group, followed by the Malays and the Indians. The island was directly controlled by the British colonial government as a crown colony until 1959 when it was granted limited self-government. Singapore subsequently merged with Malaysia in 1963, but was expelled from the federation and became an independent state in 1965. Even from colonial times, the Chinese population were divided between the English-speaking and the Chinese-speaking. Most of the Chinese-speaking belonged to the working class and were educated in the Chinese vernacular. Inspired by sentiments of nationalism and anticolonialism that prevailed in China, many students and workers were drawn to the idealism of left-wing movements.

Though Lee Kuan Yew is from the English-educated Chinese elite, the People's Action Party (PAP) under him came to power in 1959 by aligning with left-wing groups that enjoyed broad support from the Chinese-speaking population and has remained in power ever since. But while the PAP shared in the anticolonial sentiments of the Chinese, it was wary of the influence of communist idealism and Chinese nationalism. Events leading to merger with Malaya in 1963 changed the nature of the relationship between the PAP government and Chinese-speaking majority in Singapore. Concerns about communism and communalism from both the British authorities and the Malaysian government helped the PAP justify its break with the more radical left-wing element of the alliance. Merger further presented the PAP with the opportunity to promote a multiracial national ideology under the banner of a "Malaysian Malaysia" that implicitly opposed the special position of the Malays and appealed to the Chinese majority seeking equal status in the federation. However, the challenge to Malay rights and dominance eventually led to Singapore's expulsion from Malaysia in 1965.

Expulsion from Malaysia took place amidst regional instability, growing unemployment, communal tensions, and social unrest. The precarious situation of the new state, combined with strategic mistakes by the opposition, enabled the PAP government to engage in a series of tough actions that put an end to effective opposition politics and to overcome powerful trade and student unions in the name of political and economic survival. In protest, the opposition engaged in street demonstrations and undertook not only to boycott parliament altogether but the 1968 elections as well. As a result of this the PAP was able to win all 58 seats in parliament. The self-destruction of the opposition in effect enabled the PAP leadership "to create, as if on a tabula rasa, a political regime in its own desired image, untroubled by any effective challenge" (Khong 1995, 115).

In order to resolve pressing socioeconomic problems confronting the newly independent state, the PAP government needed the cooperation of the civil service. Accordingly it set out to reform civil servants through reeducation and to co-opt them by raising their salaries and improving their reputation with the people (Quah 2010). At the same time the PAP government enhanced the powers of its corruption agency to stamp out corruption (ibid.). These early policies laid the foundation for the reputation of the PAP government as clean and efficient, an enduring aspect of its legitimacy. The integration of the civil service also signalled the transformation of the PAP. As S. Rajaratnam, a founding member of the PAP and one of its long-serving ministers, recalled, "[i]t did not take long before we established a close link between us and the civil service. In fact, after the first two elections, the PAP became really an administration. It was no longer a party. And the civil service became a part of that" (Vasil 2000, 59). As the administrative or managerial state evolved, its leadership would be recruited from among the elites in the civil service, the military and the business sectors, to a point where it would become "hard to say whether a particular member of Singapore's governing elite is a private or public actor" (Hamilton-Hart 2000, 197).

With the aid of the technocratic elite, the PAP government was able to exercise comprehensive control over key areas of political, economic, and social life of the country. The success of the PAP government in transforming and modernizing Singapore has not only reinforced its pragmatic and rationalistic approach to policymaking, but has also served to validate the paternalistic and authoritarian character of its relationship with the people. The PAP government has been unapologetic about its extensive intrusion into the lives of citizens. Speaking about the early period of his government Lee Kuan Yew remarked, "I say without remorse that we would not be here, would not have made the economic progress if we had not intervened in every personal matter—who your neighbour is, how you live, the noise you make, how you spit, or what language you use" (Vasil 2000, 51).

Economic Performance

Before independence the PAP government was primarily legitimized by the provision of employment and social services to a predominantly proletarian population. Its legitimacy was reinforced by rapid socioeconomic development in the first two decades of independence. Since the government continues to be fundamentally legitimized by its provision of security and prosperity, this requires a single-minded pursuit of sustained economic growth.

To understand the economic and political vulnerability of Singapore at the time of its independence, it is important to note that Singapore is a very small island with limited natural resources. Unemployment in 1965 was at a high of 9%–10%. And in 1967 the British announced that it was withdrawing its military base, thus exacerbating the precarious economic and security situation of the country (Rodan 2006). These circumstances compelled the PAP government to accelerate its programme of industrialization. With the loss of access to a hinterland after the expulsion from Malaysia, the PAP government embarked on an export-oriented industrialization program. This program required it to attract foreign MNCs by offering generous tax breaks and subsidies, cheap land, compliant labor, and efficient infrastructure. At the same time the PAP government also embarked on a number of programs to provide the people with affordable housing and other social services. The success of its housing policy mitigates otherwise unpopular social policies carried out by the PAP government and is a major factor in sustaining its political legitimacy (Hill and Lian 1995, 123). These and other related economic measures proved to be extremely successful, unemployment was gradually brought down to below 4% by 1974, and the annual growth rates of the country from 1966 to 1973 were in the double digits (Lim and Lee 2010; Rodan 2006). Overall, the economic success of the country is nothing short of miraculous having achieved the highest national income growth in the world from 1960 to 2006, with GDP per capita going from S$1,320 in 1960 to S$53,143 in 2009 (Verweij and Pelizzo 2009, 20).

Singapore underwent further economic restructuring in the 1980s to improve productivity by shifting the economy toward more capital and skills intensive activities (Lim and Lee 2010; Rodan 2006). Since the 1990s the government has invested huge sums in R&D and has lately promoted life sciences as the fourth pillar of the economy after electronics, chemicals, and engineering. The Asian financial crisis of 1997 pushed the government toward a policy of external economic expansion. Through the development of Government Linked Corporations (GLCs) and the establishment of the Government Investment Corporation (GIC) the PAP government has become increasingly active internationally to access cheap labor and to attract top talent to help increase its global competitiveness (Goldstein and Pananond 2008). In more recent decades the PAP has had to liberalize both economically and socially to make Singapore a desirable place for talented foreigners, yet this did not compromise the PAP political dominance. On the contrary, the liberalization measures adopted by the party have further softened the authoritarian image of the government, thus enhancing both its domestic as well as international legitimacy.

Nonetheless, Singapore paid a hefty social price for its economic success. With perhaps the exception of South Koreans, Singaporeans work far longer than workers of the OECD countries (Verweij and Pelizzo 2009, 22–23), and they are currently expected to do even more in terms of improving productivity. The push toward greater productivity would aggravate the already stressful conditions of working life in Singapore. Singapore, moreover, is a rich country with many citizens struggling to make a decent living. The poorest 20% of workers in Singapore earn about S$749 a month (Li and Hussain, 2010, A40). Economically, it is the most unequal among the developed countries. Though economic inequality has been increasing since the 1980s, it has gone up more sharply since 2000.[2] Singapore thus appears to be "a First World Economy with what is closer to a Third World wage structure" (Chia 2010b).

One of the major reasons for this inequality has been attributed to the large influx of foreign workers. There are two categories of such workers: low skilled and high skilled. The low skilled foreign workers place a cap on the earning power of lesser skilled Singaporeans, while the high skilled foreigners stretch the upper limits of compensation (Li and Hussain 2010, A40). The influx of foreign workers and along with it the expansion in the numbers of permanent residents have caused widespread unhappiness among citizens. With a population of slightly over 5 million on an island a mere 710 km^2 in size, Singapore is one of the most densely populated countries in the world. Making up over a third of the population, noncitizens have been blamed for a host of issues ranging from competition for employment and school places, to rising costs of home prices as well as congestion on the roads and public transportation.

A recent survey showed that two in three Singaporeans felt that large numbers of foreigners would compromise national unity (Kok 2010, A4). The survey also revealed that those most concerned about the presence of foreigners are low-income earners. Although the PAP government has been outwardly hostile to welfare, the growing inequality has forced it to maintain an elaborate system of support for workers and their families. The Workfare Income Supplement Scheme (WIS), for example, was implemented in 2007 to supplement the income of low-wage workers. Following the financial crisis of 2008, the Jobs Credit

Scheme and the Skills Program for Upgrading and Resilience aimed to help employers retain workers and improve their productivity. For the poor and disadvantaged there are schemes like the Community Care Endowment Fund (ComCare) as well as government-supported ethnic-based self-help organizations to assist them. But it is not clear if these provisions are sufficient to overcome problems relating to the high cost of living and the diminished social mobility of poorer citizens.

At a recent speech by Senior Minister Goh Chok Tong, an undergraduate told the minister that with the influx of foreigners, "I really don't know what I'm defending any more...I feel there is a dilution of the Singapore spirit in youth...We don't really feel comfortable in our country any more" (Lin 2010, A14). Noting that this was a matter of deep concern, the senior minister said, "This is one early sign of danger...If this is happening, it is very serious" (A14). The government is acutely aware of the general unhappiness associated with the influx of foreign workers, and has made attempts to sharpen the distinction between citizens and noncitizens. But even the recent introduction of the National Service Recognition Award to reward national servicemen was greeted with a notable degree of cynicism (Ho, S. H. 2010, A 28). Although the government is trying to reduce reliance on foreigners, the problem of growing inequality associated with policies to attract top talent will not be resolved in the near future and will continue to challenge the government's legitimacy.

Democracy

The Singapore political system has been variously described as an illiberal democracy (Lam 1999), an electoral autocracy (Diamond 2002), and a semidemocracy (Vasil 2002). All these labels fall under the rubric "hybrid regimes," that is, regimes that variously combine authoritarian rule with elements of democracy (Diamond 2002; Case 2005). Accurate or otherwise these labels imply that the PAP government lacks legitimacy when judged by the standards of liberal democracy. The PAP government, however, has always maintained its opposition to liberal democracy as a yardstick of political legitimacy. Moreover, it rejects the label of authoritarianism on the grounds that it governs with the consent of the people (Plate 2010, 182). What is important for the PAP government is that it is able to "offer what every citizen wants—a good life, security, good education, and a future for their children" (Kampfner 2009, 30). For this reason each election is treated as "a public demonstration of undivided support for the government's policies" and as a means "to secure a renewal of a mandate that enables policy to be enunciated in a didactic manner" (Khong 1994, 132). With reference to the upcoming election Senior Minister Goh Chok Tong has once again warned younger Singaporeans about the dangers of liberal democracy and reminded them that democracy "is a means to select a government to look after [their] lives like a guardian or a trustee" (Chang 2010, A1).

Though the PAP clearly has a commanding position in Parliament, the government nevertheless has put up considerable obstacles to impede the opposition. In addition to its control of the media and its use of libel action against opposition members, the government has in place a range of measures that severely constrain the activities of the opposition (Au 2010).[3] All these measures have been used in spite of the fact that opposition parties are small, fragmented, and poorly funded. Furthermore, since losing two seats to the opposition in 1984, it has introduced fundamental modifications to the parliamentary system. The Non-Constituency Member of Parliament (NCMP) scheme ensures that a number of seats will be set aside for the best performing defeated opposition candidates. To help raise the level of debate, nine nonpartisan members were introduced into Parliament through the Nominated Member of Parliament (NMP) scheme. To ensure that there would be adequate minority representation in Parliament, multimember constituencies called Group Representation Constituencies (GRCs) were introduced. Critics charge that these modifications serve to further impede the opposition in contesting elections. The NCMP and NMP schemes, for example, have the effect of "weakening the sentiment for *electing* more opposition members" (Muazy and Milne 2002, 144). GRCs, on the other hand, stretch the human and financial resources of opposition parties (Au 2010, 105–106).

In spite of the many obstacles placed in its way, the opposition has been able to garner between 30 and 40% of the votes since 1988 though an economic downturn coupled with the events of 9/11 gave the PAP an unusually high share of the vote in 2001 (Au 2010, 104). The government, in spite of its dominance over Parliament, has not always reacted well to the decline in its share of votes and the loss of Parliamentary seats. During the 1997 elections the PAP government threatened to deprive housing estates that voted for the opposition of state-funded upgrades to their facilities. As 85% of the population live in public housing, this was clearly a very serious threat. Yet the government failed in its attempt to win over all the opposition wards, and the elections did not bring about a major shift in votes for the PAP. The use of such hardball tactics by the government and its intimidation of opposition members inspire not only fear but but also resentment in the people, and so compromise the kind of validation it seeks from the people. The upgrading strategy, for example, only served to harden the resolve of those opposed to the PAP government. On the other hand, those who voted for the PAP out of fear or self-interest do not feel obliged or grateful to the government for the benefits of upgrading. Such strategies merely reinforce the instrumental relationship between the people and the government.

Analyses of elections since 1988 show that issues of class, culture, and race have variously contributed to the decline of government's share of votes (Au 2010; Vasil 2000; Chua 1994; Rodan 1993). For example, working-class perceptions of a middle-class bias in government policies affected PAP votes in 1991. And since most working-class Singaporeans are Chinese-speaking, issues of language and culture also contributed to the decline of PAP votes. And it is worth recalling that working-class grievances have their roots in the government's restructuring of the economy in the 1980s, a policy that contributed to the widening income gap in Singapore. About half the voters in the next election would be citizens born after 1965. Apart from being more exposed to the West through travel and education, this generation of the voters are adept in using the Internet to share their views and criticisms of the government. As they tend to be more liberal minded, they seem to be pushing the government toward greater political liberalization, in spite of the government's aversion to it. These younger voters might be the reason why the government has made gestures to allow for greater diversity of views and political contestation by passing legislation that would increase the number of non-PAP members in Parliament to 18. Whether such gestures are sufficient to satisfy these younger voters remain to be seen. On the other hand, greater openness to a diversity of views may serve to strengthen the PAP government's role as a "neutral" intermediary.

Multiracialism and Asian Values

Over the years the government has experimented with a variety of nation-building projects to reinforce its legitimacy. At first it explored the possibility of a Singaporean identity that would transcend racial differences, but this proved difficult and so the prevailing policy has been to acknowledge Singapore's multiracial character within a larger vision of common objectives and purposes, usually spelt out in economic terms.

But because of its experience with communal conflict, the government has always been mindful of the problems that can be posed by divisions of race and religion. Since coming into power the PAP government has pursued a policy of multiracialism to assure the different races that their interests would be protected, while at the same time ensuring that issues relating to religion, language, and race are not politicized. The country has four official languages: English, Mandarin, Malay, and Tamil. Malay is the national language, and English the lingua franca as well as the language of administration. In education the policy of bilingualism ensures that students retain their cultural traditions through the study of their mother tongues. The government has also sponsored ethnic-based self-help organizations to attend to the educational and social needs of low-income families. Public housing where some 85% of Singaporeans live, is carefully managed to encourage social integration and to prevent the formation of racial or socioeconomic enclaves. These measures have enabled the various races to coexist peacefully.

But the principle of multiracialism also has paradoxical effects that complicate the PAP government's efforts to set the agenda for its nation-building projects. For one thing it encourages people to identify more closely with their ethnic group and culture rather than the common good (Hill and Lian 1995, 104). For another it causes confusion about the relation between ethnicity and nation building. Take, for example, the daily routine of students reciting the Singapore Pledge and singing the National Anthem. The pledge and anthem are major symbols of national identity. But most of the Chinese and Indian students would not understand the anthem, which is in Malay. In 2009 an attempt was made by an NMP to affirm the principle of equality contained in the Pledge. It was, however, roundly rebuffed by Minister Mentor Lee Kuan Yew, who maintained that the argument for equal treatment of the races in Singapore's context was "false and flawed" (B6). MM Lee reminded the House that it is a duty of the government not to treat all races equally as there are explicit provisions in the constitution recognizing the special position of the Malays, the indigenous people of Singapore. As far as MM Lee was concerned, the Pledge was at best an aspiration, the attainment of which would take decades, if not centuries. And because the government has a duty to protect the rights and interests of Malays it is now confronted with a new problem. Economic policies that led to the influx of foreign workers mainly from China and India are now responsible for a drop in the percentage of Malays in the Singapore population. Leaders from the Malay community are acutely concerned that the slide in numbers might make Malay culture and language less important in the future (Hussain 2010a, B2). While the prime minister has assured the community that the current mix of the population would not be changed, it is not clear how this will be accomplished.

A recent attempt by the minister of education to review the demands of the Chinese language component of the Primary School Leaving Examination created an unexpected public uproar, requiring the prime minister's intervention to resolve it. Many took the review as a sign that the government was lessening its commitment to Chinese language and culture. The concerns of Chinese-speaking Chinese are partly based on the fact that more and more Chinese children are speaking English at home. In an interview with the press, an academic offered the following explanation of the eruption of emotion from Chinese Singaporeans: "The government, which is controlled by the English-educated elite, has always been trying to push this through, to make sure the Chinese language is being made much easier for the English-speaking families. What you have here is that they have reached a stage where they (the Chinese-speaking elite) are not able to tolerate the advances of the English-educated elites anymore" (Au Yong and Cai 2010, A6).

Toward the late 1970s as economic and material conditions improved, the PAP government became concerned about the unhealthy and undesirable influence of Western liberal ideas and values. The government responded by advocating a "communitarian" ideology grounded in traditional "Asian Values" such as Confucianism. The PAP government's version of Confucianism was promoted in the 1980s, and this was superseded by Shared Values (1991) and Singapore 21 (1999).[4] By emphasizing a person's duty to the state, community as well as family, these various versions attempt to subordinate the individual to society. Critics argue that the Asian Values were introduced to support the values necessary for economic development as well as to maintain the hierarchical and paternalistic character of PAP rule (McCarthy 2006; Barr 2002). Others, however, have maintained that aspects of Asian Values do resonate with segments of Singaporean society that are culturally and religiously conservative (Mauzy and Milne 2002; Barr 2002). At any rate the problem is that the social aspects of current economic policies clash with the traditional Asian values defended by the PAP government. To maintain the country's global competitiveness the PAP government was prepared to liberalize socially to make Singapore a more attractive place for talented foreigners. This policy entailed a more liberal and tolerant attitude on the part of the government toward forms of entertainment and lifestyle choices, including homosexuality, much to the dismay of social and religious conservatives. The decision to set up two casinos to boost tourism and employment also caused considerable consternation among conservative-minded Singaporeans. These policies have been "interpreted by many Singaporeans as signs of a government that is betraying its conservative heartland constituency and thereby losing its moral authority" (Tan KP 2007, 305).

Meritocracy and Ministerial Salaries

The political attitude of the PAP government has been from the very outset realistic, pragmatic, and above all elitist (Tan 2010; Barr and Skrbiš 2008). For Lee Kuan Yew the future of Singapore always depended on the rare gifts of a few talented men: "I am sorry if I am constantly preoccupied with what the near-geniuses and the above average are going to do. But I am convinced that it is they who ultimately decide the shape of things to come" (Barr 2000). As leader of the country Lee Kuan Yew would set the precedent of cultivating elites and empowering them to effect fundamental social and cultural changes to transform the country into an economic powerhouse. This attitude with slight modification has persisted throughout the course of PAP rule, and may even have intensified in its later phases.

The principle of meritocracy, a crucial pillar of PAP governance, requires that individuals be rewarded on the basis of ability and effort and not on the basis of race, class, or other ascriptive factors. More importantly it serves to justify economic inequalities. The principle is applied in education where considerable resources are dedicated to the selection and training of talented students, many of whom are offered prestigious government scholarships to study at top universities in the West. The most promising of these scholars would later be groomed to become top officials and even ministers. In 1989, then prime minister Goh Chok Tong boasted that nearly every minister in his cabinet "was among the top students of their year" (Quah 2003, 151). In 1994, 8 out of 14 cabinet ministers were scholars; and in 2005 there were 12 scholars in a Cabinet of 19. In the current cabinet 13 of the 21 ministers are scholars.

Since 1994, the principle of meritocracy has also been invoked to justify the fact that the top government officials and ministers in Singapore are the highest paid public servants in the world. This reflects the view of Prime Minister Lee Hsien Loong that "in a meritocratic society, earning power corresponds to ability" (cited in Barr and Skrbiš 2008, 208). Government salaries have been steadily increasing since 1972, but as the economy continued to improve, it became more difficult for the government to recruit and retain its ministers and top officials. The government, therefore, decided in 1994 to benchmark the salaries of ministers and civil servants to the average salaries of top earners in the private sector. This decision institutionalized the practice of "matching public pay to the private sector, dollar for dollar" (Quah 2003, 154). As for the high salaries of ministers, the government takes the view that it must "ensure that after having sacrificed their privacy, leisure and family time, such people do not also have to make too large a financial sacrifice" (153). In 2007 the government revised the salaries of ministers and civil servants with ministers at the starting grade getting a hefty pay rise of 33%. The pay of these ministers went up from S$1.2 million to S$1.6 million. The prime minister's salary was increased by 25% from S$2.5 million to S$3.1 million (Lim, L. 2007).

Salaries of ministers and permanent secretaries are based on a formula that pegs their pay to two-thirds the median income of the top eight earners in six professions ("Ministerial Salaries Well Below Benchmark" 2007). While the formula is intended to remove the need to justify future pay increases, the government is invariably obliged to defend the policy each time salaries for its ministers and top officials are increased. Regarding the debate over the revision of salaries in 2007, K. Shanmugam, the minister for law and second minister for home affairs, said, "I cannot think of another issue where there is such a disconnect between what is clearly the right policy, and how the public react to that policy" (Shanmugam 2007, H5). The policy is clearly not a popular one, and Shanmugam may be right in indicating that it is a fundamental issue that shapes the nature of the relationship between the people and the government. The people's reaction suggests that they were not prepared to accept the kind of politics entailed by the policy. As Chua Beng Huat (2008, 56) has observed, "the logic of government is the logic of big business is an unavoidable consequence of the salary system, this mode of reasoning has become an integral part of PAP's economy-driven political and administrative pragmatism."

In response to the debate, Prime Minister Lee Hsien Loong maintained that he and the government do value people "to whom an income is irrelevant and who will do what they feel they want to do regardless of pay. When we find them, we will field them if they are suitable" (Lee, H. L. 2007). This statement reflects a particular difficulty with the PAP leadership. The prime minister cannot identify himself as such a person without offending or undermining the other ministers—in fact, the speech does not give any examples of people in this category. At the same time he has to concur with those who defend the ideal of noble sacrifice in public life:

> Many MPs have raised…the question of moral authority. They have made the argument that public office requires selflessness and sacrifice, that Ministers especially must have moral authority to lead, not just manage. Therefore, you cannot expect wages comparable to the private sector…I agree with these propositions in principle. You must be selfless, you must have some sacrifice, you must have the moral authority to lead, to get people to follow you and therefore it cannot be exactly the same as the private sector. (Lee H. L. 2007)

Having conceded that some sacrifice is necessary, the prime minister then concluded that "[y]ou need a bit of financial sacrifice. Some, but this is not an auction" (Lee H. L. 2007). For his part the prime minister decided to hold his own salary at the previous level for five years, with the increment going to charity. This apparently constitutes his "bit of financial sacrifice" so that it would give him the "moral standing to defend the policy with Singaporeans" (ibid.).

The speech is a little confusing because it fails to clarify the nature and place of "selflessness and sacrifice" in the system of governance in Singapore. In this connection it is worth noting that the sacrifice of the prime minister is somewhat paradoxical, he sacrifices his pay in order to justify a policy that says that such sacrifices are ultimately unnecessary. The speech thus leaves ambiguous the ideas of duty and sacrifice in the political life of Singaporean ministers. It is this ambiguity about the place of duty and sacrifice in the political culture of Singapore that may help to explain the apparent "disconnect" between the people and the government. And this in turn would seem to limit the moral character of the political legitimacy enjoyed by the government.

Over the years there have been several widely publicised issues concerning the problems posed by elitism (Wong and Huang 2010, 535–538). In dealing with the concerns of the public some political leaders have "often shown themselves to be arrogant, insensitive, and lacking in compassion" (Tan 2010, 280). The public expression of moral outrage in such cases suggests that the public does not believe that privileges enjoyed by the ruling elites are fully deserved. Because the relation between the government and the people is fundamentally one of exchange, both parties are particularly sensitive to any perceived tilt in the established balance of fair exchange. The political leadership's faith in meritocracy, which justifies the policy of amply rewarding the talented, commits it to the view that those who succeed in enriching others, as measured by economic growth, should not be poorer for it. The belief in meritocracy leads the ruling elites to dismiss the public's moral resentment against the ruling elites as manifestations of envy aimed at depriving them of their just rewards. This is reinforced by the fact that the public is widely regarded as incapable of producing good policies, especially those promoting economic growth. The historical memory of a more equitable income distribution in the early decades of independent Singapore and the subsequent growing income gap seem to have made the public deeply suspicious of the ruling elite's claim to fulfil their end of the bargain, the provision of security and prosperity.

Conclusion

The political legitimacy of the PAP government rests on its ability to sustain economic growth and to provide for the material well-being of its citizens. As a consequence of its economic success, Singapore society has become more diverse and complex. The PAP government is, therefore, confronted by a range of socioeconomic problems that constantly challenge its ability and capacity to address and resolve competing demands of its citizens. Hitherto it has been able to accommodate but not fully satisfy these demands. The lingering dissatisfaction of the citizens occasionally breaks out into public expressions of unhappiness that do not seriously endanger the government's dominant position. To be sure, no government is able to fully satisfy the diversity of competing demands in society. But the ability of the PAP government to sustain economic growth has convinced a majority of Singaporeans that there are no better alternatives to PAP rule. And by virtue of its control of state resources, the PAP government has been able to regulate the expression of political dissent as well as to mitigate public criticisms of its policies and practices. Indeed, the PAP government has been so successful in neutralizing problems and disarming its critics that it has reduced the country to "a nation of complainers" (Lim, W. C. 2006). As Minister Mentor Lee Kuan Yew has said, Singaporeans are "champion grumblers" (Lee KY 2010, A19). And lately Senior Minister Goh Chok Tong has coined the term "Singapore Gripe" to characterize the prevailing passion of Singaporeans (Hussain 2010b, I). These complains, however, have the potential to threaten the legitimacy of the PAP government and the most serious of them are related to the system of market-based compensation of ministers and top officials. In a recent speech to scholars, the chairman of the Public Service Commission noted that "[some] of our citizens are now beginning to expect the government to do the impossible. Many citizens are now less prepared to give the government room to make mistakes and are less forgiving and more demanding. They tend to regard explanations as excuses... Every time something goes wrong in Singapore, citizens ask, 'If our public servants and ministers are smart and paid so well, why can't they prevent the problem from occurring, or solve it for good after it occurs?'" (Teo 2010, 34).

In his defense of the salary increase of ministers, Prime Minister Lee Hsien Loong compared the median income of ministers ($2.2 million) with the median income of the top 55 earners of companies ($1.75 million) listed on the Singapore stock exchange. The salary of $1.75 million coincides with companies with market capitalization of between $4 and $5 billion dollars. The prime minister made the comparison in order to imagine what Singapore would be like if it were turned into a corporation. "If Singapore Inc were a listed company, what would its market capitalization be ...My GDP, which is the profit earned by Singapore Inc is $210 billion. The average price earnings ratio on the Singapore exchange is now 20. So if I calculated a market capitalization-if Singapore Inc. went for an IPO-- this is a $4 trillion dollar company." On the basis of this calculation the pay of the minister should be about a thousand times the median income of the top 55 private sector earners. The purpose of the comparison may have been to show that the cost of government to Singaporeans is still relatively "cheap" (Chua 2008, 56). But, on the other hand, it also reveals the immense gulf separating ministers from most Singaporeans, both rich and poor alike.[5]

The Singaporean bargain has involved the political acquiescence of the people in exchange for security and development produced by a meritocratic elite ostensibly dedicated to serving the best interests of all citizens. But the market-based compensation of ministers and top officials leaves unclear what it is that motivates the political leadership. Members of the ruling elite cannot say that they are not motivated by the desire for wealth and prestige. They cannot be characterized as individuals who are selfless in their devotion and dedication to the country. Accordingly, they cannot unambiguously command the deep respect and honor they believe they deserve from the people. Prime Minister Le Hsien Loong, moreover, has conceded that sacrifice is somehow necessary in politics to attain moral standing. But as the chief representative of the government he has only gone as far as to make "a bit of financial sacrifice." Such a sacrifice would not, therefore, command great moral authority. The market-based system of compensation only serves to reinforce the instrumental relationship between the government and the people, thus frustrating the regime's quest to cultivate a deeper sense of legitimacy with the people.[6]

Notes

1. Cited in Ho (2010, 72).
2. The Gini coefficient for Singapore is measured at 0.425 in 2009. Among the developed economies, only Hong Kong is higher at 0.434. In comparison, the United States stands at 0.408, while the Japan and the Nordic states are under 0.3."
3. Some noteworthy legislation include the Internal Security Act, the Societies Act, the Public Entertainment and Licensing Act, the Undesirable Publications Act, the Maintenance of Religious Harmony Act, and the Political Donations Act.
4. Mauzy and Milne (2002, 64) note that the reception to Shared Values was "muted and rather unenthusiastic."
5. The comparison, however, reveals how close the imagined compensation of Singaporean ministers is to CEOs of top corporations in the world. The highest paid CEO in the United States in 2008 was Steven Schwarzman of the Blackstone Group. He received US$702.4 million dollars (S$1 billion) just as the global recession deepened. ("US' highest-paid CEO earns $1b," *Straits Times*, August 15, 2009).
6. The PAP retained its dominant position in Parliament after the General Election held on May 7, 2011. It won 60.1% of the votes and secured 81 out of 87 parliamentary seats. However, this was widely held to be a watershed event. Though it gained a modest six seats, this was the most seats the opposition has won since independence. Moreover, the opposition achieved this by winning a GRC, displacing three PAP ministers, including the highly regarded Minister of Foreign Affairs George Yeo. During the election, several ministers acknowledged that there was widespread anger and resentment toward the PAP government. PM Lee Hsien Loong even took the unusual step of publicly apologizing for the mistakes of his administration. Research and submission of this chapter was completed at the end of 2010 and so did not cover the events surrounding the General Election. Nonetheless, the unhappiness with the PAP government during the election revolved around the socio-economic issues identified and discussed in this chapter. Furthermore, events immediately following the election lend support to the main argument of this chapter regarding problems with the market-based system of compensating ministers and top officials. The first initiative the PM undertook with his new cabinet was to call for a major review of minister's salaries. This is an indication of how unpopular the salary

system is with many Singaporeans. Still, it is not clear how this issue will be resolved as it is so intimately linked to the principle of meritocracy and the government's belief about the need to compete with the private sector to attract and retain its most talented ministers and officers.

References

Au, Alex Waipang. 2010. "The Ardour of Tokens, Opposition Parties Struggle to Make a Difference." In *Management of Success, Singapore Revisited*, edited by Terence Chong, 100–122. Singapore, Institute of Southeast Asian Studies.

Au Yong, Jeremy, and Cai Haoxiang. 2010. "Why Mother Tongue Is Such an Emotive Issue." *The Straits Times*, May 12, A6.

Barr, Michael, D. 2002. *Cultural Politics and Asian Values: The Tepid War.* London, Routledge.

———. 2000. *Lee Kuan Yew: The Beliefs behind the Man.* Washington DC: Georgetown University Press.

Barr, Michael D., and Zlatko Skrbiš. 2008. *Constructing Singapore, Elitism, Ethnicity and the Nation-Building Project.* Denmark: Nordic Institute of Asian Studies Press

Case, William. 2005. "Southeast Asia's Hybrid Regimes." *Journal of East Asian Studies* 5: 215–237.

Chang, Rachel. 2010. "A Watershed Election for Youth, SM." *The Straits Times*, October 30, A1.

Chia, Sue-Ann. 2010a. "Why Unions Back Productivity Push." *The Straits Times*, March 4.

———. 2010b. "World Country, But Not First World Wages?" *The Straits Times*, May 18, 2010B. Accessed on http,//www.asiaone.com/Business/News/Office/Story/A1Story20100517-216611.html

Chua, Beng Huat. 1994. "Arrested Development, Democratisation in Singapore." *Third World Quaterly* 15 (4): 655–668.

———. 2008. "Singapore in 2007, High Wage Ministers and the Management of Gays and Elderly." *Asian Survey* 48 (1): 55–61.

Diamond, Larry. 2002. "Thinking about Hybrid Regimes." *Journal of Democracy* 13 (2): 21–35.

George, Cherian. 2007. "Consolidating Authoritarian Rule: Calibrated Coercion in Singapore." *The Pacific Review* 20 (2): 127–147.

Goldstein, Andrea, and Pavida Pananond. 2008. "Singapore Inc Goes Shopping Abroad, Profits and Pitfalls." *Journal of Contemporary Asia* 38 (3): 417–438.

Hamilton-Hart, Natasha. 2000. "The Singapore State Revisited." *The Pacific Review* 13 (2): 195–216.

Hill, Michael and Kwen Fee Lian. 1995. *The Politics of Nation Building and Citizenship in Singapore.* London: Routledge.

Ho Khai Leong. 2003. *Shared Responsibilities, Unshared Power, the Politics of Policy-Making in Singapore*. Singapore: Eastern University Press.

Ho Shu Huang. 2010. "Consider a Coherent Structure for Rewards." *The Straits Times*, September 8, A28.

Hussain, Zakir. 2010a. "Malay Leaders Worry about Numbers, Nation's Largest Minority Group Is Shrinking as Percentage of Population." *The Straits Times*, September2, B2.

———. 2010b. "SM Goh Recasts the 5 Cs." *The Sunday Times*, August 8, 1.

Kampfner, John. 2009. *Freedom for Sale, How We Made Money and Lost Our Liberty*. London: Simon & Shuster.

Khong Cho-Oon. 1995. "Singapore, Political Legitimacy through Managing Conformity Political Legitimacy." In *Southeast Asia: The Quest for Moral Authority*, edited by Muthiah Alagappa. Stanford: Stanford University Press.

Kok, Melissa. 2010. "Two in Three Concerned about Impact of Foreigners." *The Straits Times*, August 2, A4.

Lam, Peng Er. 1999. "Singapore, Rich State, Illiberal Regime." In *Driven by Growth, Political Change in the Asia Pacific Region*, Revised Edition, edited by James W. Morley, 255–274. Singapore: Institute of Southeast Asian Studies.

Lee, Hsien Loong. 2006. "Securing Home Base." *The Straits Times*, December 5, 23.

———. 2007. Speech by the Prime Minister Lee Hsien Loong at Parliamentary Debate on Civil Service Salary Revisions. Prime Minister's Office, Singapore, April 11.

———. 2009. "A System in Sync with Aspirations of S'poreans." *The Straits Times*, May 28, A14.

Lee, Kuan Yew. 2004. "The Culture that Makes a Nation Competitive—or Not." *The Straits Times*, April 22, 2.

Lee, Kuan Yew. 2009. "Dangerous to Let Highfalutin Ideas to Go Undemolished, Edited Transcript of MM Lee Kuan Yew's Rebuttal of NMP Viswa Sadasivan." *The Straits Times*, August 20, B6.

Lee, Kuan Yew. 2010a. "My Job Is Really as a Long-Range Radar." Part Two of edited excerpts of an interview of MM Lee Kuan Yew with Mark Jacobson of the National Geographic. *The Straits Times*, January 6, 2010, A19

Lee Kuan Yew. 2010b. "Singapore Is a Nation in the Making." Part One of edited excerpts of an interview of MM Lee Kuan Yew with Mark Jacobson of the National Geographic. *The Straits Times*, January 5, A16.

Li Xueying, and Zakir Hussain. 2010. "Widening Wage Gap. Does It Matter?" *The Straits Times*, December 11, A40 & A 42.

Lim, Linda Y. C., and Lee Soo Ann. 2010. "Globalizing State, Disappearing Nation: The Impact of Foreign Participation in the Singapore Economy." In *Management of Success, Singapore Revisited*, edited by Terence Chong, 139–158. Singapore: Institute of Southeast Asian Studies.

Lim, Lydia. 2007. "Ministers and Civil Servants Get Pay Rise of Up to 33%." *The Straits Times*, April 10.

Lim, Wei Chean. 2006. "Stop Whining and Whingeing, MPs Urge." *The Straits Times*. November 10.

Lin, Rachel. "A Disempowered Generation?" *The Straits Times*, October 30, 2010, A14.

Low, Aaron. 2010. "Aussie Backlash a Given, Analysts." *The Straits Times*, October 27, A7.

Mauzy, Diane K., and R. S. Milne. 2002. *Singapore's Politics under the People's Action Party*. London: Routledge.

McCarthy, Stephen. 2006. *The Political Theory of Tyranny in Singapore and Burma*. Oxon: Routledge.

"Ministerial Salaries Well Below Benchmark." 2007. *The Straits Times*, March 23, H14.

Narine, Shaun. 2004. "State Sovereignty, Political Legitimacy and Regional Institutionalism in the Asia-Pacific." *Pacific Review* 17 (3): 423–450.

Plate, Tom. 2010. *Conversations with Lee Kuan Yew*. Singapore: Marshall Cavendish.

Quah, Jon S. T. 2010. *Public Administration Singapore Style*. Singapore: Talisman.

Quah, Jon S. T. 2003. "Paying for the 'Best and Brightest,' Rewards for High Public Office Singapore." In *Rewards for High Public Office, Asia and Pacific Rim States*, edited by Christopher Hood and B. Guy Peters with Grace O. M. Lee, 145–162. London, Routledge.

Rodan, Garry. 1993. "Preserving the One-Party State in Contemporary Singapore in Southeast Asia in the 1990s." In *Authoritarianism, Democracy and Capitalism,* edited by Kevin Hewison, Richard Robison, and Garry Rodan, 77–107. St. Leonards NSW: Allen & Unwin.

———. 2006. "Singapore, Globalisation, the State, and Politics." In *The Political Economy of Southeast Asia, Markets, Power and Contestation*, 3rd ed., edited by Garry Rodan, Kevin Hewison, and Richard Robison, 137–169. Victoria, Australia: Oxford University Press.

Shanmugam, K. 2007. "Why Do We Demand Financial Sacrifice from Those Going into Public Service?" *The Straits Times*, April 11, H5.

Sim, Soek-Fang. 2006. "Hegemonic Authoritarianism and Singapore, Economics, Ideology, and the Asian Economic Crisis." *Journal of Contemporary Asia* 36 (2): 143–159.

Tan, Eugene K. B. 2010. "The Evolving Social Compact and the Transformation of Singapore, Going Beyond Quid Pro Quo in Governance." In *Management of Success, Singapore Revisited*, edited by Terence Chong, 80–99. Singapore, Institute of Southeast Asian Studies.

Tan, Kenneth Paul. 2007. "Singapore's National Day Rally Speech, A Site of Ideological Negotiation." *Journal of Contemporary Asia* 37 (3): 291–308.

————. 2010. "The Transformation of Meritocracy." In *Management of Success, Singapore Revisited*, edited by Terence Chong, 272–287. Singapore: Institute of Southeast Asian Studies.

Tan, Netina. 2009. "Institutionalised Leadership, Resilient Hegemonic Party Autocracy in Singapore." Paper presented at CPSA Conference, 28 May 2009, Ottawa.

Teo, Eddie. 2010. "Idealistic Citizens Help Push Bar for Public Servants." *The Sunday Times*, October 24, 34.

Vasil, Raj. 2000. *Governing Singapore, A History of National Development and Democracy*. St Leonards, NSW: Allen & Unwin.

Verweij, Marco, and Pelizzo Riccardo. 2009. "Singapore, Does Authoritarianism Pay?" *Journal of Democracy* 20 (2): 18–32.

White, Lynn, ed. 2005. *Legitimacy, Ambiguities of Political Success or Failure in East and Southeast Asia*. Singapore, World Scientific.

Wong, Benjamin, and Huang Xunming. 2010. "Political Legitimacy in Singapore." *Politics and Policy*, 38 (3): 523–543.

CHAPTER 8

From Coup d'état to "Disciplined Democracy" in Burma: The Tatmadaw's Claims to Legitimacy

Stephen McCarthy

B urma has experienced continuous military rule for almost half a century.[1] For much of this time, the military has been occupied with fighting separatist insurgencies and suppressing civil unrest. It is remarkable that the Burmese armed forces (*Tatmadaw*) should be at all interested in their own political legitimacy, given that they came to power through the most illegitimate of means—force—and have retained this power by silencing all opposition. That the generals have tried to justify their rule in a number of ways may suggest that force alone is insufficient to hold on to power for a prolonged period of time. Indeed, Burma presents a unique example in the region where a military seeks legitimacy while ruling through fear. The study of legitimacy, in turn, takes on greater significance in Burma as it undergoes possibly more manipulation than elsewhere in the region.

Political legitimacy in Burma can be examined historically, through different periods of rule, or by themes and transitions from one source of legitimacy to another. This chapter attempts to blend the historical and thematic as it concentrates on the sources of legitimacy relied upon by the Tatmadaw since it first came to power. The Tatmadaw's early claims to legitimacy rested upon their success in the battle against insurgency during the postindependence democratic period (from 1948 to 1958, and from 1960 to 1962) and for many years following their coup of 1962. On both occasions, the survival of state unity was a paramount objective. In time, they also came to rely upon some of the same claims to legitimacy that were made during Burma's only experiment with democracy. The most significant of these was based in Burma's historical Buddhist traditions, a claim that all rulers have had to make in this devout Buddhist country. When civil unrest has arisen on a number of occasions due to their own economic mismanagement, however, the generals have been forced to shed these claims and to revert to the inevitable use of force, followed by the offering of elections and constitutional referendums to placate the people—a cycle that has emerged over their long tenure of rule and which we have recently witnessed again. That the Tatmadaw should attempt to ground their rule in sources of legitimacy that stem from Burmese traditional culture rather than any modern democratic theory is not surprising, given the way they came to power. Such a process involved them in reinvigorating and reinterpreting for themselves an authoritarian system of government—absolute monarchy—that has existed for centuries before the onset of colonial rule and the country's brief experiment with democracy.

The chapter also discusses foreign perceptions of legitimacy and the influences that the international community have had on the regime's search for legitimacy in recent years. Sustaining authoritarian rule over long periods of time is not an inexpensive exercise. Expanding and modernizing the Tatmadaw to quash ethnic insurgencies and civil unrest for half a century has demanded a continual drain on the country's resources. In a world where democratic progress is monitored far more closely and authoritarian rule is routinely questioned, the generals have reluctantly found that their own survival may require more democratic initiatives on their part. This may not lead to the solution that would satisfy the West, but it may produce a more stable, and less costly, alternative to direct military rule.

The Path to Military Rule

Although Burma's monarchical heritage can be traced to the early kingdoms of the Mon, the first great kingdom of the Burmans was founded in Pagan in the eleventh century with Theravada Buddhism established as the main religion. A succession of dynasties, kingdoms, and new capitals followed, with the last great dynasty, the Konbaung, founded in the late eighteenth century. After three Anglo-Burmese wars with the British, the whole of Burma was annexed in 1885 and the Burmese monarchy was abolished. One consequence of the end of the monarchy was that the Buddhist monasteries and monks (*Sangha*) became the country's most powerful and most organized indigenous institution. Although British colonial rule was interrupted by the invasion of Japan, who also trained Burma's first Independent Army (BIA, which would later become the Burmese National Army), the British would return to claim their losses and restore their economic domination after the war. Burma's wartime hero, Aung San, negotiated independence from Great Britain for 1948 but was assassinated along with his cabinet in 1947. Because he was instrumental in creating the BIA during the war, Aung San was considered to be the father of the Tatmadaw, which has ruled the country since General Ne Win's coup of 1962.

From 1948 to 1958, Burma adopted a parliamentary system of government, with representation for ethnic minorities. Insurgencies, factional conflict, and communist movements were prevalent during the entire period. In 1958, citing the army's mistaken fear of a communist takeover and facing rumors of an imminent military coup, Prime Minister U Nu resigned and invited the army's senior general, Ne Win, to install a military caretaker administration. Military officers were appointed to senior executive positions, and Ne Win was briefed to prepare the country for elections. Ne Win duly followed the constitutional formalities of resigning as prime minister, and parliamentary democracy returned to Burma in 1960. U Nu's faction of the Anti-Fascist People's Freedom League (AFPFL) was elected with the support of the majority of the Sangha, though the Tatmadaw would have preferred a victory by the rival faction. When serious differences again arose between the AFPFL, the Tatmadaw, and ethnic minority leaders in 1962, Ne Win, encouraged by the Tatmadaw's achievements under the caretaker administration, seized power in a coup d'etat. Ne Win arrested the civilian political leaders, dissolved the national parliament and state legislatures, dismantled the court system, suspended the 1947 constitution, and created a Revolutionary Council comprising 17 military officers with himself as chairman.

The military's Revolutionary Council created its own cadre party, the Burma Socialist Programme Party (BSPP) in July 1962. Modeled along Leninist lines, the BSPP was intended to become a mass political organization providing social, political, and economic indoctrination. Ne Win was elected party chairman when the BSPP held its First Party Congress in 1971, and he resigned his army commission in 1972. A new constitution creating a single party system was introduced in 1974. From 1962 to 1988, therefore, Burma was ruled by the military, both directly—under the Revolutionary Council, and indirectly—under the BSPP through the 1974 constitution. In reality, the country merely moved from direct military rule to indirect constitutional military rule.

In 1988, the daughter of Aung San, Aung San Suu Kyi, returned to Burma to care for her sick mother. She was coerced to join the prodemocracy movement and became the general secretary of the National

League for Democracy (NLD). Although Ne Win retired as chairman of the BSPP at an extraordinary party congress in July 1988, he played an instrumental role in violently suppressing the prodemocracy demonstrations that peaked later that year. As a result of these demonstrations, a military coup led by Senior General Saw Maung but under the direction of Ne Win ended the 14-year period of constitutional military rule on September 8, 1988. A 19-member State Law and Order Restoration Council (SLORC) placed Burma once again under direct military rule by assuming comprehensive executive, legislative, and judicial powers. Composed entirely of military officers, SLORC declared martial law and ruled by decree. Although Ne Win remained in the shadows well after the SLORC came to power amid the political crisis of 1988, the ruling generals had been distancing themselves from his influence long before his death in 2002. Hence, though the senior generals today are a product of Ne Win's legacy, their claims to political legitimacy are somewhat different from his reflecting changes in the regime's outlook in response to domestic and international pressures. The Tatmadaw ruled the country directly under the auspices of the SLORC from 1988 to 1997, and thereafter as the State Peace and Development Council (SPDC).

The Legitimacy of the Tatmadaw

Among the reasons offered to support the Tatmadaw's rule in 1962 were its claims to possess the unique ability to suppress both communist and ethnic-based insurgencies, while at the same time, effectively managing the economy. The Tatmadaw has also sought to placate domestic strife and to gain legitimacy by occasionally proposing elections, referendums, and constitutional reforms, and by drawing on historical and cultural interpretations of the traditional relationship between Burmese rulers and their subjects. The military have tended historically to realign their focus strategically among these broad alternatives, depending upon the changing conditions and circumstances. Each of these themes is discussed in turn in this chapter, along with some more general attributes that have pervaded all arguments for legitimacy in Burma throughout the postwar period.

State Unity and Ethnic Insurgencies

The Tatmadaw invested the major proportion of their time and effort following independence in suppressing ethnic and communist insurgencies and preserving the unity of the state. Indeed, the question of political autonomy for the minority groups in Burma has proved to be a source of tension and conflict since 1948. Under Great Britain's Indian-style divide-and-rule policy, the British played off the competing interests of various ethnic groups in and around the frontier areas. Resentment fueled by missionary activities and the British practice of recruiting Indians into key administrative positions also paved the ground for separatist claims among the minorities by the end of British rule. Although Aung San had declared that there could only be one nationality in Burma, he recognized distinct races and tribes within the nation. His preference was for a Union of Burma with properly regulated provisions to safeguard the rights of the national minorities (Aung San 1993, 156). Speculation over the actual concessions made to minority groups at the Panglong Conference of 1947—in particular, over the granting of statehood to the Shans, Karens, and the Kachins—helped fuel the demands for autonomy and nationhood among numerous ethnic groups for the next 50 years. These demands were forcefully expressed through many armed insurgencies by the militant wings of various ethnic minorities in addition to those of the Communist Party of Burma (CPB), capturing towns across the country. At one point, the Karen National Defence Organization, for example, had pushed to within four miles of capturing Rangoon (Smith, M. 1993, 118–121). By the time of Ne Win's caretaker administration in 1958–1960, however, the Tatmadaw claimed to have brought stability to the previously faction-ridden political environment and, with unrestrained military powers, success in the battle against insurgency. Indeed, Smith (179) believes that "in the army's official account of these years, *Is Trust Vindicated?*, Ne Win allowed the Tatmadaw's record to stand or fall more or less entirely on its successes in the battle against insurgency." Afterward, when U Nu succumbed to pressures for political autonomy from a number of ethnic minorities, including the Shan, his promise to make Burma a federation of ethnic nationalities with greater autonomy for the minority provinces became one of the reasons prompting Ne Win's return.

While much of Burma's postindependence history has been dominated by ethnic insurgency, it was the Tatmadaw's perception and promotion of its ability to quash such insurgencies and maintain peace and order that provided one of its main sources of legitimacy. Upon seizing power, however, Ne Win also used the army to suppress political opponents, protesters, students, monks, religious minorities, and other civilians on numerous occasions. He did so by arresting, torturing, and killing thousands, most particularly during the coup of 1962, the protests against the government's refusal to honor the former United Nations secretary general U Thant with an official burial in 1974 and during the popular uprising of 1988. In consequence, the size of the army, its acquisition of weaponry, and its allocation of the national budget ballooned as the Tatmadaw sought to control not only ethnic-based separatist insurgencies but also social unrest—both causes were justified by the Tatmadaw on the grounds of preserving state unity. Building the second largest army in Southeast Asia, the Tatmadaw had managed to quash all ethnic insurgencies by the mid- to late 1990s, relocate a number of religious minorities, and drive thousands of Arakanese Muslims into exile in Bangladesh. Most insurgent groups signed cease-fire agreements with the SLORC in return for local business favors or employment from the government. The two major exceptions were the Karen and the Shan, who either fled to Thailand or had their villages relocated to cut off support for their troops. The government continued to suppress ethnic minority claims to uniqueness even as it held constitutional conventions in an attempt to reengineer the Panglong Conference with handpicked representatives of the minority groups. Any claims for more autonomy were suppressed and minority cultures Burmanized. The Museum of Shan Chiefs and former palace of the last Shan lord, for example, was closed and reopened as a new Buddhism Museum displaying Buddhist artifacts and photographs of the Pagan archeological site. The Tatmadaw continue to promote their role in preserving state unity and the avoidance of disunity and the "destruction of the state"—whether by internal or external forces. These messages appear in slogans, signs, and banners across the country and in the state-run media.

Economic Performance and Infrastructure Building

The Tatmadaw have for most of their rule argued that they were the only group capable of implementing successful economic programs. They had achieved some economic success during the caretaker government period (1958–1960): the production and export of rice, for example, reached a postwar high that has not been repeated (Seekins 2002, 39). Thereafter, the military took their role as Burma's economic gurus seriously, both as an autarchic socialist state and while undergoing partial economic liberalization. Undercutting this faith in their economic credentials, however, is the fact that in modern times, Burma's economic well-being was allied to foreign interests, there being a long association with foreign investment dating back to its early trading relations with China and India. By 1941, one-quarter of Burma's capital stock was owned by foreign investors—Britain, China, and India being the dominant countries of origin. Following the end of World War II and Burma's independence, foreign companies returned and were permitted to operate through to the early 1960s, receiving official encouragement by way of Burmese investment legislation (Mason 1998, 209–210).

Socialism

The policy of reliance on foreign investment changed dramatically following the coup of 1962. Determined to defeat the political influence of the CPB, Ne Win decreed that the Tatmadaw would fight the communists in ideology as well as in the field and commissioned the drafting of the BSPP's bible, *The System of Correlation of Man and his Environment* (1973). His promotion of *The Burmese Way to Socialism* would then launch the nation toward international isolation and autarchy. Being a perversion of Aung San's ideas on socialism,[2] Ne Win's plan led to the nationalization of agriculture and industry, over a quarter-century of central economic planning, and the curtailment of almost all foreign direct investment. This ensured the destruction of the Burmese economy at a time when her regional neighbors were benefiting from large sums of anticommunist aid. It quashed any hope of a sustained economic recovery from the wartime destruction and Burma fell from its position of being the most economically promising of all the former colonial states to one of the poorest countries in Southeast Asia.

A groundswell of discontent against the military's handling of the economy reached a head in late 1987 with Ne Win's disastrous decision, based partly on numerological advice, to demonetize 60–80% of Burma's currency. Demonetization of the Kyat was used to target insurgents and black marketers operating along the Thai and Chinese borders. However, since neither group traded in Kyat because it had long been unconvertible, the demonetization hit ordinary Burmese citizens the hardest. The policy was preceded by a number of extraordinary conversions of the currency that, together, destroyed most people's savings and triggered the resentment that was eventually expressed in the mass demonstrations of 1988.[3] The subsequent crackdown by the military also led to the imposition of trade sanctions by the European Union and the United States that have been reinforced over the years.

Partial Economic Liberalization

In 1988, at Japan's urging, the SLORC embarked upon a program of partial economic liberalization that involved their deregulating many key industries and encouraging the return of foreign investment. While many Western firms were deterred by the demonstrations and subsequent coup, some of Burma's neighbors (as well as some Western oil companies) were attracted by the possibilities of natural resource extraction. Japanese companies also saw Burma as the next site for their labor-intensive manufacturing operations. Within a decade, however, the transparency of SLORC's economic liberalization policy had become apparent: any profits being made were of a short-term nature, usually going directly to the military. Seeking access to markets and foreign currency, the generals were in search of friends quickly and some Association of Southeast Asian Nations (ASEAN) members were more than happy to gain access to Burma's natural resources. But many foreign investors discovered over time that aside from intense lobbying by democracy activists at home, the country's rules and regulations (including mandatory investment arrangements with domestic state-owned partners), corruption, and lack of infrastructure severely limited their profit margins. Foreign investment over the 10-year period from 1988 to 1998 generally took the form of natural resource extraction, particularly oil, gas, and timber, while other key sectors were ignored altogether. Domestic investment was discouraged by interest rate ceilings and a reluctance to remove tight controls on the investment and banking markets. A failure to address currency complexities further discouraged investment (foreign and domestic) and encouraged a flourishing black market that preferred to trade in U.S. dollars and continued to fill shortfalls in the official economy.

In an effort to control border trade and stem the outflow of foreign currency, the SPDC in 1998 reinstated import and export controls on consumer goods and many key commodities, especially sugar and rice, thus reasserting direct control over the economy and ending their brief attempt at economic liberalization (Crispin 1998). The restrictions were largely ineffective, however, because of the wholesale hoarding of consumer goods in urban areas and the continuation of black market trading along the border. The Tatmadaw's economic liberalization policy had failed and, by implication, so too had their ability to ground their legitimacy in economic stewardship rather than popular consent after their loss in the election in 1990.

Infrastructure Building and Budget Deficits

In November 2005, the Tatmadaw began the mass relocation of government ministries and civil servants from Rangoon to its new capital,

Naypyidaw, 240 miles to the North. While the cost of its construction has continued to drain funds from the national budget, it was only one of the major projects undertaken (which included new dams, bridges, and energy projects) that geared predominantly toward new administrative hubs or future export earning deals. To avoid resentment and maintain loyalty to the regime, the salaries of civil servants and the military were also raised significantly in 2006. Government expenditures far outstripped revenues, leading to high budget deficits that the International Monetary Fund (IMF) and World Bank warned should be reduced. Since the government refused to cut expenditures on its major pet projects, it focused on raising more taxes and reducing subsidies on gasoline products, the latter reform having been strongly recommended by the IMF for some time. However, in August 2007, the generals chose to cut subsidies across the board rather than do so gradually, raising the price of diesel oil by 100% and that of compressed natural gas by almost 500%. This had an immediate impact on the cost of food, transport, and electricity generation in Rangoon and across the country, fueling a growing resentment against the SPDC's economic policies.

While there had already been numerous small protests over the rising price and availability of basic commodities and electricity in Rangoon, the new round of price hikes fueled the demonstrations of some 400–500 people led by the '88 Student Generation Group. The protesters were attacked by progovernment militia, and the ringleaders were arrested along with some 100 others including members of the NLD. The initial trigger for the mass demonstrations in 2007— economic hardship—was, therefore, remarkably similar to that in 1988. The following year the SPDC negotiated new investment agreements with the Chinese government for the construction of two pipelines carrying imported Middle Eastern and African oil as well as natural gas sourced from the Bay of Bengal from Kyaukpyu Port in Rakhine State through central Myanmar to Kunming in China's Yunnan province. The pipelines, expected to be completed by 2012, would secure a regular source of revenue for the Tatmadaw.

Regional Integration

Burma's admission to ASEAN in 1997 was an attempt by the Tatmadaw generals to gain further access to regional markets as well as attract the legitimacy associated with being a member of the region's main economic and security organization. It was proposed and backed by the former prime minister of Malaysia, Dr. Mahathir

Mohamad, who several years later would call for Burma to be expelled from ASEAN following the embarrassment it had caused by the rearrest of Aung San Suu Kyi in 2003. Indeed, more than any other member state, Burma has consistently tarnished ASEAN's credibility on a number of fronts since joining the organization. While other member states have from time to time attracted criticism from the international community, for various reasons, Burma has been subject to intense scrutiny sustained by an army of activists, the occasional influential politician or world figure, and, more recently, the mass media. The Burmese generals' actions, of course, have only intensified such criticism. The worldwide attention caused by Suu Kyi's arrest and continued detention, for example, forced ASEAN to make unprecedented statements and repeated calls for her release since 2003 (ASEAN 2003).

The prospect of Burma chairing ASEAN in 2006 caused ASEAN to note that Burma's chair could severely affect the organization's credibility. While ASEAN insisted that it would not force Burma to relinquish its chair, Burma forfeited its chair voluntarily in 2005 to the relief of ASEAN and the disappointment of the generals. Two years later, ASEAN was again forced into damage control following the mass demonstrations by the Sangha and laymen, and subsequent crackdowns by the SPDC, in September 2007. These events created unprecedented worldwide attention and criticism from foreign governments, the UN Security Council, human rights organizations, and the media. The ASEAN Chair would eventually issue a statement expressing ASEAN's "revulsion" over the violent suppression of the demonstrations only after similar statements had been issued by the UN, European Union, and other international organizations (Minister of Foreign Affairs, Singapore 2007). The demonstrations also took place on the eve of ASEAN's fortieth anniversary celebrations and before the Singapore Summit in November where the member states were to sign a charter that was to usher in a new age of regional cooperation. They proved hugely embarrassing for ASEAN and completely overshadowed the signing of the charter. All in all, the Burmese junta's actions have reduced ASEAN's credibility in recent years. On numerous occasions ASEAN has been forced to react with pronouncements and recommendations, sometimes even strongly worded criticism in order to deflect international pressure from itself. Rather than achieving some regional legitimacy and prestige, the result of Burma's entry into ASEAN has been to force the organization to adopt damage control positions, limiting the extent to which the organization's reputation could be tarnished by one of its members.

Monarchy, Buddhism, and Legitimacy

Monarchy and Legitimacy

The Tatmadaw generals have for some time attempted to reinvent the Burmese monarchy for themselves and to tap into the legitimacy associated with traditional kingship. They occasionally rely upon traditional understandings of the prerogatives enjoyed by the Burmese monarchy, along with their own reinterpretations of those prerogatives, to justify the forced conscription of corvée labor for conducting military exercises, public works, and, in general, promoting loyalty to the state. Viewed as such, their kingly rule is a reciprocal relationship with the people recognizing the authority of the king and remaining loyal to him in return for the latter's provision of public welfare (see generally Aung Thwin 1985; Lieberman 1984; Taylor 1987). Historical comparisons to the Burmese monarchy are not inappropriate because the rule of a Burmese king was a rule of absolute monarchy that lasted unchallenged in Burma until King Thibaw was exiled to India by the British. Without any serious thought given to any alternative system of government and with no alternative neighboring models with which to compare, absolute monarchy was considered to be the only form of government. There was no hereditary aristocratic class (the local nobility were appointed at the king's favor and were purged in establishing a new ruler): only a ruling class consisting of the king, his royal family, and his appointed officials on one side, and the common people on the other.

Because the king could appoint or dismiss his Supreme Court and Administrative Council ministers (*Hluttaw*) at will, the only influence over his absolute rule came from the intervention of the Sangha. Indeed, protecting the Sangha was also a primary religious function of the king (Smith, D. 1965, 27). In return, the Sangha tended to support the Burmese monarchy (Maung Maung Gyi 1983, 32; Pye 1962, 75). The Sangha also provided the only check against the tyranny and extortionate actions of powerful officials by their role in obtaining pardons for executions, remission of taxes for people in times of scarcity, temporary relief when crops failed, and their intervention for the release of prisoners. As defender of the faith, the king was bound by his duty to uphold the traditional custom of displaying reverence toward the Sangha and concern for their welfare, and as head of state, he had to set an example of good conduct and righteous behavior. Yet his concept of public welfare rarely extended beyond the confines of religion, religious needs, and institutions (Maung Maung Gyi 1983, 25–26). The Tatmadaw's promotion of and attempted association with Burma's monarchical traditions has clearly been evident since 1988. Examples include their restoration of the home of the last Burmese monarch King Thibaw— the Royal Palace in Mandalay, their use of exhibitions glorifying the traditional monarchy in the National Museum, and their nationwide promotion of Buddhism. In 2006, on Armed Forces Day, Than Shwe officially named the new capital *Naypyidaw* (royal city or the place of the royal state). By heeding the advice of astrologers and founding the new capital, Than Shwe had asserted his own "royal" legacy.

Buddhism and Legitimacy

Throughout Burmese history, promoting and defending Buddhism ultimately confirmed a king's legitimacy (Gravers 1999; Smith, D. 1965, 23; Spiro 1982). The promotion of Buddhism during times of political crisis is a long-standing cultural tradition in Burmese politics dating back to the eleventh-century kingdom of Pagan. Houtman (1999, 160) observes that whenever "a government has faced erosion of political legitimacy, whether it be Anawratha, U Nu, or Ne Win, it returns to Buddhism" (see also Smith, M. 2001, 21). Since 1948, all rulers—democratic and authoritarian—have tapped into Burma's Buddhist traditions to gain political legitimacy or to express their piety—genuine or otherwise. U Nu's democratic government, for example, blended Buddhism and the Burmese belief in spirits (*nats*) with politics throughout his troubled administration. Under pressure from senior abbots (*sayadaws*), U Nu declared Buddhism to be the official state religion in 1961, an act that antagonized the Christian minorities and the military and encouraged the subsequent coup.

The Tatmadaw began meddling in Buddhism during their caretaker administration, primarily through their Psychological Warfare Department's religious publications to mobilize anticommunist sentiment in their fight against the CPB (Smith, M. 1993, 180–182). Following their coup in 1962, the Tatmadaw focused on defining and controlling the Sangha's role in politics. Upon coming to power, Ne Win repealed religious laws enacted under U Nu, including the *State Religion Promotion Act*, and abolished government subsidies for the promotion of Buddhism. For most of his rule, Ne Win, like Aung San, believed that Buddhism was the preserve of the Sangha and that monks should avoid politics. The BSPP's guiding ideology, for example, positioned its philosophy as a purely mundane and human doctrine without any connection to religion (180–182). Attempts made in 1964 and 1965 to impose a registration of the Sangha and their associations were largely resisted, and Ne Win would arrest large numbers of monks several times, especially in 1965 and 1974. In 1980, Ne Win oversaw the registration of all monks and the creation of a Supreme Sangha Council, or *Sangha Maha Nayaka*, whose hierarchical structure aimed to tighten the state's control over the Sangha (Matthews 1993, 415–416). Sangha councils were also created at the village, township, city, and district levels, with members appointed by the government and in which retired military officers took over the handling of finances and public donations for monasteries and pagodas. The reorganization of the Sangha made sayadaws responsible for the political activities of their monks.

The Tatmadaw's relationship with the Sangha underwent a dramatic transformation following the events of 1988 and 1990 when thousands of monks came out in support of the democratic movement and took part in mass demonstrations in Rangoon and Mandalay. In 1990, the SLORC's refusal to hand over power to the NLD after the elections, as well as the Tatmadaw's shooting of a monk and several students during a prodemocracy demonstration, triggered a rebellion in Mandalay. The sayadaws subsequently called for a religious boycott in monasteries across Burma during which the Sangha refused to accept alms from the Tatmadaw or perform religious services for their families. Over 400 monks were arrested and monastery property destroyed. The SLORC chairman, Saw Maung, quoted Buddhist scriptures and king's law (*yahzathart*) to sayadaws and claimed he had the right to invade and purify the domain of the Sangha (Mya Maung 1992, 184). The SLORC soon after issued a law stipulating the proper conduct for a Buddhist monk (including the avoidance of politics) and penalties for their violation by monks or monk organizations. Thereafter the Tatmadaw sought the blessing and support of sayadaws with both carrot and stick: those who refused to cooperate had their monasteries placed under surveillance and were sometimes arrested, while those who were compliant received donations, gifts, and elaborate ceremonies in which honors and titles were granted.

Buddhist Nationalism

The entry of Aung San Suu Kyi and the NLD onto the political stage forced a strategic redirection in the Tatmadaw's search for legitimacy in the early 1990s. At that time, Aung San Suu Kyi appeared as the challenger to the royal throne (*minlaung*) in Burmese popular tradition. Given this dynamic, it was no longer enough for the generals to simply keep the Sangha quiet. They now had to present themselves as better Buddhists than Suu Kyi. By promoting the cause of Buddhism, the generals were responding to the threat of Suu Kyi—the minlaung who courted the support of the Sangha—while at the same time assuming the legitimacy of a Burmese monarch for themselves. Ironically, the Tatmadaw began to promote a similar kind of devotion to the Buddhist traditions that had ultimately toppled the U Nu government, and the ethnic minorities would be forced yet again to endure policies that promoted Buddhist nationalism.

The threat that Suu Kyi posed to the generals' legitimacy was real, and it had intensified following the Sangha's decision to side with the prodemocracy movement in 1988 and 1990. This threat also gained pace with the public overtures made by NLD candidates to the Sangha before the 1990 elections along with the publication of Suu Kyi's speeches and her Buddhist political thought, mostly compiled under house arrest, and her visits to monasteries upon her release. Suu Kyi's political rhetoric involved a conscious use of Buddhist ideas that developed into a discourse on the compatibility of Buddhist thought with a democratic society, and on the attainment of freedom through Buddhism under authoritarian rule. The grounding of her message in the union of Buddhist thought and democratic government offered a political alternative in terms of Western democracy and liberalism (see McCarthy 2004). As such, she posed a direct threat to the legitimacy of the Tatmadaw's authoritarian rule.

To negate the influence of Suu Kyi and the NLD, the generals embarked upon a massive campaign to promote its own version of nationalism and order through Buddhist culture. In 1993, the SLORC established the Union Solidarity and Development Association (USDA) that, modeled on the BSPP, represented the Tatmadaw's alternative to the NLD. The USDA offered free courses in Buddhist culture with the aim of fostering patriotism and loyalty to the government. The SLORC and SPDC have also used the state-run media to interpret Buddhist traditions in a way that conformed to their vision for an orderly society. They used museums to promote their Buddhist credentials and to reinvigorate monarchic traditions; they made public donations to monasteries; they consecrated Buddhist sites and invented prominent roles for themselves in ceremonies that were broadcast on state television and in newspapers, and they began participating in what has been dubbed "monumental Buddhism": the "building or renovating of pagodas and centres of devotion in order to acquire legitimacy" (Seekins 2005, 273). Indeed, in 1998 the SPDC introduced the *Protection and Preservation of Cultural Heritage Regions Law* to restrict the independent construction and renovation of Buddhist structures, which also effectively restricted all the accompanying merit-acquiring opportunities to the generals.

Religious Boycotts, Demonstrations, and the Loss of Legitimacy

In 2007, events would transpire that would overshadow the junta's efforts to promote Buddhist nationalism. By again overturning their alms bowls and refusing to accept donations from the military, monks participating in mass demonstrations across the country threatened to undo any shred of legitimacy that the generals had attempted to maintain internally since their election loss in 1990. The sheer size of the Sangha's involvement in the demonstrations, which have come to be called the "Saffron Revolution," along with participating laymen, indicated how out of touch the generals were with public sentiments and internal social forces. Moreover, their brutal response to the demonstrations seriously damaged their own legitimacy on Buddhist grounds. The demonstrations began as a protest by several hundred student monks at the large monastery in Pakokku against the sudden price hike in oil and gas. News of the maltreatment of several monks by the authorities rapidly spread through monasteries across the country and the SPDC ignored the demands of the All Burma Monks Association (ABMA) for, among other things, an apology and a reduction in commodity prices or face the threat of a religious boycott (ABMA 2007). As in 1990, this threat was taken very seriously as it could demoralize the Tatmadaw and affect the loyalty of its soldiers and security forces, now almost entirely composed of Burman Buddhists.

The ABMA did call for a *pattta nikkuijana kamma* (a refusal to accept alms) from the military, the militia, and all government workers and its calls for peaceful marches in Rangoon, Mandalay, and elsewhere were answered by the Sangha, joined by thousands of lay citizens. The movement became an intensely political force as a consequence of the meeting that some 500 demonstrating monks held with Aung San Suu Kyi amidst the protests in Rangoon and the protests swelled considerably overnight across the country. On the final days before the crackdown, an estimated 30,000–50,000 monks demonstrated together with the same number of civilians, many of whom were holding flags of the NLD and the banned All Burma Buddhist Monks Union. The SPDC eventually used soldiers, police, USDA, and the paramilitary *Swan Arr Shin* (Masters of Force) to violently suppress the demonstrations around the country. Rebel monasteries were invaded, desecrated, and sacked, and thousands of "bogus monks" (so labeled by the authorities) were beaten, interrogated, disrobed, and imprisoned, and an unknown number of deaths occurred. These demonstrations and the inevitable crackdown were pivotal events in terms of the regime's loss of legitimacy. In addition, it forced the SPDC to expedite its constitutional convention and once again pressured the generals to talk about holding referendums and elections.

Nationalism and Foreign Perceptions of Legitimacy

The military regime in Burma has often been labeled xenophobic for a good reason. A fear of foreign, especially Western, influence has permeated the entire period of military rule since 1962. It could be argued that such a fear was also influential during U Nu's democratic period as a response to years of British colonial rule, Japanese occupation, and the subsequent return of foreign economic domination. Yet Burmese rulers since Aung San have become skilled in adapting to changing circumstances and choosing their allies carefully, often remaining neutral in international affairs, which gives the perception that they are isolationist or inward looking. Ne Win's years of socialism and autarchic economic policies reinforced this trait in the Tatmadaw, a trait that became more obvious after 1988 when the regime's primary goal became survival. Any threat that challenged their survival, whether foreign influenced or not, would be met by nationalistic claims and accusations of undermining the unity of the state. Aung San Suu Kyi posed a threat to the Tatmadaw, hence she was accused of being a puppet of Western governments and their anarchic societies. The Tatmadaw sought to delegitimize her and the NLD by emphasizing her Western connections and discrediting her identity as a Burmese national. The SPDC also sought to delegitimize the monks who demonstrated in 2007 by accusing them of acting under the influence of foreign interests. Following the rebroadcast of amateur digital coverage of the demonstrations inside Burma, some Western foreign media outlets (especially those originating in the United States and the United Kingdom) were banned from broadcasting in Burma.

The Tatmadaw's continued distrust of foreign influence was also made obvious by the events surrounding Cyclone Nargis in 2008 where the slow access granted to foreign aid agencies was precipitated by restrictive guidelines introduced two years earlier. In 2006, the generals had become concerned about foreign aid workers having access to politically sensitive areas and introduced new guidelines for all UN, NGO, and INGO activities inside Burma (Myanmar Ministry of National Planning and Economic Development 2006)—the guidelines placed foreign workers under the direct supervision of the state. That the generals had become particularly sensitive to Western influence since 1988 reflects the West's criticism of their actions and emphasis on democratization since the end of the Cold War. The opposition's alliance with a Western perception of legitimacy, being grounded primarily in the holding of elections, meant that the Tatmadaw were forced to delegitimize the opposition on other grounds until it finally held an election in 2010. The West, in turn, have delegitimized the military regime, not only by pointing to its lack of democratic processes and inability to provide for basic human needs but also by labeling Burma a "narco state" or even a "rogue state." Facing foreign criticism themselves, some of Burma's partners in ASEAN persuaded the generals of the merits of at least declaring some initiative toward democratic reform, if only to placate the international community. In 2003, Thailand's foreign minister proposed a five-point roadmap for democracy in Burma. This roadmap was converted by the Burmese into their own seven-point roadmap for a "disciplined democracy," which included drafting a new constitution, a referendum on the constitution, and holding free and fair elections (*The New Light of Myanmar* 2005). While they have continued to follow their roadmap for the benefit of the international community as well as some of their allies, their conducting of the referendum and elections attracted worldwide criticism not only because of the unfair electoral rules but also due to the lack of independent observers.

Elections and Constitutional Reforms

Elections are merely one element of the legitimacy equation in Burma and have rarely led to the transfer of power as they do in more established democratic regimes. The exception was when U Nu took over from Ne Win's caretaker administration in 1960. Elections and referenda held under military rule, however, potentially provide the generals with another tool in its arsenal of self-legitimization and semblance of constitutional legality. The holding of elections is designed not only to placate foreign influences but also the domestic population, especially when other sources of legitimacy have failed. Since independence, the people have voted in national elections on five occasions, and it would be difficult today for any government in Burma to claim full legitimacy without staging an election, whether or not the election itself was a contrived event.

National multiparty elections were held for a democratic parliament in 1951, 1956, and 1960, and there were allegations of widespread intimidation, ballot rigging, and other anomalies on each occasion (Smith, M. 1993, 124). Under military rule, the draft of a new constitution creating a single party system (the BSPP) was put to a national referendum in 1974. The new constitution was approved by a remarkable 90.19% of the voting population, including a majority of voters in states with insurgencies against the government: the Shan, Kachin, Kayah, and Karen. Although the results of the referendum were questionable, the fact that the Tatmadaw saw any need at all to stage a referendum showed that there was still a desire on their part to be perceived as acting in a constitutional manner so as to give some legitimacy to the document.

Following the unrest of 1988 and pressured by the possible withdrawal of Japanese aid, the SLORC announced that they would schedule a general election for 1990 (Seekins 1999). Allowing largely free and fair elections to take place was a major miscalculation by the Tatmadaw, which had convinced themselves that their own party, the National Unity Party (NUP, formerly the BSPP), would win. Although the campaigning before the election was controlled tightly, it was comprehensively won by Aung San Suu Kyi's NLD.[4] Before the election, both parties understood that the election results would not immediately lead to a transfer of power, but that power would be transferred only after the approval of a constitution. Yet the NLD's claim for power was met by the SPDC's disbelief and reluctance to relinquish it, and eventually, the arrest and detention of most successful NLD candidates followed. The generals downplayed the importance of the election results. They explained that the election was merely a signal for constitutional change and that all major parties would be invited to attend a National Convention with the purpose of writing a new constitution. This Convention, first convened in 1993, would reconvene at irregular intervals for the next 14 years with most of the participating representatives from the minorities being handpicked by the government. It provided the generals with the means to placate international pressure by appearing to facilitate the democratic process and demonstrate their willingness to work toward a negotiated resolution. The SPDC announced the completion of its Convention amid the demonstrations in 2007 and claimed that the protesters were undermining their "roadmap to democracy."

In 2008, with the Convention completed and another mass demonstration successfully quashed, the generals sought to diffuse the unrest of the previous year by announcing that a referendum on a draft of their new constitution would be held and that general elections would be scheduled for 2010. Upholding their promised referendum, however, would again draw international criticism. The draft constitution was already viewed as a contrived entrenchment of military rule. The referendum, being unmonitored, was now seen as being neither free nor fair and it also drew resources away from dealing with the aftermath of Cyclone Nargis that had struck the Irrawaddy Delta only a week before the date scheduled for the referendum. The official results for the referendum were in the end remarkably similar to those of 1974: the new constitution, a 235-page document containing 15 chapters of detailed provisions, was passed by 92.4% of the voting population. Following Suharto's example in Indonesia, the new constitution secured a permanent role for the military in the national and regional legislatures— one-quarter of the seats in both the lower house (*Pyithu Hluttaw*) or People's Assembly and the upper house (*Amyotha Hluttaw*) or House of Nationalities were reserved for the military, as well as one-quarter of the seats in the 14 state and division assemblies. It also disenfranchised the entire Sangha community (SPDC "Constitution" 2008).

The legitimacy of the 2010 elections was affected by the arrest and trial of Aung San Suu Kyi for breaking the terms of her house arrest in 2009 when a U.S. national swam across Inya Lake to her house on University Avenue and stayed for two nights before being caught by the authorities upon his departure. Her continued detention and possible exclusion as a candidate received worldwide criticism including from ASEAN (ASEAN Secretariat 2009). Eventually the NLD chose to boycott the 2010 election on the grounds that the rules were too unfair—hundreds of its members and potential candidates were disqualified from running as they had served or were still serving prison sentences at the time of registration— and this decision led to their disbanding. Before the 2010 election, the SPDC converted the USDA into a political party (the Union Solidarity Development Party or USDP) along the lines of Suharto's Golkar. On November 7, 2010, it held its first election in 20 years, securing a victory across the board and indirect rule for the next five years—the USDP won 76.5% of the contested parliamentary seats nationwide (Thar Gyi 2010). Aung San Suu Kyi was released the following week.

Conclusion

Since seizing power in 1962, the Tatmadaw have sought political legitimacy on a number of fronts, making transitions as key events and changing circumstances forced them to do so. The Tatmadaw's early claims to legitimacy were based on their successes in the battle against ethnic separatist and communist insurgencies. These claims were carried through to the late 1980s, by which time cease-fires had been negotiated with most ethnic minority groups. Under military rule, the Tatmadaw also claimed to have solid plans for the economic management of the country. Their experiment with socialism and autarchy, however, caused widespread poverty, while their partial economic liberalization produced mainly short-term foreign investments in resource extraction with few gains being distributed to society. Attempts at regional integration aimed at securing prestige and international legitimacy has merely caused embarrassment for ASEAN and unwelcome "roadmaps" for the generals. Moreover, the generals' economic mismanagement on two occasions led directly to mass demonstrations and the inevitable crackdowns by the military, both of which caused a significant loss of legitimacy and precipitated the holding of referendums and elections.

The Tatmadaw generals since 1988 also set about reinvigorating the monarchy and promoting their piety. Yet the events of 2007 were an assault on their legitimacy, not only because they threatened cohesion within their ranks, but also because it exposed the intent behind their public acts of piety—survival—and challenged their claim to traditional legitimacy as rulers in a devoutly Buddhist country. The Tatmadaw lost an enormous amount of legitimacy in the subsequent crackdown against the Sangha because they committed violence against the very institution they were meant to support. The Sangha remains the only sizeable, potentially rapidly organizable, and morally dangerous opposition in Burma. The demonstrations of 2007 also pressured the generals into making some progress on their roadmap to democracy—offering a referendum in 2008 and elections in 2010. This cycle repeats the events of 1988 and 1990. But in the eyes of the West, these elections were neither properly monitored nor assessed to be free and fair, and hence the regime remains illegitimate. Because their main aim is simply survival, the Tatmadaw's claims to legitimacy may be discarded at will and replaced by force when the need arises. At the same time, the government will continue to appeal to nationalism while subverting foreign influences and delegitimizing their opposition.

As the generals make the transition toward "disciplined democracy," the country's need for unity, stability, and independence will likely remain core arguments for a strong central government in the future, demanding the continued presence of the military. The Tatmadaw have now secured electoral legitimacy to justify their continued presence in influencing and running the political institutions of the country. Any new understanding of legitimacy, even a more liberal one, will need to take on Burmese characteristics and this invites the possibility of reverting to authoritarian interpretations and manipulations of Burmese historical traditions in the future, as well as their counterinterpretations by democratic challengers to the throne. A Burmese style of disciplined democracy may not please the West as any opening to democracy will surely be tightly controlled by the Tatmadaw. Nevertheless it represents a step forward from the alternative, direct military rule, and this kind of mixing of the democratic and oligarchic elements in the Burmese manner may be the only option available for securing some stability in the foreseeable future, and for opening the regime to the possibility of improvements in justice. It may also be all that is possible under the current generation of the Tatmadaw.

Notes

1. Burmese refers to both the people of Burma and the predominant language spoken in Burma, while Burman refers to the ethnic majority of Burma. The Burmese, therefore, include both Burmans and non-Burmans (the ethnic minorities comprising, among others, the Shan, Karen [Pao, Kayan, Karenni], Kachin, Chin, Rakhine, Naga, Lahu, Akha, and the Mon-Khmer [Mon, Wa, and Palaung]). In 1988, the military government changed the name of the country to Myanmar, which is a closer transliteration of the country's name in the Burmese language. For consistency, this book retains the use of Burma rather than Myanmar throughout unless referring to government sources or titles since 1988.
2. Aung San (1993, 153–155) described his "New Democracy" as somewhere between capitalism and socialism.
3. The 75 and 35 Kyat notes, for example, had been introduced in 1985 and 1986, respectively, because they were said to be, according to Ne Win's numerological advisers, luckier than the 100 and 50 Kyat notes, and the 75 Kyat note was also introduced on Ne Win's 75th birthday. The 75 and 35 Kyat notes were then replaced with the 90 and 45 Kyat notes in 1987 because 9 was Ne Win's lucky number.
4. The NLD received 59.9% of the popular vote and 392 of the 485 contested seats (80.8% of the total seats), while the army-backed NUP won approximately only 21.2% of the popular vote and 10 seats (2.1% of the total seats) (see Seekins 2002, 210).

References

All Burma Monks Association (ABMA). 2007. "Announcement of All Burma Monks Alliance, 12 Waning Day of Wagaung, 1369 BE, Letter No. (1/2007)." *The BurmaNet News* (September 10). Accessed February 18, 2010. http://www.burmanet.org/news/2007/09/10/announcementof -all-burma-monks-alliance-12th-waning-day-of-wagaung-1369-be-sunda yletter-no-12007/.

Association of Southeast Asian Nations (ASEAN). 2003. "Joint Communique of the 36th ASEAN Ministerial Meeting, Phnom Penh." *Aseansec.Org*, June 16–17. Accessed February 18, 2010. http://www.aseansec.org/14833.htm.

Association of Southeast Asian Nations (ASEAN) Secretariat. 2009. "ASEAN Chairman's Statement on Myanmar." August 11. Accessed February 18, 2010. http://www.aseansec.org/ PR-090812-1.pdf.

Aung San. 1993. "Bogyoke Aung San's Address at the Convention Held at the Jubilee Hall, Rangoon on the 23rd May, 1947." In *The Political Legacy of Aung San*, edited by Josef Silverstein, 151–161. Ithaca, NY: Cornell University Press.

Aung San Suu Kyi. 1991. *Freedom from Fear*. London: Viking Press.

Aung Thwin, M. 1985. *Pagan, The Origins of Modern Burma*. Honolulu, HI: University of Hawaii Press.

Burma Socialist Programme Party (BSPP). 1973. *The System of Correlation of Man and His Environment*. Rangoon, Myanmar: BSPP.

Crispin, Shawn W. 1998. "Heading for a Fall: Burma's Economy Edges towards Collapse." *Far Eastern Economic Review* 161: 56.

Gravers, Mikael. 1999. *Nationalism as Political Paranoia in Burma*. London: Curzon Press.

Houtman, Gustaaf. 1999. *Mental Culture in Burmese Crisis Politics: Aung San Suu Kyi and the National League for Democracy*. Monograph Series No. 33. Tokyo, Japan: Institute for the Study of Languages and Cultures of Asia and Africa, Tokyo University of Foreign Studies.

Lieberman, Victor B. 1984. *Burmese Administrative Cycles: Anarchy and Conquest, c. 1580–1760*. Princeton, NJ: Princeton University Press.

Mason, Mark. 1998. "Foreign Direct Investment in Burma." In *Burma, Prospects for a Democratic Future*, edited by Robert I. Rotberg, 209–230. Washington, DC: Brookings Institution Press.

Matthews, Bruce. 1993. "Buddhism under a Military Regime: The Iron Heel in Burma." *Asian Survey* 33: 408–423.

Maung Maung Gyi. 1983. *Burmese Political Values*. New York: Praeger.

McCarthy, Stephen. 2004. "The Buddhist Political Rhetoric of Aung San Suu Kyi." *Contemporary Buddhism* 5: 67–81.

Minister of Foreign Affairs, Singapore. 2007. "Statement by ASEAN Chair, Singapore's Minister for Foreign Affairs George Yeo in New York." *MFAS*, September 27. Accessed February 18, 2010. http:// app.mfa.gov.sg/2006 /press/view_press.asp?post_id=3125.

Mya Maung. 1992. *Totalitarianism in Burma: Prospects for Economic Development.* New York: Paragon House.

Myanmar Ministry of National Planning and Economic Development. 2006. "Guidelines for UN Agencies, International Organizations and NGO/INGOs on Cooperation Programme in Myanmar." *BurmaLibrary.Org,* February 7. Accessed February 18, 2010. http:// www.burmalibrary.org /docs3/guidelines-English-official.pdf.

The New Light of Myanmar. 2005. "Implementing the Seven-Point Road Map for the Future Nation." December 28, 8–9.

Pye, Lucian W. 1962. *Politics, Personality, and Nation Building: Burma's Search for Identity.* New Haven, CT: Yale University Press.

Seekins, Donald M. 1999. "The North Wind and the Sun: Japan's Response to the Political Crisis in Burma, 1988–1998." *The Journal of Burma Studies* 4: 1–34.

———. 2002. *The Disorder in Order: The Army State in Burma since 1962.* Bangkok: White Lotus Press.

———. 2005. "The State and the City: 1988 and the Transformation of Rangoon." *Pacific Affairs* 78: 257–275.

Smith, Donald E. 1965. *Religion and Politics in Burma.* Princeton, NJ: Princeton University Press.

Smith, Martin. 1993. *Burma, Insurgency and the Politics of Ethnicity.* Oxford: Zed Books.

———. 2001. "Burmese Politics after 1988: An Era of New and Uncertain Change." In *Burma: Political Economy under Military Rule,* edited by Robert H. Taylor, 15–39. New York: Palgrave.

Spiro, Melford E. 1982. *Buddhism and Society: A Great Tradition and Its Burmese Vicissitudes.* Berkeley, CA: University of California Press.

State Peace and Development Council (SPDC). 2008. *Constitution.* Accessed February 18, 2010. http://www.scribd.com/doc/2592218/SPDC-Constitution -Burmese-n-englsih-version712kb.

Taylor, Robert H. 1987. *The State in Burma.* Honolulu, HI: University of Hawaii Press.

Thar Gyi (2010), "USDP Wins 76.5 Perecnt of Vote." *The Irrawaddy,* November 18, Accessed November 31, 2010. www.irrawaddy.org.

CHAPTER 9

Legitimacy Deficit in Japan: The Road to True Popular Sovereignty

Haruko Satoh

Japan's path of political renewal offers a long and interesting story, complete with epilogue, of the relationship between economic development and political legitimacy in Asian states. It reveals how economic development and social change can eventually bring about democratic evolution, even in a society inclined to be hierarchical, collective, and resistant to the spread of liberal values.

To tell this story, the recent fall of the 1955 regime (55 *nen taisei*)—the conservative regime that guided Japan's rapid economic recovery after World War II and created the miracle of "Japan, Inc."—needs to be placed within the longer narrative of Japan's modernization since the late nineteenth century. The key lies in recognizing that both prewar Japan and postwar Japan were driven by an urge to acquire international status. Both regimes were politically pragmatic and opportunistic but also ideologically nationalistic, harboring antiliberal (anti-Western) views about society. Indeed the main elements of Japanese conservatism can be detected today across Asia in regimes resisting fully Western-style liberal democracy.

This article argues that old sources of Japanese state legitimacy—geared toward rapid, catch-up modernization, and industrialization—are now being quietly contested, replaced, or absorbed by others, especially popular sovereignty and international community. In order to make this case, however, we must first address some general questions about legitimacy in Japan.

Problems of Legitimacy in Japan

Japanese rarely use the word "legitimacy" to discuss problems in the political system. One reason is that there is no exact Japanese equivalent of the word. A possible translation, *seitosei*, is not commonly used in domestic political commentary and is rarely found in the index of books about contemporary Japanese politics. More common phrases used to imply a weak mandate to rule are "not reflecting *min'i*" (popular will) or "not listening to *kokumin no koé*" (the voice of the nation). Another reason is that postwar Japan has been formally a representative democracy, with popular sovereignty as an important pillar of legitimacy. All governments, however unpopular, are presumed legitimate to the extent they have been elected by the people.

Just because problems with the political system are not described as problems of legitimacy does not mean, however, that the latter do not exist. The slow decline of LDP dominance since the 1990s has been a long-term phenomenon of failing legitimacy of the 1955 regime that emerged with the birth of the LDP. Although the Socialist Party—the LDP's ideological archrival in the regime—maintained just over a third of parliamentary seats during the Cold War period, the LDP was able to rule continuously on its own throughout mainly because of its economic policies. After a brief hiatus in 1993 the party came back to power in 1994 and sat on the governing seat for another 15 years (although this time in coalition with smaller parties). So long as things were booming, there seemed no compelling reason, despite concern about a democracy with no real change of power for four decades, to challenge the LDP's single-party rule (McNeil 1993; Maull 1990).[1]

But the economic success of the regime obscured the reality that sources of political legitimacy in postwar Japan—some reaching back to the era before Japan became a modern state in the nineteenth century— were deeply contested and not securely articulated. The American-authored postwar constitution, in particular, gave rise to a cluster of legitimacy issues because of LDP objections to parts of it, especially to Article 1 (that altered the status of Emperor [*tenno*] from sovereign to symbol of the nation) and Article 9 (that banned the use of military force as a state instrument).

Revising this 1947 constitution was an important objective for the conservative leaders who formed the LDP in 1955. Central to the revisionist aim was the perceived need to regain state freedom, seen as restricted by Article 9. Rearming was the main objective, but restoring the structure of the prewar Prussian-style monarchical state, with the *tenno* as sovereign, and modifying liberal reforms believed to be alien to Japanese tradition (such as individual rights and gender equality) were all part of the so-called reverse course conservatism (*hando hoshu*) that the LDP represented. However, when the first attempt failed in 1960, the LDP refused to drop the idea, with the consequence that defending the constitution became a prime cause of the opposition. During the Cold War, the Socialist Party represented the strong antiwar sentiment of a public that largely supported the pacifist orientation of the state and held the position (until the 1990s) that both the Self-Defense Forces (SDF) and the U.S.–Japan security treaty were unconstitutional. Article 9 continues to cause disagreement over the purpose and mode of Japan's international engagement, especially regarding the use of the SDF in or beyond UN peacekeeping missions.

If the word *seitosei* were ever to be used, it would be over these matters of nation-state identity. While the resolution of such issues is a domestic matter, how they are discussed and resolved, especially Article 9, has always had bearing upon how Japan is perceived by the outside world— particularly by Japan's Asian neighbors—because they are tied to the history of Japan's aggression in Asia. After all, the postwar constitution was intended to demilitarize and democratize an authoritarian, militarist prewar state. It is important to Japan's international credibility as a peaceful democracy that it not be perceived as returning to this past. The recent rise of right-wing nationalism and the LDP's reignited drive to revise the constitution in the post–Cold War era may be a reactionary response to the rise of China, something new in Japan's modern history, but over the longer term it should be seen as part of a muddling through process of political renovation driven by historically embedded forces competing to shape national identity.

However, these national identity issues, though important, are somewhat removed from the day-to-day political, economic, and social concerns of most people, whose faith in the domestic system was closely tied to its economic success. Any complacency the public may have felt was badly shaken after the sudden economic downturn in 1992, when the market crashed with severe political consequences. The decision-making process went into paralysis and, in the words of an astute observer of Japan, persistent economic stagnation "more or less killed people's trust in the LDP System" (Buruma 2004, 2).

The arrival of the iconoclast Koizumi Jun'ichiro in 2001 appeared to bring real change to the political process. Koizumi pitted himself against the old, corrupt LDP machinery—promising radical reforms to end pork-barrel politics, to slim down the government and make it more accountable—and won massive popular support by doing so. Popular support, in turn, gave Koizumi the power to control party elements resisting change. His critics called him "populist" and his style of politics "theatrical," but by appealing directly to the electorate through the media he imparted a sense that the people were more in control of their destiny than before, and thus able to displace the three pillars of Japan, Inc.: big business, the faceless bureaucracy, and the LDP (Ohtake 2003).[2]

But Koizumi proved no substitute for a real change of power, which at last occurred on August 30, 2009, when Japanese voted in the lower house elections. The Democratic Party of Japan (DPJ) overwhelmed the LDP by winning 306 out of 480 seats in parliament, the most significant demonstration of popular will against the LDP thus far. According to *Nikkei* (2009, 1), Japan's leading financial daily, the result expressed "a powerful no to LDP politics that represented the post-war economic model of growth." Hatoyama Yukio, then DPJ's leader, characterized the victory as the beginning of three significant changes in Japanese politics: change of power; change of the old ways of profit-driven politics in the service of vested interests; and change from bureaucratic rule to popular sovereignty.[3] In foreign policy, the DPJ began to stress the importance of ties with East Asia to counterbalance the LDP's excessive focus on the United States in the past.

This political development marked, at the very least, a formal end to the drawn-out unraveling of the 1955 regime. There were immediate as well as long-term, structural causes for this demise that cannot be explained by economic downturn alone. The regime had after all relied not only on the overall performance of Japan, Inc. but also on the strategic stability that Japan enjoyed during the Cold War as America's main Asian ally. The end of the Cold War, the emergence of new powers, especially China and India, and the global expansion of capitalism presented new challenges that a postwar political order devoted exclusively to economic growth was not equipped to meet. Furthermore, Japan itself had changed since the regime's heyday, when it had effectively mobilized society to support Japan, Inc.'s quest to catch up and overtake the more advanced industrialized economies of the West.

The momentous political changes of the early twenty-first century thus seemed to augur profound changes in the bases of legitimacy that had supported Japan's postwar economic modernization. I now examine these changes more closely within the broader historical context, looking at the emotive issue of Japanese nationalism before tracing the course of the political crisis provoked by economic and social change.

Constructing and Defending the Japanese Nation

The Japanese have long perpetuated the view that they are more nationalistic than others as an ethnically homogenous nation (*tan'itsu minzoku*) within a single state (*tan'itsu kokka*). To this day, Japan strikes the foreign observer as being under the spell of the single-nation-state idea, arguably with good reason (Buzan 1991, 75; Hobsbawm 1990, 66).[4] As David Williams (1994, 108) wrote, "Japan is a nationalist polity. What then is a nation? The answer is important because the 'nation' is simultaneously the cause, the means and the end of Japan's modernization drive."

Japan hastily fashioned itself into a nation-state in the first 60 years of modernization after the Meiji Restoration of 1868 with the Emperor (*tenno*) as sovereign. The political order of the *shogun* and the *samurai* (warrior) class that ruled Japan from the twelfth century, and during the Edo period (1603–1868) under the Tokugawa *bakufu* (shogunate), was particularly stable and enduring. The significant point is that, until 1868, the *tenno* was one step removed from ruling over the people, obscured behind the veil of the imperial palace in Kyoto for nearly seven centuries. Devoid of political power, *tenno* only retained the formalizing (in one sense legitimizing) power to confer titles, such as the title *shogun*, on the *samurai* class while the *samurai* feudal lords actually governed the country in the *bakufu* system (Wakita 2003). The succeeding Meiji state fused political power and authority hitherto held separately by two institutions, the *bakufu* and *tenno*'s imperial court.

To legitimize the *tenno*'s historical claim to absolute power in the process of engineering the Japanese nation-state, the Meiji state created the national narrative known as *kokoku shikan* (imperial state history) and gave birth to the foundation myth that the *tenno* was the progenitor of the nation and had divine power to rule as the descendant of the ancient Shinto gods. This "invention" seemed necessary to transform a loosely federal structure of over 300 fiefdoms (*hans*) under the *bakufu* system into a fully centralized state and also to impart a sense of national consciousness among the people. The nation imagined under this new Meiji state comprised the monoethnic Yamato people, who were all supposed to be blood-related to the *tenno*. The religious character of the prewar imperial state's Shinto-based nationalism, institutionalized by the Yasukuni Shrine and later usurped to disastrous effect by the military regime, fortified the sense of common destiny between the *tenno* and his imperial subjects.

The driving urge behind Japanese modernization during the Meiji period was the search for international status. Japan has consistently measured itself in terms of how others see it, an attitude that persists to the present day. As in Isaiah Berlin's (1969, 155) words about individual status affirmation, Japan has been seeking to avoid "being ignored, or patronized, or despised, or being taken too much for granted."[5] Once Japan had become the first modern state in Asia, the Meiji leaders set out to revise the unequal treaties forced upon Tokugawa Japan and to acquire "great power" or first-class power (*itto-koku*) status.[6] Their ambition was displayed in wars waged and won against Qing China and Tsarist Russia, and in their pride at Japan's place among the victors at Versailles after World War I. Of course, Japan was not alone in those days in placing high priority over gaining status or in driving domestic resources to this end (Samuels 2003)—in the interwar years it competed strenuously with other colonial powers, and in the course of this competition stern militarists used the *tenno* system to gain control over central authority.[7]

Although the Meiji reforms had dismantled the feudal system and imported some liberal ideas—emancipating commoners from the rigid class system, introducing a German justice system, recognizing property rights, and allowing a degree of representative politics—the relationship between state and society was hardly enlightened since the Edo period, and the ruling elites maintained the view of the nation as being in the service of the state, which meant the sovereign *tenno*.

The American occupiers after 1945 tried to replace the *tenno*-centric notion of sovereignty with rule of law and a democratic system by injecting liberal values that had had little room to grow in prewar Japan. Dismantling the institutions that legitimized the organic conception of the militarist state was an important objective of the postwar reforms. Most significantly, the *tenno* was stripped of any political role and became the symbol of the Japanese nation, a move that Miyazawa Toshiyoshi, an influential postwar constitutional scholar, called "revolutionary." At the time, the question of *tenno*'s status was a bigger issue than Article 9 because Japanese leaders were concerned on the one hand to protect Hirohito, whose integrity as sovereign was perceived to be threatened by possible prosecution as a war leader, but deeply disturbed, on the other, by the fact that accepting Article 1 would mean foregoing the idea of *tenno* as sovereign (Kyodo 2007; Hando 2006; Iokibe 1997). But over time, Article 9 proved to be a more enduring source of division.

After seven years of occupation, Japan's status-seeking began again when independence was restored in 1952 by the San Francisco Peace Treaty. Then leader prime minister Yoshida Shigeru took a pragmatic decision to first focus Japan's resources on economic recovery rather than rearming fully as an independent state. For security, Japan armed only lightly and entered into a military alliance with the United States.[8] What became known as the Yoshida Doctrine contributed greatly to Japan's subsequent economic take-off and success. The international environment was favorable because the region was strategically stable, Japan's security was guaranteed by the U.S. nuclear umbrella, and competition was essentially economic and among the like-minded industrialized democracies in the free world of the Western alliance. The 1955 regime could concentrate on the smooth running of Japan, Inc.

Nevertheless the Yoshida Doctrine was extremely unpopular among the conservative forces—including some prewar leaders—wishing to revise the 1947 constitution.[9] Although the constitution gained considerable legitimacy over time, its authority as supreme law of the nation was vitiated by the deep divisions perpetuated by this conservative reaction. Yet even as these reactionary views percolated, Japan was steadily rebuilding its international status. In 1956 it rejoined the world formally as a member of the UN. Many Japanese felt that their country was more securely received back into the international community when Tokyo hosted the 1964 Summer Olympic Games. Others noted the significance of different dates, such as 1972 when Okinawa was returned to Japan from the United States; or 1973 when a rather exclusive community, the Trilateral Commission, was established among the policy elites and public intellectuals of North America, Western Europe, and Japan; or 1975 when the G-7 brought together the leaders of the industrialized powers (Britain, Canada, France, Italy, Japan, United States, and West Germany) in the Western Alliance.

Despite these triumphs, and despite Japan's burgeoning economic success, Article 9 remained an existential dilemma for status-conscious leaders who deeply wished for Japan to be more than a "soft" economic power. Although Japan had effectively rearmed with the establishment of the SDF (following upon an American decision to make the country a forward base in the Cold War's Asian theater), this did little to alter political leaders' sense of Japan as a quasi-independent state. America essentially retained the authority of an occupying force under existing security treaty arrangements. However, the public had become decidedly averse to the idea of constitutional revision, which it construed as the ultimate act of "reverse course" that would take the country back to the bad old days of the war-mongering state. The Socialist and Communist Parties stood to gain by posing as the fort against this reactionary "reverse course." Even the LDP was not totally united on the issue. Nakasone Yasuhiro and Miyazawa Kiichi, two former prime ministers and elder statesmen, represented the two schools within the party about the constitution. Miyazawa consistently expressed caution about discussing revision in terms of Article 9 alone (Mikuriya and Nakamura 2005, 332–323). Nakasone (2000) had always stressed the importance of a constitution written by the Japanese themselves in order to restore a fully independent, independent-minded state—or in Japanese, *shutaisei*.

One might ask, however, "independent from what?" The LDP's right-wing nationalist rhetoric about restoring Japanese independence asserted that the right to war was essential for state freedom. Yet what relevance has such an objective in an increasingly interdependent, globally connected world where the state, never mind military force or war, is not the only expression of power and in which very few states can claim to be fully responsible for their own security?[10] The answer lies in the abstract realm of repossessing a sense of self and control over one's own destiny, or what Nakasone and others like him speak of as *shutaisei*. In other words, it is about the sense of identity.[11] But as Masaru Tamamoto (1999, 124–125) writes, the problem with nationalist rhetoric is that "[t]here is no precise equivalent of the word 'identity' in Japanese; some use the English word. Others prefer the word *shutaisei*, commonly defined as subjectivity, independence, identity of existence, or the rule of individualism. But nobody seems to have a satisfactory idea of what a Japan with *shutaisei* would be like, or what it would take to bring *shutaisei* to Japan."

Unfortunately for Japan, its national image was taking something of a beating by the turn of the twentieth century as the "miracle economy" of the 1970s and 1980s entered the doldrums. It was perhaps not surprising that the mesmerizing rise of China and Japan's own economic stagnation and worries about declining international influence would make conservative Japanese feel more assertive and hawkish. But this was following a period of reforms that aimed to reconstruct a moribund political system in order to put Japan once more on a healthy economic course.

The Slow Path to Political Reform

Were Japanese voters in August 2009 saying "no" just to the incompetence of the LDP or to something more? The path of democratic evolution from Koizumi's rise to the LDP's spectacular defeat suggests there might be "something more."

To say "democratic evolution" in the Japanese case—or to hear Hatoyama declare popular sovereignty's triumph—may strike the nonspecialist as odd, since Japan has been constitutionally a democracy since shortly after World War II. However, Western critics of Japanese democracy often pointed out the need for a change of power to demonstrate that Japan had shed the authoritarian impulses of the past and become truly democratic. It is doubtful, in fact, whether the Americans during the Cold War would have welcomed the anti-U.S. Socialist Party in government. Some argued, too, that the factions within the LDP are quasi-political parties, providing choice and change by proxy.[12]

At any rate, LDP dominance was popularly accepted in the early phase of postwar recovery and development. People were, on the whole, satisfied with a politics—however dirty—that delivered jobs, improved their living standards, and gave them a role in the country's rapid recovery from war devastation to become the second richest nation in the world. The 1955 regime was geared precisely to achieve these goals, and it was extremely successful in running a quintessential developmental state in which formal democracy became, in words of a former American diplomat Frank McNeil (1993, 2), "the enabling element for domestic progress." Democracy to the Japanese meant wealth creation and redistribution.

In the bubble years of the 1980s, there was naive optimism that the economy would continue to grow. Meanwhile the opposition Socialist Party proved unable (or unwilling) to mount any serious bid for power. The regime thus went virtually unchallenged until the Cold War ended, the speculative bubble burst, and the economy slumped into recession.[13] Even then the Japanese—both voters and political leaders—collectively chose to overlook the flaws in the system, however corrupt and scandal-ridden it had become. I quote here at length from a study of Japanese politics by McNeil (1993, 49), just before the LDP lost power for the first time in 1993. It captures as well as any political commentary from that time the emerging problems of the regime.

Today, Japan's political institutions have declined significantly in effectiveness. Their decline is responsible for the corruption that undermines public confidence and for the policy gridlock—for lack of a better phrase—that hampers domestic and international decision making...By the late 1980s, the deficiencies were highly visible: a dysfunctional electoral system for the dominant Lower House in Japan's parliament; a talented, powerful, but increasingly hide-bound central bureaucracy;

a ruling LDP in thrall to money and faction; and an "eternal opposition" unready to take power...Disgusted with cascading scandal and no longer certain of the relevance of electoral politics to their lives, many citizens stayed at home [for the July 1992 Upper House elections]; at 51 percent the voting rate for those elections was the lowest in post-war history.

The problems McNeil identified, and that he thought might be resolved sooner rather than later, persisted and plagued the Japanese political economy beyond the 1990s. The 1955 regime had corrupted the political process to such an extent that cleaning it up proved difficult. The "lost decade" of the 1990s was so called because deregulation and administrative and electoral reforms (introduction of single-seat constituencies to encourage change of power) came slowly and in piecemeal fashion. Postponing decisive political reform and economic liberalization had only exacerbated the crisis by the time Koizumi arrived on the scene. His neoliberal structural reforms were, therefore, inevitably double-edged and painful. They cut public spending and bureaucratic largesse to slim down a government already impoverished and heavily in debt, diminishing its capacity to provide a "social safety net" for people now thrown into a more competitive market society.

Koizumi's priority was to confront anything standing in the way of domestic political reform. His main aim was to cut the political machinery's access to the massive public savings in the postal system, thus choking the main channel of the endemic pork-barrel politics that so distorted Japanese policymaking.[14] To this end, he called a snap election in 2005 over the bill to privatize the postal system, and even expelled LDP members who opposed it. This drastic measure confirmed to the public Koizumi's determination to destroy the old LDP by untying the party from its traditional powerbase—the farmers, construction companies, and postal workers—and to create a new party with a broader support base, including the urban swing voters who constituted about a third of the electorate.

The DPJ, meanwhile, had been building its identity as a new opposition party, presenting itself as an alternative conservative voice among urban voters in an effort to counter the LDP's traditional strength in the rural districts. It was, therefore, a major blow to the DPJ when, in the 2005 elections, it lost all but one of the 25 seats in the Tokyo district to the LDP. The LDP's victory, however, was more a demonstration of the all-round appeal of Koizumi's popular leadership than of the comparative weakness of the DPJ.

So, what happened in the four years between 2005 and 2009 to effect a dramatic reversal? Koizumi had provided a lifeline for the enfeebled LDP to reinvent itself as a party attuned to the diverse needs of an affluent, postindustrial society. Unfortunately, his immediate successor, Abe Shinzo, squandered that possibility following his ascent to the prime ministership in September 2006. Instead of bread-and-butter issues, he focused on the old politics of Japanese identity, revisiting the party's right-wing roots in an effort to sort out the embedded legitimacy issues of postwar Japan. For the LDP, his timing could not have been worse.

Abe, Identity Politics, and the LDP's Epilogue

Kenneth Pyle (2006) wrote quite optimistically that Abe represented an emergent new generation of Japanese leaders that would catapult Japan into the twenty-first century in a style different from that of his postwar, Cold War predecessors. Pyle (9) argued that Abe's appeal both to younger members of his party and the public was due to "his assertive stance toward North Korea over issues of abduction of Japanese citizens and missile tests and toward China over issues of territorial dispute and the Yasukuni war memorial. After years of self-effacement in international political matters, many Japanese are finding this new assertiveness liberating."[15]

As spelled out in his preelection campaign pamphlet, *Toward a Beautiful Country* (Abe 2006), Abe tried to pursue the path of postwar Japanese conservatism, restoring proper independence to the Japanese state and reasserting tradition and patriotism. To this end, he declared he would "cast away the post-war regime" based on the American design for a demilitarized and democratic Japan, and told the Diet in no uncertain terms of his ambition to realize "revision." He was the first prime minister to mention revision in a Diet speech since Hatoyama Ichiro, the first LDP president, 51 years earlier. That he could put constitutional revision on the cabinet agenda without much opposition indicated that the Constitution was no longer the taboo subject it had been throughout the Cold War, due mainly to the decline of the Socialist Party.[16] Public attitude became increasingly realistic about the need to articulate more clearly the status of the SDF, which after 1993 had begun to participate in UN peacekeeping.

The futility of Abe's leadership was demonstrated, however, only after a year in office. He abruptly resigned in October 2007 after losing the July upper house elections to the DPJ. The defeat was a serious set back for the LDP. Although it still held sway in the lower house, the gridlock in the Diet slowed down government business.[17] This drastic turnaround in fortune could be attributed to several factors, each with cumulative force.

First, Abe's relative inexperience had caused him to rely on old-style factional politics to form his cabinet (he held no cabinet post in his portfolio) (*Shukan bunshun* 2007). Koizumi had done exactly the opposite, ignoring the factions in order to keep his cabinet clean and independent from party/money politics.[18] Abe's cabinet turned out to be a "department store of scandals," with four ministers resigning and one committing suicide. Agricultural Minister Matsuoka Toshikatsu hanged himself before he was due to face a parliamentary hearing about his shady political financing. Health Minister Yanagisawa Hakuo resigned for causing uproar among legislators and attracting negative publicity for commenting that "women are baby-producing machines." Abe had not the resourcefulness to run background checks on colleagues, even as the public grew increasingly intolerant of dirty politics.

Second, Abe made a tactical error by allowing the return of former LDP members expelled from the party by Koizumi, further tarnishing his popular image as Koizumi's heir. The voting public had expected Abe to carry on in the same fighting spirit as Koizumi, to "destroy the LDP if it could not change" its old ways. His decision to bring back the "postal rebels" was construed as backtracking on what Koizumi had doggedly fought to achieve.

Third, revelation of the scandalous mismanagement of the national pension scheme, and Abe's poor handling of the situation, deepened public skepticism toward the LDP and further dented Abe's popularity.[19] His approval rating plunged from an initial height of around 70% upon succeeding Koizumi to around 30% within a few months.

Yet Abe himself was perhaps most responsible for his undoing. The pedigreed conservative proved to be hopelessly out of touch as he tried to gain ground in identity politics even as the voting public became acutely anxious over the national pension scheme fiasco. The fact that he kept constitutional revision on the July upper house election agenda even after a scandalous year revealed his profound misreading of the public mood.

With Abe's departure, the LDP chose the moderate Fukuda Yasuo, the son of Prime Minister Fukuda Takeo and Koizumi's first chief cabinet secretary, to lead the party. A foreign policy moderate, Fukuda quietly shoved constitutional revision off the table and shifted the government's focus onto bread-and-butter issues to win back public support and regain credibility as a ruling party. Notably, he announced the establishment of a new government agency for consumers, a move indicating a departure from the old ways of protecting business interests first. Fukuda's successor Aso Taro, another pedigreed politician as the grandson of Yoshida Shigeru, followed this same pragmatic line, though neither of these leaders was able to restore the failing fortunes of the LDP. The party under Abe, Fukuda, and Aso increasingly suffered the criticism that it was out of touch with the *min'i* (popular will).

After the 2007 victory of the DPJ in the upper house elections, the voices calling for constitutional revision quieted down, and the LDP was forced to tone down its nationalist-revisionist image. Indeed the advent of the DPJ might be said to have partially solved the Article 9 controversy, mainly because the two parties now dominant in parliament are, in essence, conservative. When the Socialist Party was in opposition, strict adherence to the constitution's restraint on the use of force was the main issue. The LDP and the DPJ, however, are mainly in opposition over the *conditions* of Japan's use of force, not the act itself. The domestic debate about the SDF in general has been sobering and maturing in this respect. Importantly, the public has come to accept the role of the SDF as part of Japan's contribution to international peace.

Moreover, the world to which Japan must adjust itself has changed. Arguments over Article 9 used to be couched exclusively in terms of relations with the United States, so much so that Japan lost the habit of strategic thinking about wider international politics. The rise of China and the maturity of regional international politics in Asia have enlarged the "audience" that takes note of the parochial discussions about revising Article 9 to remilitarize politics as a way toward "independence." It has been clear since Koizumi's trouble with China over his controversial visits to the Yasukuni Shrine that the LDP could not manage relations with China. For the LDP, the last war meant the war with the United States that began with Pearl Harbor in 1945 and ended with the two atomic bombs later the same year. For the Chinese Communist Party, it meant the longer, 15-years war that began with the Manchurian Incident in 1931. So long as the LDP insisted on putting pressure on the U.S. alliance by harking back to the war, it was bound to raise offense in China. There was clearly a pressing need to come up with a new formula that would work with both the United States and China, but the LDP's hands were tied by the reactionary identity politics that it had unleashed in the guise of a more "assertive" Japan in the past decade.

The legacy of Japan's nation-making process has thus lingered long enough to undermine the LDP. Abe Shinzo wrote in *Beautiful Country* (2006, 85): "It is a fact that in Japan, an enormous tapestry of history was woven with the *tenno* as its warp." Countering this, a new, politically neutral narrative is emerging that reflects a more scholarly attempt to understand what and who exactly wove this "tapestry of history." This narrative is geared toward explaining the "whys" of Japanese history, tradition, and culture in an effort to escape the parochial trappings of *Nihon-jin ron* (Japanese thought) (Amino 2004, 6). These issues of state identity have been an integral part of Japan's so-called history problem—the refusal to confront its Asian war past, the history textbook whitewashing, and the Yasukuni shrine controversy, to mention a few. How these issues are settled now that the LDP is out of power will have a bearing on Japan's international relations—especially on its standing in the region.

Breaking Apart for the Better

The nation-state project of national purpose now seems to have arrived at a crossroads, or at least reached the limit of its usefulness as a system. However, focusing on central political developments alone is rather like seeing the tree and not the forest. The latter might be described as a repository of various historical, subnational forces that were kept from the political limelight while the "national" issue reigned supreme.

The growing defiance of prefectural governors toward the central government in recent years demonstrates vividly the felt need of local governments to gain more freedom from the administrative stranglehold of the center. In 2008, reformist prefecture governors banded together to create a nation-wide movement—*Sentaku*—that seeks to change Japan from the periphery by setting the pace and agenda of reform. In fact, regional and local initiatives over educational reform, welfare programs, public works, town planning, and taxation have run into contention with the central government, but it is clear that there is an emergent idea from the periphery about how the country should be governed.

The fact that Japan's democratic deficiency gap has begun to be filled at regional and local levels reflects the changing concerns of Japanese citizens. Japan's engagement with the globalizing international economy over the past 30 years or so has created a vast "middle-class" society that identifies with global, middle-class values. It is concerned with "quality of life" issues such as the environment, education, welfare, and the reappraisal of regional diversity and identity—all issues that affect people immediately or are identified as "global" trends or concerns. It seems clear to these citizens that the central state is no longer capable of running the country in the fashion familiar to Japan's traditional conservative political leadership. A law on special economic zones passed in 2002 was an attempt to stimulate the economy by encouraging local initiatives, local business models, and the development of regional identities. Decentralization and rationalization of the complex web of bureaucratic control and regulations are seen as the key to reform.[20] A more federal structure of governance looms on the horizon.

There is some historical irony in the rise of regionalism today. Modern Japan sought and achieved success as a highly centralized state, but the acquired centralizing habit turns out to be the obstacle on Japan's route to economic recovery and social and political revitalization. The Meiji leaders sought to make a modern state out of a feudal country, and the key was centralization of power (Wigen 1998, 229–242; Gluck 1985).[21] The Meiji restoration was technically about transferring power from the *hans*, that is, the regions, to the new central state apparatus. Fukuzawa Yukichi, one of the most influential thinkers of the early Meiji era, had already likened the newly born Meiji state to a large tree with no root system, making it thus unstable. He worried about the fragility of a centralized structure of governance that tried to take over all of the functions that were dispersed among *hans* and *bakufu*.

Political decentralization today attempts to address this fragility by reversing the process. Outspoken governors of Osaka and Miyazaki thus make demands on both the LDP and DPJ to consider including the governors' decentralization manifesto in their party manifestos. Meanwhile, Okinawa, Fukuoka, or Niigata all look away from the center and try to assert their geographical proximity to the region's other economies; cities like Kobe and Osaka regard their history as open ports as strengths in the international economy. Do they represent a new paradigm in the way Japan defines its role in the globalizing Asian economy?

The Shifting Grounds of Japanese Legitimacy

Chalmers Johnson once wrote that, in Japan, the politicians reign but the bureaucrats in fact rule. Japan under the 1955 regime was all about slicing the fat pie of state under processes that were corrupt and, in the long run, counterproductive. The 2005 and 2009 elections were both about saying "no" to an excessively regulatory administrative structure and "a political class grown fat on a broken system" (*The Economist* 2008, 13). These were two legacies from a developmental state whose centralized structure of governance had not only outlived its usefulness but turned parasitical upon a political economy in need of revitalization.

Even if Japanese has no exact equivalent for "legitimacy," it is clear that this has not absolved it from problems, even a crisis, of political legitimacy. The long unraveling of the 1955 regime represented the unfolding of this crisis, and marked an often faltering and uncertain attempt to refound legitimacy on grounds other than those that had informed Japan's modernization. This chapter has tried to show that the old bases of legitimacy, which supported Japan's long-term push for international status, had roots deep in the earliest period of modernization and in prewar politics. The LDP's stubborn adherence to reactionary values in the postwar period could be tolerated on the international stage so long as Japan acted as a frontline state against Asian communism, and domestically so long as government policy fostered growth and high employment for a basically quiescent population. With the end of the Cold War, the stagnation of the economy, and the rise of a more sophisticated and demanding citizenry, the cracks in the legitimacy structure of the 1955 regime became apparent.

A crucial part of the attack on this structure relied on transforming the democratic charade of postwar Japanese politics into the real thing. Koizumi tried to change the LDP, the DPJ sought to replace it, but both depended on a vitalization of Japanese democracy. Each of the elections of 2005 and 2009 registered a higher voter turn out than during the 1990s. People were basically sick and tired of anything that hinted at the old ways after years of being disappointed by political and economic reforms that seemed to promise little and change things even less.[22] They made their feelings felt through the ballot box, and reforming leaders had a political base that was independent of the traditional power brokers of Japan. With the DPJ's victory, popular sovereignty became a genuine foundation of legitimacy, marking the beginning of a new political life in Japan. The process is still underway, as demonstrated by the politically contentious but popular so-called *shiwake* (administrative restructuring) carried out by the DPJ government against forces of resistance within the old "bureaucracy-industrial complex." Meanwhile, the efflorescence of regional initiatives and moves toward the decentralization of administration has both reflected and deepened the shift toward popular participation.

With the absence of a strong state to look after everything, from economic security to social welfare, there is bound to be confusion. Many economic and social problems remain to be managed, and how the Japanese will cope is anyone's guess. As for the question of international status, it seems that Japan's foreign policy decision-making paradigm has become as "normal" as in any mature democracy, with a cultivated preference for peaceful methods. Certainly, the Japanese public has been ambivalent about America's recent wars, particularly in Iraq, but has understood the need for Japan to be seen as a reliable ally. Its emotional support for Article 9 remains but should be less of a political minefield for decision makers and more of an opportunity to explore Japan's policy options and carve a unique "pacifist" identity among the powers.

Thus in Japan, democratic participation is replacing quiescent citizen obedience, the desire to be a responsible member of the international community is replacing an assertive nationalism. The grounds of Japanese political legitimacy have decidedly shifted and, perhaps truly for the first time since the Meiji restoration, a new national path beckons.

Notes

1. As diplomat Frank McNeil wrote in 1993, "Japan has operating democratic institutions, elections are honestly counted, and individual rights are protected by law...In Japan, as here and in Europe, it is the performance of democratic institutions, not their existence, that deserves critical examination" (2). German scholar Hanns Maull also noted back in 1990 that Japan had not yet passed the "ultimate test, a peaceful change of government" unlike Germany, which had experienced it twice already in 1969 and 1982 (91).

2. Koizumi was popular because of his un-politician-like character. He freely shared his love of the opera (he wrote a book on it after he stepped down) and Elvis Presley, speaking in the "vernacular" and not reading rigid and formal speeches prepared by the bureaucracy, and generally posing as one of the people and not a professional politician. For an analysis of Koizumi's early years and Japanese populism, see Ohtake (2003).

3. Hatoyama delivered this message at the post-DPJ victory press conference in the early hours of September 1, 2009. (The Democratic Party of Japan 2009).

4. The Japanese claim for being nationalistic than others has currency to the extent that Western scholars have also recognized Japan as model case of a nation-state. For example, Barry Buzan wrote: "A pure model of the nation-state would require that the nation precede the state, and in a sense give rise to it, as in the case of Japan, Germany, Poland, Swaziland and others" (75). Eric Hobsbawm also notes that Japan is (together with China and Korea) one of the "extremely rare examples

of historic states composed of a population that is ethnically almost or entirely homogeneous." (p. 66)

5. It is notable still today how frequently Japanese leaders and diplomatic commentators speak of how far Japan lives up to the expectations of the United States, or more broadly, the major Western countries.

6. One could argue that the conservative argument to revise the post-war constitution is in a similar vein, in that the conservatives want to restore full sovereignty robbed by Article 9 and make Japan "independent" again.

7. See Richard Samuels's (2003) comparative study of the role of Italian and Japanese leaders in the late nineteenth and early twentieth centuries.

8. Yoshida (1995) himself has regretted the impact of his decision in later years. Also see Nagano (2004).

9. This is not to say that the conservatives were the only party against the constitution. When the draft was being debated the Communist Party expressed strong reservations about Article 9.

10. Arguably, only states like the United States, China, or India can claim to be "fully" independent. States in the European Union or like Japan and South Korea are ultimately dependent on U.S. extended deterrence.

11. Quite revealingly, those who speak of cutting the umbilical cord tying Japan to the United States *as the progenitor* of postwar Japan would never contemplate a Japan without a U.S. security guarantee.

12. LDP factions represented different interest groups—such as the large corporations, the construction industry, the agricultural sector, and postal workers—and policies that benefited them, as Kitaoka Shin'ichi describes: "Factions are old, big, formal, and ideologically consistent. They are, in reality, political parties. If factions are parties…the LDP…is a coalition government." Shin'ichi Kitaoka, "Japan's Dysfunctional Democracy," *Asia Program Special Report*, No. 117 (Woodrow Wilson International Center for Scholars, January 2004), 6–8.

13. The LDP fell from power for the first time in 1993, and though returning to power the following year was not able thereafter to rule on its own.

14. It is said that Koizumi's main target was the Hashimoto faction, or the former Tanaka faction, the largest LDP faction founded by Tanaka Kakuei in the 1970s that was known to be the hotbed of pork-barrel politics.

15. Abe had the right conservative pedigree, as the grandson of Prime Minister Kishi Nobusuke (1956–1960), son of former foreign minister Abe Shintaro, and nephew of Prime Minister Sato Eisaku (1965–1972), all from Yamaguchi prefecture that also produced the main architects

of modern, Meiji Japan. Pyle wrote (2006, 7): "[n]o political leader in Japan has deeper roots in this elite than Abe."

16. The Socialist Party had already made a series of ideological sell-outs since 1989, when its main supporting union, Sohyo, joined the moderate unions of Rengo. In 1992, it changed its English name to Social Democratic Party of Japan (SDPJ) to tone-down its "socialist" image. In 1993, its then-leader, Yamahana Sadao, spoke of *soken* (creative evolution of the constitution), thereby breaking away from the traditional party-line of *goken* (defence of the constitution). All these moves had resulted in alienating traditional Socialist voters. The decision by Murayama Tomiichi—the first Socialist leader to become prime minister in nearly half century—to reverse in 1994 his party's long-held interpretation that the SDF was unconstitutional effectively killed the party.

17. The House of Representatives (lower house) holds legislative power over the House of Councillors, much like the power balance between the House of Commons and the House of Lords in the United Kingdom. Even if a bill is struck down in the upper house, the lower house can override it with a two-thirds majority when the bill returns to the lower house. If the upper house refuses to deliberate, then after 90 days the bill automatically becomes law.

18. Koizumi was said to have run background checks of potential ministers, looking out for seeds of potential scandal. His five years in power were relatively scandal-free in spite of Japan's flourishing "gutter" press.

19. Some 50 million pension records could not be matched to those entitled and Abe promised to match all of them within a year, which was simply impossible. Many thought that Abe could not grasp the gravity of the crisis for the ordinary folks because of his privileged upbringing.

20. The government has been seriously contemplating the introduction of larger units of regional administrative system by merging the existing prefectures (47 in all, including Hokkaido, Kyoto, Osaka, and Tokyo that are not called prefectures) into roughly 7 domains (*doshu* system). Such remapping of regional administrative units would be a major historical event, matching what took place with the Meiji restoration, when some 300 feudal domains (*han*) were merged into the present prefectures.

21. The Meiji leaders proceeded to ensure that old, feudal loyalties would be diluted or dispersed by laying down new administrative units, the prefectures (*ken*) to make a clear break from the past regime and to "render prefectures blank slates that could more easily be inscribed with the modern state's priorities" (Wigen 1998, 237; see also Gluck 1985).

22. The voter turnout for the 2009 general elections was 69.28%, the highest since single-seat districts were introduced in 1996. In fact, the

voting rate had been declining since 1993, the lowest being 59.65 in 1996. At Koizumi's *yusei* (postal reform) snap elections the rate leapt to 67.51% (voting rate date is available from the Ministry of Home Affairs and Communications website [2009]).

References

Abe, Shinzo. 2006. *Utukushi-i kuni-e* [Toward a Beautiful Country]. Tokyo, Japan: Bungei-shunju.

Amino, Yoshihiko. 2004, *Nihon-ron no shiza: retto no shakai to kokka* [Viewpoint of Nihon-ron: Society and State of the Archipelago]. Tokyo, Japan: Shogakukan.

Berlin, Isaiah. 1969. *Four Essays on Liberty.* New York: Oxford University Press.

Buruma, Ian. 2004. *Inventing Japan: 1853–1964.* New York: Modern Library.

Buzan, Barry. 1991. *People, States & Fear,* 2nd ed. Colchester, UK: ECPR Press.

Democratic Party of Japan. 2009. "Toward an Even Greater Victory for the People." *DPJ.* Accessed on March 3, 2010. http://www.dpj.or.jp /news/?num=16918.

The Economist. 2008. "Japain." February 21.

Gluck, Carol. 1985. *Japan's Modern Myths: Ideology in the Late Meiji Period.* Princeton, NJ: Princeton University Press.

Hando, Kazutoshi. 2006. *Showa-shi: sengo-hen 1945–1989* [History of Showa: Post-war Volume 1945–1989]. Tokyo, Japan: Heibon-sha.

Hobsbawm, E. J. 1990. *Nations and Nationalism since 1780.* Cambridge: Cambridge University Press.

Iokibe, Makoto. 1997. *Senryoki: shusho tachi no shin nihon* [Occupation Period: The Prime Minister's New Japan]. Tokyo, Japan: Yomiuri Shinbun-sha.

Kyodo, Tsushin-sha, ed. 2007. *Kaiken no keifu: 9 jo to nichibei domei no genba* [The Genealogy of Constitutional Revision: The Scene of Article 9 and Japan–U.S. Alliance]. Tokyo, Japan: Shincho-sha.

Maull, Hanns W. 1990. "Germany and Japan: The New Civilian Powers." *Foreign Affairs* 69: 91–106.

McNeil, Frank. 1993, *Japanese Politics: Decay or Reform?* Washington, DC: Carnegie Endowment for Peace.

Mikuriya, Takashi, and Takahide Nakamura, eds. 2005. *Kikigaki: Miyazawa Kiichi Kaikoroku* [Oral History: Miyazawa Kiichi Memoirs]. Tokyo: Iwanami Shoten.

Ministry of Home Affairs and Communications. 2009. "Voting Rate Date." Accessed February 20, 2010. http://www.soumu.go.jp/senkyo/senkyo_s /data/.

Nagano, Nobutoshi. 2004. *Yoshida seiken: 2616 days* [Yoshida Government: 2616 Days], vol. 2. Tokyo: Gyoken.

Nakasone, Yasuhiro. 2000. *21 seiki Nihon no Kokka Senryaku* [Strategy for the Japanese State in the 21st Century]. Tokyo: PHP Kenkyujo.

Nikkei. 2009. "Michinaru yoto ni takusu mono" [The Mandate for a New Ruling Party]. *Nihon Keizai Shimbun (Nikkei).* September 1.

Ohtake, Hideo. 2003. *Nihon-gata popurisumu* [Japanese-Style Populism]. Tokyo: Chuokoron.

Pyle, Kenneth B. 2006. "Abe Shinzo and Japan's Change of Course." *NBR Analysis* 17: 5–31.

Samuels, Richard. 2003. *Machiavelli's Children: Leaders and Their Legacies in Italy and Japan.* Ithaca, NY and London: Cornell University Press.

Shukan bunshun. 2007. "Hayakumo aoiki toiki Abe seiken: hosakan 5-nin wa nani yatteruno?" [Abe Government Out of Breath Already: What Are the 5 Aides Doing?] *SB*, February 1. Accessed March 3, 2010. http://bunshun.jp.shukanbunshun/thisweek_pol/070201.html.

Tamamoto, Masaru. 1999. "The Uncertainty of the Self: Japan at Century's End." *World Policy Journal* 16: 119–128.

Wakita, Haruko. 2003. *Tenno to chusei bunka* [Tenno and Medieval Culture]. Tokyo: Yoshikawa Kobunkan.

Wigen, Kären. 1998. "Constructing Shinano: The Invention of a Neo-Traditional Region." In *Mirror of Modernity: Invented Traditions of Modern Japan*, edited by Stephen Vlastos, 229–242. Berkeley, CA: University of California Press.

Williams, David. 1994. *Japan: Beyond the End of History.* London and New York: Routledge.

Yoshida, Shigeru. 1995. Reprint. "Nihon gaiko no ayundekita michi [The Path Travelled in Japanese Diplomacy]." In *Sengo Nihon gaiko ronbunshu* [Postwar Japanese Works on Diplomacy], edited by Shin'ichi Kitaoka, 99–113. Tokyo: Chuokoron-sha. Originally published in *Kaiso junen* [Ten Years of Recollection], vol. 1. Tokyo, Japan: Shincho-sha, 1957.

CHAPTER 10

Political Legitimacy in an Unconsolidated Democratic Order: The Philippines

Noel M. Morada

The legitimacy of the democratic state in the Philippines remains stable and strong despite a number of political crises that that nation faced for over two decades since 1986. Prior to the restoration of the democratic order, the country operated under the authoritarian regime of Marcos who drew much of his legitimacy from the support of the military, political clans, and business cronies. Marcos, who came to power in 1965 under an American-inspired 1935 democratic constitution, declared martial law in 1972 to suppress both legitimate opposition and armed rebellion in the country. He was ousted in a joint civilian-military "people power revolution" in February 1986. Filipinos still have faith in their imperfect political system founded on democratic principles that protect their basic freedoms and civil rights even though they are also cognizant of the failure of their government to improve their quality of life.

This chapter examines the nature and dynamics of political legitimacy in the Philippines since the democratic order was restored 25 years ago. The chapter argues that the democratic system in the country—though still largely unconsolidated and suffering from deficits in performance legitimacy—remains stable because Filipinos in general are principled believers in democracy and do not favor authoritarian alternatives. Even so, the legitimacy of the Philippine state will continue to be challenged by armed rebellions and poverty, both of which have persisted under the restored democratic order.

Restored Democratic Order after 25 Years

Twenty-five years after President Ferdinand E. Marcos' removal from power in 1986, democratic governance in the Philippines is far from consolidation. Briefly, the "yellow revolution" led by Corazon "Cory" C. Aquino and supported by the Roman Catholic Church, reformist elements in the Armed Forces of the Philippines (AFP), and civil society groups sought to bring down the authoritarian rule of Marcos, who arguably lost his legitimacy amidst abuse of power, human rights violations, cronyism, poverty, and corruption. Aquino promised that her government would be based on transparency, rule of law, and protection of human rights. These principles were later incorporated in the 1987 constitution, which restored the three coequal branches of government under an American-inspired presidential system. Likewise, the constitution limited the president's tenure to a single six-year term and significantly clipped the powers of the executive. For instance, the president cannot declare martial law in the country or any part thereof without the consent of congress, and this can be done only under conditions of external invasion or rebellion. These provisions were clearly aimed at preventing another dictator from emerging under the restored democratic order. Even so, the optimism that greeted Aquino's ascent was short-lived as her government faced several failed coup attempts by restive elements in the military, apart from the armed rebellion of communist insurgents and the Moro separatist movement in southern Philippines that challenged the authority and territorial integrity of the democratic state.

Despite the relative peace and stability achieved under the administration of President Fidel V. Ramos, the euphoria of the first civilian-backed uprising in 1986 appears to have evaporated as many Filipinos became more cynical of leadership changes in the country, whether through "people power" or elections. Indeed, these changes have failed to bring significant improvement in their living conditions. It must be recalled that in 2001, the six-year term of former president Joseph E. Estrada was cut short by another "people power" uprising over corruption charges involving illegal gambling money. Just like in 1986, the support of the Roman Catholic Church and the military played a critical role in forcing Estrada to step down, which enabled then vice-president Gloria Macapagal-Arroyo to take over as president of the country. At the time, there were high hopes for the new administration of Arroyo, a trained economist, to do a better job of steering the country toward sustained economic growth and development. However, despite achieving higher economic growth rates under the nine-year term of Arroyo, the legitimacy of her government was undermined by two major political crises. These stemmed mainly from allegations of her cheating in the 2004 elections and the corruption scandal in 2008 surrounding the over US$300-million ZTE national broadband project and the US$600-million North Rail project, both of which involved investments from China.

Benigno "Noynoy" C. Aquino III, son of democracy icons "Ninoy" and "Cory" Aquino, took over from Arroyo as the fifteenth president of the Philippines after he won 42% of the votes cast in the first automated elections in the country in May 2010.[1] Some pundits in the Philippines have attributed Aquino III's landslide victory to what they call a revival of the spirit of "people power" uprising in 1986 and outpouring of sympathies to the Aquino family after his mother passed away in August 2009. Though a reluctant candidate from the start, Aquino III was persuaded to run for president by influential religious, business, and civil society leaders who considered him as the best candidate to succeed Arroyo as he was perceived to be carrying on the legacy of his late mother's transparent and moral leadership.[2] In his inaugural speech, Aquino III promised to wage war against corruption and promote transparency in government. He also announced the creation of a truth commission tasked to investigate corruption committed by the Arroyo administration. The Supreme Court, however, declared the creation of the truth commission unconstitutional, as it violated the principle of equal protection under the law because it focused only on the Arroyo administration, and duplicated the authority and functions of other constitutional bodies, and usurped the power of the legislature in creating offices (Philstar.com 2010).

This brief overview shows that after 25 years, the restored democratic order in the Philippines is far from consolidated for a number of reasons. First, clans or families continue to dominate politics in the country all the way down at the local government level. Although the 1987 constitution mandates the legislature to pass a law that should put an end to "political dynasties," congress thus far has failed to comply with this mandate, in part because many of its members are from traditional political families who continue to dominate the legislature.[3] Indeed, under Cory Aquino, the revival of the premartial law political order simply brought back the dominance of the oligarchy. Second, elections in the Philippines have been more about the popularity of individual personalities than about policy differences or ideologies of political parties. In fact, political parties in the country are essentially loose coalitions of individual politicians whose primary interest is to secure national or local positions than make a commitment to any agenda, platform, or ideology. Third, violence, vote buying, and allegations of cheating or vote rigging remain constant features of elections in the Philippines. Over 100 private armies are reportedly maintained by several political clans that contribute to the persistence of political killings, especially in the run-up to elections. This was clearly demonstrated in the Maguindanao massacre of November 2009 perpetrated by some members of the ruling Ampatuan clan. Part of the Autonomous Region of Muslim Mindanao (ARMM), Maguindanao has long been reported in the Philippine media as the hub of election fraud in the country. Finally, the legitimacy of the central government under the democratic order is continually being challenged by armed rebellion, specifically by the communist insurgents and Muslim separatist movement in Mindanao. Since 1986, attempts to forge a peaceful settlement of these internal conflicts have failed for a number of reasons as is discussed in a separate section of this chapter.

Beyond democratic consolidation, the apparent lack of a shared vision for the country among the Filipino political elite has resulted in more than two decades of wasted opportunities for the Philippines to catch up with its neighbors in the region. Electoral competition—which has been limited to fractious traditional politicians and the landed elite—has rendered the *cacique* democratic system ineffective in moving the country forward and achieve sustainable economic growth and development that would improve the quality of life of Filipinos. As one scholar had pointed out, the 2010 elections in the Philippines suggest that the long dominant political narrative of "rich-versus-poor" has been challenged by "reformist" appeals for good governance (Thompson 2010). Even so, the reformist Aquino III administration must have the political will to address the structural problems of the country to improve the economic conditions of many poor Filipinos, which would only enhance the performance legitimacy of the political system and deepen the Filipinos' commitment to the democratic order. The next section of this chapter discusses the sources and dynamics of political legitimacy in the Philippines over the past 25 years, focusing mainly on public perceptions, the role of religious groups, the military, civil society, and the external environment.

Sources of Democratic Legitimacy

Support for Democratic Order

Recognition and support for the democratic order in the Philippines remains high even as Filipinos are generally able to assess variations in the quality of regimes that existed in the country since the administration of Marcos. For instance, Filipinos consider the current political regime as democratic compared with the previous order under Marcos, which is largely perceived as a dictatorship. It was only during the term of Arroyo that a significant proportion of the public in 2002 viewed the political system to be authoritarian, largely because of the crackdown that was undertaken by her government against Estrada supporters following the latter's ouster in 2001 (Guerrero and Tusalem 2008, 67–68). The Social Weather Stations (SWS) reported that satisfaction with the way democracy works in the country reached 69% in September 2010, with 56% of respondents expressing preference for democracy over other kinds of governments. Also, overall satisfaction with how the Philippine democratic system works reaches its peak after elections in the country, such as those in 1992 (70%), 1998 (70%), and 2010 (68%). The lowest satisfaction rating was registered in 2004 (44%) following the controversial elections that year (SWS 2010b).

Amendments to the 1987 constitution have been proposed by succeeding administrations after Cory Aquino, arguing for a shift to a parliamentary system to overcome the so-called gridlock character of the current presidential system.[4] Each time that such charter amendments were made or revived, however, it was met with strong resistance from mainstream opposition parties, civil society groups, the Catholic Church, and the general public. Indeed, charter change proposals were viewed with suspicion as an attempt to extend the incumbent's terms of office. Thus far, public opinion has been consistently opposed to charter change and extension of terms of office of national and local government officials (ABS-CBNnews.com 2008).

Overall, Filipinos believe in the importance of political participation and score favorably on perceptions of political efficacy compared with their East Asian neighbors. Notwithstanding their ambivalence about individual capacities, Filipinos have apparently developed a sense of "collective strength" because of successful uprisings in the past, which could potentially be used to effect political change (Guerrero and Tusalem 2008, 71). Exercising their right to vote is the main manifestation of political participation for most people in the Philippines as demonstrated by consistent high voter turnout particularly during presidential elections. Even so, more Filipinos feel that they do not have the capacity to either understand or influence the political process in the country, or believed that they are capable of understanding but not influencing it, than those who thought that they are capable of both (71).[5]

Confidence in Democratic Institutions and Good Governance

In the Philippines, institutions of representative democracy (e.g., legislature, political parties, national and local governments) are trusted less compared to societal institutions (e.g., newspapers, television, and nongovernment organizations or NGOs) and government institutions (e.g., civil service, military, courts). Guerrero and Tusalem (2008) reported that societal (57%) and governmental (51%) institutions scored higher than political institutions (46%) as far as public trust among Filipinos are concerned. In particular, newspapers and NGOs have gained good reputations, respectively, through exposure of corruption in government and advocacy on behalf of marginalized social sectors. NGOs have also played a significant role in interest articulation and aggregation, for example, through endorsement of certain platforms of party-list groups in the legislature. Political parties (35%) were the least trusted given their lack of discipline, as well as their personality-oriented and elitist character (73–75). In 2006, public opinion polling indicated that 67% of Filipinos believed that none of the existing political parties was concerned about their welfare. Also, there were more people (29%) than believers in particular political parties who thought that there was no political party with realistic platforms and noble leaders that interacted with marginalized sectors and sought to benefit citizens (SWS 2006).

Meanwhile, control of corruption continues to be a major problem in the country, particularly in the public sector. Majority of Filipinos perceive that corruption occurs in the national government in almost all or most officials but less so among local officials. To some extent, political corruption stems mainly from the way candidates for national positions, for example, finance themselves during elections, which creates higher stakes and financial rewards after they win (Guerrero and Tusalem 2008, 71–72). In 2008, the Philippines scored 71 (moderate) in the Global Integrity Index that measures several dimensions of good governance and corruption. While it scored strongly in administration and civil service (86), and moderately in oversight and regulation (76) and anticorruption and rule of law (71), the country scored weak in government accountability (70), civil society, public information, and media (68), and very weak in elections (59), and received very low scores in rule of law (51) and law enforcement (60) (Global Integrity 2008).

Overall, corruption issues are likely to influence the Filipinos' trust and confidence in their government, although these may not necessarily undermine continuing support for the legitimacy of the democratic order. In the short term, Aquino III faces an uphill battle in dealing with this issue given the animosity between his administration and the judicial branch. For one, he does not have a good rapport with the chief justice of the Supreme Court, whom he considers a "midnight appointee" of Arroyo. He had also accused the Supreme Court of putting obstacles to his reform program after it declared unconstitutional the creation of a truth commission that will investigate corruption allegations of the Arroyo government (Porcala 2010). For its part, the Supreme Court resented Aquino III's decision to significantly reduce its budget for 2011 and even threatened at one point to stage a "judicial revolt" against his administration. Undoubtedly, this would be a setback to its judicial reform program and efficient delivery of justice. For example, the hiring of new judges and court personnel to improve the speed of disposing cases cannot be undertaken even as court facilities are in dismal conditions (Dalangin-Fernandez 2010a). Based on its past record, the the democratic state's ability to contain corruption in the long term is very much in doubt. For example, efforts to regain the reported ill-gotten wealth of the Marcos family have not been successful more than two decades after it was ousted from power. Although Estrada was placed under house arrest for six years, Arroyo immediately pardoned him "for humanitarian reasons" less than a month after he was convicted of plunder. This enabled Estrada to run again for president in the May 2010 elections and received a sizable number of votes. More recently, the Ombudsman allowed a former military general, who was the comptroller at the AFP—charged with plunder, to plead guilty to a lesser charge enabling him to post bail and was set free (Dalangin-Fernandez 2010b).

Religious Groups

The support of the Catholic Church in the two "people power" uprisings against Marcos in 1986 and Estrada in 2001 was crucial in the downfall of the two presidents. Jaime Cardinal Sin in particular was one of the central figures in these two historic events as he called on the Catholic faithful to join massive protest along the main highway EDSA. As the voice of the Catholic Church, Cardinal Sin's pronouncements on political issues influenced the legitimacy of political leaders and their policies. He not only denounced abuse of power, human rights violation, and corruption in government but also opposed government policies pertaining reproductive health, family planning, and attempts to make divorce legal in the Philippines. The Catholic Church also opposed the death penalty, which was again abolished in 2006 after it was reinstated in 1994. Since Cardinal Sin passed away in 2005, however, the unity of the Catholic hierarchy appears to have weakened. To some extent, this enabled Arroyo to survive her worst political crisis that took place in 2005 that stemmed from allegations of cheating in the 2004 general elections. Even so, some members of the Catholic Church opposed to the Arroyo administration remained steadfast in denouncing extensive corruption in her government.

Apart from the Catholic Church, other religious groups have also been influential in Philippine politics. The Iglesia Ni Kristo (Church of Christ) or INK and the Catholic charismatic group El Shaddai vote as a bloc during elections and their respective support are very much sought after by candidates at the national and local levels. The INK also played a critical role in the second EDSA[6] "people power" in 2001 that ousted Estrada and even demanded a role in the "coordination committee" that included another lay religious group called Couples for Christ (Abinales and Amoroso 2005, 277). It was also the head of the INK who negotiated with Arroyo to grant amnesty to Estrada as early as 2001, apparently in exchange for its withdrawal of support for anti-Arroyo protests a few months after the ouster of Estrada that was staged by his supporters (dubbed also as EDSA 3, which was sparked by the arrest of the former president in April 2001 on plunder charges) (GMAnews.TV 2007). El Shaddai leader Mike Velarde, a former adviser to Estrada, supported EDSA 3 initially but later played a role of mediator between Arroyo and Estrada supporters following the bloody attack against Malacañan Palace in May 2001. El Shaddai also opposed government-sponsored charter change initiatives that were aimed at, among others, shifting the country's political system to a parliamentary form of government, which was largely perceived by many as an attempt to extend her rule.[7]

The Military and Politics

Article II, Section 3 of the 1987 constitution states that "civilian authority is, at all times, supreme over the military" and that the AFP "is the protector of the people and the state" whose goal is "to secure the sovereignty of the State and the integrity of the national territory." In 2001, former AFP chief of staff Angelo Reyes invoked this provision of the democratic constitution to justify the withdrawal of support from his commander-in-chief president Estrada and transfer allegiance to the then vice-president Arroyo as the constitutionally mandated successor to Estrada. Likewise, the coup plotters against Arroyo during the 2003 Oakwood mutiny invoked the same constitutional provision to justify their uprising against her government. Indeed, the AFP as "protector of the people" posed a dilemma for the Philippine military at the height of calls for Arroyo's resignation in 2005 even as many of her trusted generals refused to heed calls to withdraw support from her government. Some alumni members of the Philippine Military Academy (PMA) were even, reportedly, in favor of abolishing this provision of the constitution as it has been misinterpreted to mean the right of the AFP to intervene in politics (Cabreza 2008).

An important downside to the 2001 "people power" uprising is that Arroyo became dependent on the support of the military and traditional politicians to ensure her political survival. This became even clearer after the Oakwood mutiny in 2003 and the subsequent political crisis in 2005 when there were clamors for her resignation after allegations of her cheating in the 2004 elections surfaced (Abinales and Amoroso 2005, 278). The Arroyo administration's efforts to reform the AFP in response to some of the valid grievances raised by the mutineers may be one positive outcome of the failed coup. Even so, some of the gains made by the AFP under Arroyo in preventing future military adventurism in the country have been undermined by her successor, Aquino III. Specifically, the latter's decision to grant amnesty to the rebel soldiers not only sends the wrong message to the AFP about the consequences of military adventurism but also complicates further any existing rift within the defense establishment on this issue. Without even waiting for the verdict of the lower court on the criminal charges filed against the Oakwood mutineers, the executive branch went ahead with the amnesty proclamation that did not even contain conditions, such as admission of guilt on the part of soldiers, before they could avail of the amnesty. However, the implementing rules and regulations released by the Department of Defense stipulates that rebel soldiers must first recognize their guilt before they could avail of the amnesty, though some prominent rebel soldiers have strongly opposed this condition (Pazzibugan 2010). This is clearly an indication that there is resistance within the AFP to the grant of unconditional amnesty to the rebel soldiers.

To be fair, former president Ramos also granted amnesty to rebel soldiers of the Reform AFP Movement (RAM) who staged several failed coups against Cory Aquino as part of his national reconciliation policy. But what makes Aquino III's amnesty proclamation especially controversial is that it comes out clearly as part of political retribution against Arroyo, rather than a credible attempt to foster national reconciliation as he claimed. The decision cannot be a political payback to the military rebels as the group did not endorse Aquino III in the May 2010 elections. Even so, during election campaign, he publicly stated that coup leader Antonio Trillanes, who was elected senator in 2007 while in jail, was a victim of injustice under Arroyo. That Aquino III took a special interest on the matter is demonstrated by his order to review the rebel leader's case within a month after he assumed office (Ramos and Ubac 2010). But because the case was already tried and the ruling of the lower court was expected, Aquino III preempted the court by announcing a grant of amnesty to the rebel soldiers.

Aquino III's apparent leniency toward the rebel soldiers is in stark contrast to his strong reaction against the plea bargain agreement between the office of the Ombudsman and a former military general charged with plunder that allowed the latter to temporarily walk free on a lesser charge. Specifically, he invoked the rule of law and criticized the prosecutors for not following proper procedures in the case (Cabiling 2010). Both cases undermine efforts in the reform of the security sector in the Philippines for which the national leadership should have an interest in promoting. Supremacy of civilian authority over the military is an important pillar of any democratic order and granting amnesty to the military rebels even before the court has made a ruling on the case undermines not only this principle but also the legitimacy of the country's judicial process.

Civil Society

Civil society emerged as a dynamic force in Philippine politics after the democratic order was restored. Its revival and growth are partly attributed to "the steady fragmentation of the Left, including its heftier national democratic wing" (Franco 2004, 109) and opening of political space after the ouster of Marcos (Abinales and Amoroso 2005, 237). The number of these registered nonstock, nonprofit organizations increased from 27,000 in 1986 to a high of about 95,000 in 2000, with some 7,000 engaged in grassroots organizations that aim to empower poor and marginalized sectors (Franco 2004, 109). The Asian Development Bank (ADB) has estimated that the number of civil society groups in the Philippines is about 500,000 but only a fraction of these are formally registered (ADB 2007). They cover a wide spectrum based on their respective advocacies, strategies, and extent of networks within and outside the country. Some focus on single-issue advocacy (e.g., human rights protection), while others have been involved in social advocacy like redistribution (e.g., land reform), sustainable development, environmental protection, women and reproductive health, and labor protection (including welfare of overseas Filipino migrant workers), as well as conflict prevention and peace building, particularly in conflict areas of Mindanao, and have been actively involved in peace talks between the national government and the rebel forces—the MILF and the Communist Party of the Philippines/New People's Army (CPP/NPA).

During the administration of Cory Aquino, the participation of civil society groups in policy decision-making process became "mainstream" and provided legitimacy to government policies and programs. This began the process of democratic consultation where government policies are presented both to the legislature *and* NGOs and people's organizations (POs) for approval (Abinales and Amoroso 2005, 237). President Ramos continued with this practice under his administration, specifically in formulating a social reform agenda and in promoting civil society involvement in development of multisector stakeholder mechanisms in the pursuit of peace in Mindanao (ADB 2007, 3). Civil society groups also supported Ramos' successor, Estrada, but were later disillusioned with his policies and bad performance in addressing poverty issues. They later joined forces with other groups in calling for his ouster following corruption and bribery scandal involving illegal gambling. Subsequently, Arroyo appointed some civil society leaders in her cabinet, notably in the social welfare and peace positions. These cabinet members, however, resigned from their posts in 2005 after allegations of Arroyo's involvement in election cheating the previous year. Although she survived the political crisis, relations with civil society groups have been strained and further exacerbated after a state of emergency in 2006 following a failed coup attempt against her government. They also supported efforts by opposition groups in the legislature to impeach Arroyo on allegations of corruption and cheating in the 2004 elections. This was further complicated by accusations of her government's tacit approval of the military's involvement in extrajudicial killings of persons associated with left-leaning organizations and community workers (3).

The contribution of civil society groups to democratic consolidation in the Philippines has been given mixed assessments by some scholars. On a positive note, they were able to "extend the reach of democratic right and freedoms to previously excluded populations" and "expanded political competition" (Franco 2004, 126). In addition, their support enabled reformist candidates win over traditional politicians in some provinces, which led to the passing of certain laws (e.g., anti-human trafficking and antiviolence against women and children) albeit with the support of traditional politicians (Abinales and Amoroso 2005,

266). On the downside, however, they remain "colonized to a significant extent by an elite-dominated, status quo-oriented political society" and have "also served (unintentionally) to revive or reinforce the
political influence of antireform elite interests" (Franco 2004, 126).
This is what Benedict Anderson calls the paradox of "the logic of
electoralism."[8] Also, civil society's influence in promoting the reformist
agenda since the downfall of Marcos in 1986 appears to have waned due
to a variety of factors, such as scarce resources, lack of professionalism,
transparency and accountability, rivalries between and among NGOs
and POs, as well as "protest fatigue" among their supporters that rendered mass mobilization less effective (Abinales and Amoroso 2005,
266). Divisions within civil society groups have also deepened due to
the three-member cap in the party list elections, which prevent incen-
tives for stable coalitions of NGOs and their political parties within and
outside the legislature (Wurfel 2004, 222).

External Sources

To some extent, the success of the first "people power" uprising in
the Philippines may also be attributed to the decision of the United
States under the Reagan administration to cut its support for Marcos
and provide a safe haven for his family in Hawaii. And, the United
States played a significant role in ensuring the survival of the restored
democratic order in the country under Cory Aquino after she faced
several aborted coup attempts. In 1989, for example, facing its bloodiest
coup that almost toppled her government, the United States granted
the request of Aquino for some fighter jets from an American air base
in the country to take persuasion flights against rebel soldiers holed
up in a hotel in Manila's financial district. However, some nationalist
Filipino politicians saw in the "military assistance" extended to Aquino
a clear manifestation of American intervention in the country's internal affairs, which consequently deepened further long-held resentment
against the United States for supporting the Marcos dictatorship in the
past as quid pro quo for continuation of American military bases in the
Philippines. The United States paid dearly for this as a majority of the
members of the Philippine Senate in 1991 rejected the extension of
the 1947 military bases agreement despite strong public support for its
renewal. Consequently, bilateral relations between the Philippines and
the United States hit a plateau until the security alliance was revived
following the tragic events of 9/11.

Under George W. Bush, the Philippines became an important non-NATO ally of the United States in the context of the latter's war against international terrorism. With Southeast Asia considered as a second front in the global war on terror, this created an opportunity for the "people power"-installed government of Arroyo in 2001 to increase its political legitimacy at home, especially after her government joined the "coalition of the willing" in support of the U.S. war in Iraq in 2003. The Philippines benefited from increased American military assistance to the AFP and continuing support for the government's campaign against the communist insurgents and the notorious Abu Sayyaf Group (ASG). It also meant unwavering moral support from Bush at critical moments when Arroyo faced major political crises at home such as the Oakwood mutiny in 2003, election-related cheating allegations in 2005, and the aborted coup in 2006. Not even the strained relations between the two countries that stemmed from Manila's decision to withdraw the Philippine humanitarian contingent from Iraq in 2004, which was deeply resented by some neoconservative advisers of Bush, seriously diminished his support for Arroyo's government.

To some extent, the Bush administration's forbearance was tested as it attempted to understand the dilemma faced by the Arroyo government whose political survival was at stake when a Filipino worker in Iraq was kidnapped by a terrorist group that demanded the withdrawal of the Philippine contingent from that country. Indeed, more than just a foreign policy issue, the protection of Filipino migrant workers turned into a crisis of political legitimacy at home when the government was perceived incapable of saving the lives of its nationals facing mortal danger abroad. President Ramos had such crisis in 1995 when the Singapore government refused to grant clemency to a Filipina domestic helper who was hanged after she was convicted of murder. To mollify public anger, Ramos fired his labor and foreign affairs secretaries, although his approval rating suffered just the same. Since then, succeeding administrations have made it an important pillar of the state's foreign policy to ensure the protection of migrant Filipino workers abroad. Arroyo, for instance, had made several trips to some countries in the Middle East to appeal for clemency of Filipinos facing the death penalty. It is against this backdrop that Arroyo decided in favor of rescuing the life of a Filipino in Iraq over the country's security commitment to the United States, which unfortunately was seen by then secretary of defense Donald Rumsfeld as a weakness that was "provocative."

Challenges to the Democratic Order

Armed Rebellions

The legitimacy of the Philippine state continues to be challenged by two armed rebellions, the communist insurgency led by the CPP/NPA and the Muslim separatist movement in Mindanao led by the MILF. Peace talks between the national government and these two groups have been stalled under the Arroyo administration for different reasons. The inclusion of the CPP/NPA in the list of international terrorist organizations in 2002 and 2004 by the United States and the European Union (EU) respectively foreclosed any peaceful negotiations to end the communist insurgency under the Arroyo administration as the rebel group made their delisting as a precondition for resumption of talks with the government. The CPP/NPA's guerrilla forces have declined steadily since the ouster of Marcos in 1986 and the terrorist tag seriously undermined its external financial support (*Manila Bulletin Online* 2010).[9] Internal rifts within its leadership also weakened the communist movement's influence throughout the country. Even so, the communist insurgency continues to inflict harm on government troops, public utilities, and private companies through guerrilla attacks and extortion activities like extracting revolutionary taxes. In areas where they have effective control or influence, they are also able to charge candidates the so-called "permit to campaign fees" during elections. These extortion activities aim to increase their domestic revenue collections, especially as external funding has substantially dwindled.[10] Communist strongholds remain in mainly poor rural areas of the country where access to basic services are almost absent (PHDR 2005). Peace talks under the administration of Aquino III are expected to resume in Norway in the first quarter of 2011 but progress toward a political settlement of the 42-year-old insurgency remains uncertain. For one, the CPP/NPA has not committed itself to a longer unilateral cease-fire despite the willingness of Aquino III to resume peace negotiations (*ABC News Online* 2010; Gomez 2010).

Meanwhile, the 12,000-strong MILF poses a more serious threat to the legitimacy and territorial integrity of the state as the group continues with its separatist objectives. The aborted signing of the MOA-AD in 2008 after the Supreme Court declared it unconstitutional has stalled peace negotiations with the central government. Although Aquino III had expressed his administration's desire for the resumption of peace talks with the MILF, the prospects for this taking place soon remains uncertain given that the issue of ancestral domain and the creation of a Bangsamoro Juridical Entity (BJE) remain on the agenda of the Muslim separatists. The BJE was declared by the Supreme Court as unconstitutional because it violates the territorial integrity of the state. The insistence of the MILF for a "state within the state" framework as part of a negotiated peace settlement will not prosper given the strong opposition to the idea at national and local levels, most especially from politicians affected by an expanded BJE, as well as from the Moro National Liberation Front (MNLF) with whom the national government signed a final peace agreement in 1996 that created the new ARMM. There is also no guarantee that all the factions within the MILF would abide by a peace agreement. In fact, the MILF was a breakaway faction from within the MNLF that opposed the 1996 final peace agreement signed between the national government and the MNLF.[11] For theMNLF, autonomy under the framework of the ARMM is the only viable option for the MILF given that the MOA-AD has been declared unconstitutional and a peace agreement with the government is not possible if the latter insists on the idea of a Bangsamoro juridical entity (Fernandez 2010). For its part, the MNLF has also been exerting pressure on the national government to fully implement the 1996 final peace agreement that should give more autonomy to the ARMM.[12]

Overall, armed rebellion against the state continues even under the restored democratic order because fundamental issues related to poverty, inequality, and justice have not been satisfactorily addressed by the central government for the past 25 years. This is complicated by the persistence of oligarchic families and traditional political clans opposed to economic liberalization and reform of the political system. Despite limited victories of reformists in some provinces in the country, autocratic rule by entrenched political clans especially in poor, conflict-prone areas of Mindanao remains the order of the day. In fact, the continuing culture of violence manifested through the practice of *rido*[13] among clans in Mindanao has exacerbated further the conflict situation in the area because "it tends to interact in unfortunate ways with separatist conflict and other forms of armed violence ... [even as] confrontations in the past involving insurgent groups and the military were actually triggered by a local *rido*" (Torres III 2007, 12).

Poverty and Economic Development

Notwithstanding widespread support for the democratic order, Filipinos generally see a disparity between democratic performance and policy performance of post-Marcos administrations in the Philippines over the past 25 years. While there have been improvements in civil liberties (e.g., freedom of speech, association) and popular participation, majority of Filipinos are still quite unhappy with socioeconomic conditions of the country. For most people, the quality of life has not improved significantly since the ouster of Marcos, particularly in alleviating poverty and creating a strong middle class, as a small oligarchy continues to control the nation's wealth (Guerrero and Tusalem 2008, 68–70). This is also reflected in the way that most households in the country consider themselves to be poor. For example, just before the end of Arroyo's term in June 2010, about 50% of Filipino households (or an estimated 9.4 million households) rated themselves as poor compared to 43% (or 8.1 million households) in March 2010. Although the general trend has been declining since 1983 (which peaked at more than 70% under Marcos and Cory Aquino), the level of self-rated poverty among Filipino families has always been much higher than the official poverty incidence reported by government. Over the past two decades, more than 50% of households that considered themselves poor were from the rural areas, mainly from the Visayas and Mindanao (SWS 2010a).

For some economists the persistence of poverty in the Philippines may be attributed to its inability to achieve sustained economic growth rate that is much higher than its population growth rate. In particular, the dismal record of poverty reduction in the country in recent years was not only the result of its low per capita GDP growth rate but also its inability to transform any growth rate into alleviating poverty. Evidently, for the past 25 years, the Philippine government has not paid particular attention to agricultural and rural development, or to investments in basic services such as health and education in the rural areas, both of which could contribute significantly to poverty reduction in the country. More importantly, the government's posture on population growth, which has been held captive by the Catholic Church's strong resistance to family planning programs, has also undermined serious efforts at poverty reduction (Balisacan 2007, 217–219). Most traditional politicians in the predominantly Catholic country are still unwilling to have direct confrontation with the Catholic Church hierarchy on the issue. On top of these are the institutional weaknesses of the state such as high incidence of tax evasion and low revenue collection, disproportionate allocation of national budget that goes to debt servicing obligations, and, of course, graft and corruption.[14] The huge remittances of overseas Filipino workers (OFWs)—at over US$17 billion in 2009 and about US$18 billion in 2010—thus far have kept the economy afloat and helped the country weather the Asian financial crisis in 1997 and the recent global economic crisis. But there are also some social costs to the phenomenon of Filipino *diaspora*, such as increase in teenage pregnancies, drug addiction, and broken families. Even so, the government seems to have relied on OFW remittances "to skirt the difficult task of policy reform that would have improved the performance of the domestic economy and reduced the need for overseas employment" (Pernia 2007, 240).

Conclusion

Over the past 25 years, the restored democratic order in the Philippines has endured a number of crises of legitimacy and armed challenges to the authority of the state. Much of this may be attributed to the abiding faith of Filipinos in upholding democratic principles that guarantee their fundamental freedoms and civil rights, even though they are also cognizant of some clear institutional weaknesses in their country's political system. Filipinos are also generally principled believers in democracy and are averse to authoritarian alternatives.[15] It is clear from the foregoing discussions that democracy in the Philippines is far from having consolidated over the past two-and-a-half decades. More than this, the political elite in the country—dominated by traditional political clans and the oligarchy—remains fractious and unable to develop a shared vision for the country and its people. Reformist Aquino III, who ran on the platform of good governance and transparency, defeated the populist and "pro-poor" former president Estrada in the 2010 elections. It remains to be seen, however, whether Aquino III would be able to muster enough political will to pursue the much-needed structural reforms in the country and address the problems of poverty, corruption, and armed rebellion. On the one hand, there is no question that a successful reformist agenda under the Aquino III administration would enhance the performance legitimacy of the democratic order; on the other hand, failure of his reformist agenda would not necessarily lead to a decline in public support for democracy in the country.

Notes

1. Aquino III won overwhelmingly (15.2 million votes) over other front-runners in the race, former president Estrada (9.4 million), former Senate president Manuel Villar Jr. (5.5 million), and former defense secretary Gilberto Teodoro (4 million) who was the Arroyo administration's candidate and a cousin of Aquino III.
2. See, for example, de Quiros (2007).

3. See, for example, Coronel (2003).

4. For a discussion of the history and debates surrounding proposals for charter change, see Abueva (2007).

5. In the 2002 survey results presented in Guerrero and Tusalem's essay, only 13% of the respondents felt capable of understanding and influencing politics in the Philippines, while 38% felt incapable of either and another 32% believed that although they are able to understand the complexities of politics, they lacked the confidence to participate in the political process.

6. EDSA is acronym for Epifanio Delos Santos Avenue, a major highway in Manila where the headquarters of the Armed Forces of the Philippines is located and site of the first "people power revolution" in 1986.

7. On the role of the Catholic Church in Philippine politics, see Jamon and Mirandilla (2007).

8. According to Benedict Anderson the paradox of the "logic of electoralism" is "when the 'educational' process of protests and demonstrations are replaced by individualized decision-making of the election booth, ties between NGOs/POs and their mass bases are undercut. When reformist social forces no longer implement effective political education programs, depoliticized voters again become vulnerable to traditional political ties and money politics (vote buying)" (Abinales and Amoroso 2005, 267).

9. The AFP by the end of 2010 claimed that the CPP/NPA forces stand only at over 4,000 guerrillas, from its peak of 25,000 in the 1980s.

10. For an examination of the political economy of the communist insurgency in the Philippines, see Magno (2007).

11. For a detailed critique of the 1996 final peace agreement between the Philippine government and the MNLF, see Bauzon (1999).

12. On the Muslim armed rebellion in Mindanao, see Abinales (2007), Sema (undated), and Santos Jr. (2001).

13. *Rido* is a term used for conflict or feuding among Moro groups in Mindanao. Torres III (2007) defined the term as "a state of recurring hostilities between families and kinship groups characterized by a series of retaliatory acts of violence carried out to avenge a perceive affront or injustice" (12).

14. Hill and Piza (2007), Sicat (2007), and Wallace (2007) provide detailed analysis of macroeconomic issues, investment climate, and economic development challenges facing the Philippines.

15. A principled believer in democracy is one who "not only expresses favorable orientations toward democracy but also rejects authoritarian alternatives" (Chu et al. 2008, 27). For them, "the greater the number of principled believers living under a new democracy, the more robust its foundation of legitimation" (27).

References

ABC News Online. 2010. "Philippine Soldiers Killed before Christmas Truce," December 15, from http,//www.abc.net.au/news/stories /2010/12/15/3094299.htm, accessed January 3, 2011.

Abinales, Patricio B. 2007. "Sancho Panza and Buliok Complex." In *Whither the Philippines in the 21st Century?*, edited by Rodolfo C. Severino and Lorraine C. Salazar, 277–312. Singapore: Institute of Southeast Asian Studies.

Abinales, Patricio B. and Donna J. Amoroso. 2005. *State and Society in the Philippines.* Lanham, Boulder, New York, Toronto, Oxford: Rowman & Little Field.

ABS-CBNnews.com. 2008. "64% Don't Want Arroyo's Term Extended, SWS Survey," November 25, from http,//www.abs-cbnnews.com /nation/11/25/08/64-dont-want-arroyos-term-extended-sws-survey, accessed January 3, 2011.

Abueva, Jose C. 2007. "Proposed Constitutional Reforms for Good Governance and Nation Building." In *Whither the Philippines in the 21st Century?*, edited by Rodolfo C. Severino and Lorraine C. Salazar, 43–77. Singapore: Institute of Southeast Asian Studies.

Asian Development Bank (ADB). 2007. "Overview of NGOs and Civil Society, Philippines," Civil Society Briefs, Asian Development Bangk, Manila, December.

Balisacan, Arsenio M. 2007. "Why Does Poverty Persists in the Philippines?" In *Whither the Philippines in the 21st Century?*, edited by Rodolfo C. Severino and Lorraine C. Salazar, 202–221. Singapore: Institute of Southeast Asian Studies.

Bauzon, Kenneth. 1999. "The Philippines, The 1996 Peace Agreement for the Southern Philippines, An Assessment," *Ethnic Studies Report* 17, 2 (July 1999): 253–280.

Cabiling, Genalyn D. 2010. "Palace to Ombudsman, Explain Garcia Bargain," *Manila Bulletin*, December 19, from http,//www.mb.com.ph /articles/293794/palace-ombudsman-explain-garcia-bargain, accessed December 29, 2010.

Cabreza, Vincent. 2008. "PMA Alumni Seek to Abolish 'Protector Clause,'" Inquirer.net, March 13, from http,//newsinfo.inquirer.net /inquirerheadlines/nation/view/20080313-124405/PMA-alumni-seek-to-abolish-protector-clause, accessed December 28, 2010.

Chu, Yu-han, Larry Diamond, Andrew J. Nathan, and Doh Chull Shin. 2008. "Introduction, Comparative Perspectives on Democratic Legitimacy in East Asia." In *How East Asians View Democracy,* edited by Yu-han Chu, Larry Diamond, Andrew Nathan, and Doh Chull Shin, 1–38. New York: Columbia University Press.

Coronel, Sheila S. 2003. *The Rulemakers, How the Wealthy and the Well-Born Dominate Congress.* Quezon City: Philippine Center for Investigative Journalism.

Dalangin-Fernandez, Lira. 2010a. "Judiciary's Woes Continue, 2011 Budget Offers No Solution," Inquirer.net, September 6, from http,//newsinfo .inquirer.net/topstories/topstories/view/20100906-290798/Judiciarys -budget-woes-continue-2011-budget-offers-no-solution,   accessed December 28, 2010.

———. 2010b. "Garcia Deal to Boost Impeachment Complaint vs. Ombudsman—Solons," Inquirer.net, December 21, from http,//news-info.inquirer.net/breakingnews/nation/view/20101221-310219/Garcia -deal-to-boost-impeachment-complaint-vs-Ombudsman--solons, accessed December 28, 2010.

de Quiros, Conrado. 2010. "Making of a President, PH Style," Inquirer. net, December 23, from http,//newsinfo.inquirer.net/inquirerheadlines /nation/view/20101223-310511/Making-of-a-president-PH-style,accessed December 23, 2010.

Fernandez, Edwin. 2010. "Mindanao, Foreign Groups Renew Support for Peace Process," Inquirer.net, September 22, from http,//www.inquirer.net /specialfeatures/mindanaopeaceprocess/view.php?db=1&article=20100922 -293763, accessed January 3, 2011.

Franco, Jennifer C. 2004. "The Philippines, Fractious Civil Society and Competing Visions of Democracy." In *Civil Society and Political Change in Asia, Expanding and Contracting Democratic Space,* edited by Muthiah Alagappa, 97–137. Stanford: Stanford University Press.

Global Integrity. 2008. "Philippines, Integrity Indicators Scorecard," Global Integrity Report 2008, Global Integrity, from http,//report.globalintegrity .org/Philippines/2008/scorecard, accessed December 26, 2010.

GMAnews.TV. 2007. "Newsbreak, Erap Pardon Arroyo's Overdue Promise to Iglesia ni Kristo," GMAnews.TV, October 26, from http,//www.gmanews .tv/story/66024/Newsbreak-Erap-pardon-Arroyos-overdue-promise-to -Iglesia-ni-Kristo, accessed December 28, 2010.

Gomez, Jim. 2010. "Communist Rebels Threaten Attacks Despite Looming Talks," *The Associated Press,* December 26, from http,//www.gmanews. tv/100days/story/209164/communist-rebels-threaten-attacks-despite -looming-talks, accessed January 3, 2011.

Guerrero, Linda Luz and Rollin F. Tusalem. 2008. "Mass Public Perceptions of Democratization in the Philippines, Consolidation in Progress?" In *How East Asians View* Democracy, edited by Yun-han Chu, Larry Diamond, Andrew J. Nathan, and Doh Chull Shin, 61–82. New York: Columbia University Press.

Hill, Hal and Sharon Faye Piza. 2007. "The Philippine Development Record." In *Whither the Philippines in the 21st Century?,* edited by Rodolfo C. Severino and Lorraine C. Salazar, 246–276. Singapore: Institute of Southeast Asian Studies.

Jamon, Grace G. and Mary Grace Mirandilla. 2007. "Religion and Politics." In *Whither the Philippines in the 21st Century?,* edited by Rodolfo C. Severino and Lorraine C. Salazar, 100–127. Singapore: Institute of Southeast Asian Studies.

Magno, Alexander C. 2007. "The Insurgency that Would Not Go Away." In *Whither the Philippines in the 21st Century?* Edited by Rodolfo C. Severino and Lorraine C. Salazar, 313–329. Singapore: Institute of Southeast Asian Studies.

Manila Bulletin Online. 2010. "Counter Insurgency, Terrorism Operations Fruitful in 2010—AFP," *Manila Bulletin Online,* December 31, from http,//www.mb.com.ph/articles/295839/counter-insurgency-terrorism -operations-fruitful-2010-philippine-military, accessed January 3, 2011.

Pazzibugan, Donna. 2010. "No Apology but Rebs Must Admit Guilt," Inquirer. net, December 29, from http,//newsinfo.inquirer.net/inquirerheadlines /nation/view/20101229-311455/No-apology-but-rebs-must-admit-guilt, accessed on December 29, 2010.

Pernia, Ernesto. 2007. "Diaspora, Remittances, and Poverty." In *Whither the Philippines in the 21*st *Century?,* edited by Rodolfo C. Severino and Lorraine C. Salazar, 222–245. Singapore: Institute of Southeast Asian Studies.

Philippine Human Development Report (PHDR). 2005. Human Development Network, from www.hdn.org.ph, accessed November 15, 2010.

Philstar.com. 2010. "SC, EO Forming 'Truth Commission' Unconstitutional," Philstar.com, December 7, from http,//www.philstar.com/Article.aspx?a rticleId=637034&publicationSubCategoryId=63, accessed December 23, 2010.

Porcala Delon. 2010. "Noy, Supreme Court Singling Me Out," Philstar.com, December 28, from http,//www.philstar.com/Article.aspx?articleId=6432 40&publicationSubCategoryId=63, accessed on December 28, 2010.

Ramos, Marlon and Michael Lim Ubac. 2010. "Aquino, Trillanes May Be a Victim of Injustice," Inquirer.net, July 17, from http,//newsinfo.inquirer .net/inquirerheadlines/nation/view/20100717-281561/Aquino-Trillanes -may-be-victim-of-injustice, accessed December 29, 2010.

Santos Jr., Soliman. 2001. *The Moro Islamic Challenge, Constitutional Rethinking for the Mindanao Peace Process.* Quezon City: University of the Philippines Press.

Sema, Muslimin. Undated. "Speech of Muslimin G. Sema, Chairman, Moro National Liberation Front," undated, from http,//www.armm.gov. ph/index.php?option=com_content&view=article&id=133&Itemid=127, accessed January 3, 2011.

Sicat, Gerardo C. 2007. "Macroeconomic Issues and Challenges." In *Whither the Philippines in the 21st Century?,* edited by Rodolfo C. Severino and Lorraine C. Salazar, 142–179. Singapore: Institute of Southeast Asian Studies.

Social Weather Stations (SWS). 2006. "Fourth Quarter 2006 Social Weather Survey, Attitudes towards Political Parties in the Philippines," Social Weather Stations for the Ateneo School of Government, with the support of the Konrad Adenauer Stiftung (undated), from http,//www.kas.de/wf /doc/kas_20518-1522-2-30.pdf?100917093912, accessed December 26, 2010.

———. 2010a "Second Quarter 2010 Social Weather Survey, Self-Rated Poverty 50%; Self-Rated Food Poverty 38%," September 8, from http, //www.sws.org.ph, accessed December 25, 2010.

———. 2010b. "Third Quarter 2010 Social Weather Survey, Satisfaction with How Democracy Works Reaches 69%," December 22, 2010, from http,// www.sws.org.ph, accessed December 25, 2010.

Thompson, Mark R. 2010. "Populism and the Revival of Reform, Competing Narratives in the Philippines." *Contemporary Southeast Asia* 32, 1: 1–28.

Torres III, Wilfredo Magno. 2007. *RIDO, Clan Feuding and Conflict Management in Mindanao*. Makati City: Asia Foundation.

Wallace, Peter. 2007. "Investment Climate and Business Opportunities." In *Whither the Philippines in the 21st Century?*, edited by Rodolfo C. Severino and Lorraine C. Salazar, 180–201. Singapore: Institute of Southeast Asian Studies.

Wurfel, David. 2004. "Civil Society and Democratization in the Philippines." In *Growth and Governance in Asia*, edited by Yoichiro Sato, 215–224. Honolulu: Asia Pacific Center for Security Studies.

CHAPTER 11

Political Legitimacy in South Korea

Hun Joon Kim

S ince Korea was forced to open its doors to Japan in 1876, Korean politics has been a microcosm of global developments. Currently, it remains the only place in the world where Cold War and post–Cold War political systems coexist. The Cold War between the USSR and the Western powers that ended with the fall of the Berlin Wall in 1989 did not end the cold war between communist North Korea and democratic South Korea. Since Germany and Yemen each became unified, the two Koreas remain the only two countries in the world referred to by their polar direction. Historically, the modern politics of the two Koreas has been marked by the collapse of the Joseon dynasty, Japanese colonialism, both Soviet and U.S. military occupation, sundry riots and revolutions, the Korean War, dictatorship and authoritarianism, coups, repression and massacres, and, most recently, democratization. Remarkably, all these events occurred within the past hundred years, suggesting that the political legitimacy of the modern South Korean state might be resting on shaky ground.

Political legitimacy is this: "The belief in the rightfulness of a state, in its authority to issue commands, so that those commands are obeyed not simply out of fear or self-interest, but because they are believed in some sense to have moral authority, because subjects believe that they ought to obey" (Barker 1990, 11).[1] In this chapter, legitimation of power is understood as a reciprocal, dynamic, multilevel, and multifaceted process. First, legitimacy is a relational concept. Legitimation of power is a "social practice" (Alagappa 1995, 11) that involves a reciprocal interaction between rulers and the ruled. Legitimacy is situated within power relationships between the state and citizens and is contingent upon both major and minor changes in power. Second, legitimacy is never constant but an ever-changing and dynamic process. Therefore, it is better to speak of "legitimation of power" than the static "legitimacy." Legitimacy is constantly made and unmade and is continuously asserted and challenged. The making and unmaking of legitimacy occur simultaneously and the enforcement of one source of legitimacy can easily endanger other sources. Third, legitimation of power is a multilevel process. Although the interaction between rulers and the ruled lies at the core, other actors—both inside and outside the state—such as great powers and markets, play a significant role in the process. Sometimes, decisive support or opposition to existing legitimacy claims comes from outside forces and this is more likely so in small and weak countries like South Korea. Fourth, legitimation of power is a multifaceted process occurring at various social interfaces. Legitimacy has traditionally been understood as the rightful acquisition and use of power.[2] Habermas (1984, 138), however, challenges this view by seeing legitimation as an intrinsic process between the state and the markets. Furthermore, he sees other factors apart from politics: the economy, culture, education, and health and welfare as part of the legitimation process in a developing society (146–147).

In this chapter, I explore the South Korean experience with these four aspects of political legitimacy in mind. In the first section, I provide an overview of the traditional Korean politics that shaped the modern and contemporary discourse of legitimacy. In the next section, I examine four major, rather stable, sources of legitimacy: security and ideology, the economy, nationalism, and democracy. I study how governments (both authoritarian and democratic) relied on these four sources of legitimacy to seize and secure the moral high ground of political power. In addition, I explore major challenges to political legitimacy in this period and study how the governments responded to these political and socioeconomic challenges. I end my analysis with the Kim Dae Jung administration (1998–2003) since the two administrations that follow that are too recent to study. I conclude with a summary and a few observations on current changes.

Historical Context of Legitimacy Debate

Modern South Korean politics is deeply rooted in the political and socioeconomic legacies of traditional Korea. The first political entity to rule the entire Korean peninsula was the Silla dynasty in 676, which conquered two rival kingdoms with the help of the Chinese Tang dynasty. The Silla dynasty ruled until 918 and was followed by the

Goryeo dynasty, which ruled from 936 to 1392. The Goryeo dynasty lasted 400 years with 100 years of military rule by 12 different generals. The dynasty was eventually overturned by another military coup in 1392 led by General Lee Seong Gye. The Joseon dynasty created by Lee lasted for 500 years. In the late nineteenth century, the Joseon dynasty encountered major internal and external challenges: invasions from powerful neighbours, the *Imo* riot (1882), the *Gapsin* coups (1884), the *Kapo* peasant uprising (1894), and annexation by Japan in 1910.

In traditional Korean culture, legitimacy (*jeongdangseong*) was understood to be primarily a relationship between rulers and the ruled. Debates about legitimacy occurred among a small circle of the ruling elites, the royal family, and Confucian scholars with every political transition, given that such transitions tended to pose serious existential threats to their status. Internally, these debates were settled by the moral support of traditional religion. For instance, the generals who staged a coup against the Goryeo dynasty claimed themselves to be the protectors of the true Buddhism, the state religion of the Goryeo. Likewise, General Lee made continuous efforts to secure support from Confucian scholars by promoting Confucianism and suppressing Buddhism upon establishing the Joseon dynasty. Some even argue that "without the literati he [Lee] could not have established legitimacy for his new regime" (Oh 1999, 9). Internationally, legitimacy debates in Korea were resolved by the formal recognition of new regimes by the Chinese emperors, either by accepting tribute from or by sending envoys to the new regime.

The 35 years of Japanese colonialism (1910–1945) were marked by coercive sociopolitical repression and economic exploitation. The colonial authorities relied exclusively on coercion, terror, and surveillance to rule the Korean population between 1910 and 1919 (Robinson 2007, 43). However, following the first national independence movement of 1919, the colonial authorities skillfully invented and used various ideological ploys to reduce its reliance on coercion, control, and surveillance. For example, Japan pursued an assimilation policy aimed at effacing Korean national identity and incorporating Koreans as second-class citizens of the Japanese polity. The idea that the Koreans and the Japanese share a common ancestry, which was claimed by pro-Japanese historians, was used to facilitate assimilation and even to conscript Koreans into the Japanese army. In due course, the colonial authorities effectively used Korean collaborators from different walks of life: politicians, businessmen, scholars, journalists, religious leaders, writers, and artists to induce voluntary submission to their rule. Even the Japanese colonial authorities realized that coercion and control alone could not be effective to rule Koreans.

The debate over legitimacy peaked with liberation from Japanese colonialism in 1945. An interim authority was set up to keep law and order until the establishment of a new Korean state. However, this interim authority lasted only a mere 20 days until the arrival of the U.S. Army in early September. The U.S. Army soon set up a U.S. military government and declared it the only legitimate power. The presence and rule of the U.S. forces was justified by their having liberated the Koreans from the Japanese occupation but this justification did not find acceptance. South Koreans strongly resisted major policies of the U.S. military government: first, to revive and deploy the repressive colonial state apparatus and reemploy Korean collaborators of the Japanese; second, not only to ban the communist party but also to suppress any progressive social movements; third, to hold a separate election in the South and set up a separate government headed by Rhee Syng Man. Peasants violently expressed their objection to major socio-economic policies of the U.S. military regime such as the delayed and partial land reforms in 1948 and unrealistic rice collection and distribution policies. Popular uprisings such as the October uprising of 1946 and the Jeju uprising of 1947 were brutally suppressed, leaving many intended and unintended civilian casualties. After three years of U.S. military rule, the UN monitored separate elections in the South that created the Republic of Korea in 1948. This government declared itself to be the paramount indigenous and legitimate political entity on the Korean peninsula. The new state even symbolically allocated congressional seats for Northern representatives and appointed a governor for the Northern provinces.

Sources of Political Legitimacy in South Korea

However, "the politics of the vortex" (Henderson 1968)—the term often used to refer to Korean politics at that time—was not over yet. The invasion by North Korea in 1950 can also be seen as a challenge to the legitimacy claimed by the new state in the South. Successive South Korean governments challenged the legitimacy of the Northern regime and pursued aggressive and militaristic unification policies against the North after the war. A series of undemocratic regimes ruled South Korean until 1993: the patriarchic dictatorship of Rhee Syng Man (1948–1960), the military dictatorship of Park Chung Hee (1961–1979), and the authoritarian regimes of Chun Doo Hwan (1980–1988), and

Roh Tae Woo (1988–1993). The first government headed by a civilian president was that of Kim Young Sam in 1993. Since then, South Korea has had four democratic regimes: that of Kim Young Sam (1993–1998), Kim Dae Jung (1998–2003), Roh Moo Hyun (2003–2008), and Lee Myung Bak (2008–present). Throughout this period, authoritarian and democratic governments of South Korea alike relied on four sources of political legitimacy: security/ideology, the economy, nationalism, and democracy.

Security/Ideology

National security and anticommunism have been the most important sources of legitimacy in South Korea since the period of U.S. military rule. The anticommunist policy of the U.S. occupational government became official in 1946 when the U.S. authority smashed counterfeiting rings in which 16 communists were allegedly involved. Communism since then has been regarded as the main enemy of the state and deterring communist aggression the number one policy priority of every administration. Anticommunism provided a convenient raison d'être for the sometimes oppressive actions of the South Korean governments; national security depended on successfully deterring both internal and external communist threats. Nondemocratic regimes justified their rule by citing the need for national security, and an anticommunist stance and democratic regimes were often accused of overlooking communist threats or sometimes being too sympathetic to communism. Anticommunism has been, since the end of World War II, at the center of South Korean politics.

Even before the outbreak of the Korean War in 1950, the Rhee regime (1948–1960) relied on the fear of communism to overcome political crises. In 1948, the Korean congress set up a special court to investigate and punish pro-Japanese collaborators. The court consisted of 16 judges who had the authority to sentence former collaborators to death for crimes of treason. Within four months, the court investigated 682 cases, indicted 221, and convicted 14 collaborators. Rhee, whose domestic political support came exclusively from the colonial elites, criticized the court and refused to remove identified collaborators from his administration. Rhee and his supporters accused court members of being communists who threatened national security by instigating social dissension out of hatred and vengeance. Judges were threatened with assassination, and the police, with the tacit consent of Rhee, raided the courthouse, injuring many and destroying documents. The court gradually withered and was eventually dissolved. The failure of the court shows how, in South Korea, even the most agreed upon national-istic agenda can easily be thwarted by anticommunist ideology.

The dependence on anticommunism for legitimacy intensified with the outbreak of the Korean War. For Rhee, the war was not only a war between two states but also a civil war between his new government and the communist fifth column in South Korea. The sheer number of war victims validates this view: During the war, massacres of at least 300,000 civilians suspected of being communists occurred at the hands of the South Korean authority (Seo 1999, 613) and persons suspected of having even a hint of communist sympathy were purged by the police, military, congress, and public offices, and many of them were executed. In comparison, the war left approximately 138,000 combat deaths for the South Korean army. This period marked the height of civilian mas-sacres committed by the South Korean police and military.

As Rhee saw it, the war was a twofold challenge to his regime with communists attacking both inside and outside the country. But Rhee successfully overcame the crisis with the significant assistance of the United States.

Rhee continued using anticommunism as a reason to consolidate and justify his extraordinary presidential power after the war. He strength-ened his anticommunist stance by referring to it as a *myeolgong* (defeat-ing communism) policy rather than a simple *bangong* (anticommunist) policy. He vehemently opposed the U.S.-led armistice talks and cam-paigned for the total defeat of North Korea. With citizens terrified by their war experience and fearful of further civilian massacres commit-ted by the government, a perfect environment was in place for enforcing the political legitimacy of Rhee's regime. The National Security Law provided a convenient tool for punishing any political opponents by charging them with having procommunist sympathies (Robinson 2007, 122). Due to the notorious guilt-by-association system, people directly or indirectly related to alleged communists were placed under close sur-veillance and socially ostracized. Ordinary citizens were deprived of their civil and political rights and prominent opponents such as Jo Bong Am of the Progress Party were found guilty of espionage on fabricated charges and were executed. Democratic ideas and values were easily trumped by security and anticommunist imperatives under Rhee, and, unfortunately, this precedent left a lasting legacy on South Korean poli-tics. Anticommunism became a tempting and easily available political tool to suppress popular demand for democracy.

Despite his criticism of Rhee as an incompetent and corrupt leader, Park Chung Hee emulated the latter by appealing to anticommunism and national security to bolster his rule (1961–1979), silence his political opponents and generally terrorized citizens to make them submit to his dictatorial rule. The Anticommunism Law of 1961 declared any criticism or challenge to the regime as an act of communism. The logic was clear and simple: any criticism of the South Korean government, which was officially still at war with the North, would cause social dissension in the South and thus endanger national security by benefiting the North (Park 1994). Many opposition leaders, students, and social movement activists were arrested, tortured, and disappeared. In 1973, Kim Dae Jung was also kidnapped by the secret service and almost drowned in the Pacific Ocean. The situation was similar under the Chun Doo Hwan (1980–1988) and Roh Tae Woo (1988–1993) regimes. The brutal suppression of protestors in the 1980 Gwangju massacre, which left 154 dead, 70 missing, and 3,028 injured, was again justified by anticommunism and national security. Popular desire for democracy after the assassination of Park was blamed on just a few troublemakers sympathetic to the communist North (Oh 1999, 83). In addition, the governments provoked anticommunist sentiment among the public to win popular support for their rule. In some cases, communist-inspired terrorism such as the shooting down in 1983 of the Korean Airliner by the USSR, the 1983 Rangoon bombing, and the 1987 Korean Airliner bombing, provided perfect grounds for claiming legitimacy. At other times, the regime deliberately created anticommunist fervor in the population either by exaggerating the threat (e.g., 1986 Peace Dam incident) or picking the scabs off the wounds left by the Korean War and thus reminding the population of the evil face of communism (e.g., 1983 KBS [state television station] campaign for finding internally displaced persons and promoting family reunion).

In summary, for the military and authoritarian regimes lacking a democratic source of legitimacy, anticommunism and national security were the most important sources of legitimacy. The Rhee dictatorship, which was created by an illegal constitutional amendment in 1954, and the Park and Chun regimes, created by military coups, had to rely exclusively on national security and anticommunism for their popular support. In part, this was possible because there was actually a continuous threat from the state-sponsored terrorism of North Korea. The threat was real and consistent and the possibility of war was ever-present. Nevertheless, the perception of communist threats were delicately manipulated and used to overcome political crises or win major elections (Park 2006, 313). In this regard, the so-called North wind was the most effective way to unite conservative political groups and garner votes from ordinary citizens. The findings from the recent Truth and Reconciliation Commission show that many political opponents and civilians were falsely convicted on the basis of forced testimonies and trumped-up evidence. Many spy scandals were fabricated by the authoritarian regime to obtain popular support for "the nondemocratic but effectively functioning regimes in deterring North Korean threats." It was impossible to challenge the government's manipulation of perception because of the ban upon civilian contact with North Korea (Bleiker 2009, 18). All of the regimes had effective and powerful intelligence agencies monitoring every segment of society, and over time, anticommunism became a way of life and citizens internalized the government's norms and standards (Choi 1993, 23). In short, the government policy of anticommunism was sustained by state control as well as public acquiescence.

Economy

The transition from an agrarian to an industrial economy began in the early 1960s when Park Chung Hee instituted an export-oriented economic growth policy. Coercive but effective economic planning resulted in an average annual gross domestic product (GDP) increase of 8.3% under the Park's administration. Similar export-oriented policies continued under Chun Doo Hwan and Roh Tae Woo, but the focus was moved from light and labor-intensive industries to the heavy and chemical industries. Despite the negative growth rate in 1980, the Chun and Roh administrations fared well and recorded an average 8.4% annual GDP growth rate between 1981 and 1993. Economic growth served as the second most important source of political legitimacy in the period of authoritarianism and into the early years of democracy. But all this changed after the Asian financial crisis of 1997, when a record low annual GDP growth rate of −6.9% was recorded for 1998. Economic recovery and the redistribution of wealth became the focal point in the economic policies of the Kim Dae Jung administration. In order to understand how the economy served as a major source of legitimacy, both the pre-1960 agrarian and post-1960 industrial economy should be considered.

The most important economic policy under Rhee was the land reform act of 1950: any individual can own a maximum of 7.35 acres of agricultural land as long as he cultivates it only for himself. Tenancy and land-renting activities are illegal. This reform had far-reaching socioeconomic consequences: First, land reform alleviated inequality and achieved income redistribution (Amsden 1989, 38). In 1945, 80% of the rural population were tenants and landlords; 3% of the population owned 60% of the land (Shin 1998, 1313). As a result of the reform, one-third of farm land changed hands affecting two-thirds of farming households (Lie 1998, 11). By 1951 the ratio of owner-cultivated land to total arable land is about 96% (Jeon and Kim 2000, 253). Second, land reform destroyed the traditional landlord class and forced them to become capitalist, paving the way for industrialization (Shin 1998, 1314). Many landlords purchased enterprises and became early entrepreneurs in key agro-businesses such as sugar, flour, and cotton (Lie 1998, 33).

Land reform had significant political consequences. First, land reform created a strong popular support for Rhee, who had previously spent most of his lifetime in the United States and did not have a popular domestic following (Lie 1998, 11). However, despite his fame and strong support from the United States, Rhee lacked a stable political base. Land reform made Rhee "one of the few nationally known figures in a predominantly rural country" (25). Second, land reform added a thick layer of conservative farmers who, for the first time, enjoyed "the freedom of democracy and rights of ownership in rural areas" (Pak 1956, 1021). Political support from them was so strong that farmers could never be organized to resist Rhee's dictatorship (Lie 1998, 38). Third, land reform removed any longing for communist-style land reform and contributed to eradicating any residual sympathy for communism. Nevertheless, the positive impact of the reform did not last long due to the failure of the Rhee administration to develop effective and sustainable long-term agricultural policies. Farmers faced a dual pressure because they had to pay for the land and struggle to compete in grain markets with virtually no support from the government. As a result, by the late 1950s, about 90% of rural households fell into debt, and between 1960 and 1980, 11 million of the rural population left for the cities (111).

After the coup of 1961, which brought him to power, Park suffered serious challenges to his legitimacy due to his "illegal usurpation of power and extralegal exercise of authority" (Shin 2006, 103; Oh 1999, 52). Challenges to his authority came from both outside and inside. On the one hand, the United States was seriously concerned with Park's previous involvement in communist activities. On the other, the elites and the public questioned Park's intentions because he overturned the new democratic government created after the successful popular uprising against the Rhee dictatorship. Park overcame the opposition by justifying his rule with the need for national security and economic growth. Park's emphasis on economic development can be found in his own writing: "The purpose of this revolution is to reconstruct the nation and establish a self-sustaining economy, and its essential purpose is to restore to all the people the political and economic systems which had become the possession of a few privileged classes" (cited in Oh 1999, 52). Accordingly, five-year economic development plans were started in 1962 and Park himself headed the Economic Planning Board. The Korean economy experienced a rapid growth and this led to popular support for Park.

However, economic growth was not a linear process. Due to the heavy dependence on exports, the Korean economy was vulnerable to external shocks. In the 1973 oil crisis, Park made a bold move to change the economic focus from light and labor-intensive to heavy and chemical industries, designating five strategic sectors: steel, automobile, electronics, shipbuilding, and petrochemical. The new policies overcame the crisis and created an average annual GDP growth rate of 8.3% between 1974 and 1979. However, the 1979 oil crisis was more devastating because it coincided with critical misjudgments in the government's macroeconomic policy and political turmoil triggered by the assassination of Park and the subsequent military coup by Chun and Roh. For the first time since 1961, South Korea experienced a negative annual GDP growth rate of −1.48% in 1980. For Chun and Roh, who took power in the 1979 coup and brutally suppressed civilian protestors in the 1980 Gwangju massacre, securing political legitimacy by successfully overcoming economic crisis was vital to the survival of the regime (Moon and Lim 2001, 209). The Chun and Roh administrations pursued various neoliberal economic reforms to stabilize the economy: fiscal austerity, wage freezes, currency devaluation, and privatization of state enterprises (209). These measures turned out to be successful and the average GDP annual growth rate under the combined Chun and Roh administrations (1980–1993) was 7.7%. Thus, economic growth became a key source of legitimacy and provided strong popular support for the military and authoritarian regimes.

Ironically, economic growth had the unintended consequence of ultimately destabilizing the authoritarian regimes. First, due to rapid industrialization in the 1960s and 1970s, the agricultural sector quickly dissolved and released a large number of unskilled labor and urban poor who were largely dissatisfied with the regimes. The rapid economic growth of this period was based on low wages, which was possible due mainly to the government's low grain price policy (Shin 1998, 1314).

Workers, farmers, and the urban poor emerged as important political actors against the authoritarian regimes. Second, rapid economic growth intensified income inequality, which made the authoritarian regimes more vulnerable to demands for greater equality. South Korea up until the early 1970s was a highly egalitarian society both in income and land distribution but inequality significantly worsened since the mid-1970s (Koo 1984, 1029). Third, economic growth led to the rapid expansion of a well-educated middle class, which became increasingly vocal and resistant to the authoritarian regime (Koo 2002, 109). Here, we can see the complicated role of the economy as a source of political legitimacy: the economic forces that strengthened the authoritarian regimes were at the same time sowing the seeds of their destruction.

Nationalism

Koreans strongly believe in their common ancestry and ethnic homogeneity and nationalism lies at the core of Korean politics. In a recent survey, 93% of respondents agreed that the nation has a single blood line and 95% agreed that North Koreans are part of the same family and nation (Shin 2006, 2). This is also reflected in the address made by Kim Dae Jung at the 2000 historic summit with Kim Jong Il: "We are one people. We share the same fate." Many believe that ancient Korea was created by *Dangun*, a grandson of God, in 2333 BC. Even today, South Koreans celebrate *gaecheonjeol* as a national holiday commemorating *Dangun*'s creation (Shin 2006, 99). The native name of the country *Daehanminguk* literally means "the State of the Great Korean Nation," which again affirms the belief in ethnic homogeneity. But while Korean nationalism may be partly an outcome of the actual relative ethnic homogeneity of the population—something made possible by the country's rather secluded geographic position—it is undoubtedly also a historical construct, with foreign invasions and Japanese colonialism playing a decisive role in shaping its modern form.

The 1905 *Eulsa* Treaty, which made Korea a protectorate of Japan, engendered modern Korean nationalism. The period between 1905 and the 1910 annexation was an era of awakening Korean identity. Many organizations emerged with the aim to achieve national independence and there were nationwide armed uprisings against the Japan authorities. Historians rewrote ancient and modern history to bolster the national spirit and heighten national pride. These efforts continued throughout the repressive colonial period and exploded in the 3.1 Movement of 1919. Inspired by the principle of self-determination of

Woodrow Wilson, 33 representatives declared independence from Japan and the public participated in peaceful demonstrations nationwide. Japanese reprisals ended with 7,500 killed, 15,000 injured, and 45,000 arrested (Robinson 2007, 48). The movement left a significant legacy, including the establishment of a provisional government in China from which later governments will trace their legitimacy. Even the current constitution states: "We, the people of Korea...upholding the cause of the provisional government born of the 3.1 Movement." Japan, shocked by the magnitude of the movement, adopted a conciliatory policy known as "the culture rule" (1920–1930) allowing cultural autonomy. Koreans used this brief window of opportunity to promote nationalism by starting newspapers and studying history, language, and literature.

The First Republic headed by Rhee had two critical hurdles to overcome in order to establish itself as the representative of the Korean nation. First, despite his involvement in the independence movement, Rhee seized power by aligning himself with former collaborators. Second, Rhee was the only politician to support the U.S. policy of creating a separate government in the South. In sum, Rhee was viewed as an antinationalistic and opportunistic politician who aligned himself with collaborators and responsible for the division of Korea. To overcome this perception, Rhee, after securing popular support as a result of land reform, disassociated himself from the collaborators and created his own party. Second, Rhee actively pursued "anti-Japanism" (Shin 2006, 100) and relied on popular anti-Japanese sentiment to secure his political legitimacy. Rhee rejected continuous demands from the United States to normalize diplomatic relations with Japan. Instead, he demanded a sincere apology and proper restitution from Japan throughout his tenure. Third, Rhee constructed his version of nationalism, called *ilminjuui* (ideology of one people), by skillfully combining anticommunism with political nationalism (100). He proposed that the Korean people had always been one throughout history and thus the communist state in the North was illegitimate and South Koreans must achieve national unification through a northward advance. This anticommunist nationalism was the basis of Rhee's unification policy and provided firm grounds for his objection to the 1953 armistice to end the conflict on the Korean peninsula. In addition, *ilminjuui* spilled over into Rhee's foreign policy by his adhering to the Hallstein doctrine, which stated that South Korea had the exclusive right to represent the Korean nation, and would not establish diplomatic relations with any state recognizing North Korea.

After the 1961 coup, Park relied on the combination of nationalism and economic growth as summarized in his vision of *jogukgeundaehwa*, or modernization of the fatherland (Shin 2006, 103). For him, economic growth was understood to be a national and historic mission in which state control, planning, and intervention were inevitable. Everyone was to participate in this historic mission and to make sacrifices (e.g., putting up with longer working hours, lower wages, poor working conditions, restricted union activities, low grain prices, increased household savings, buying only Korean products, restricting international travel) for the good of the nation. Citizens, forcibly and voluntarily, followed the government's lead and, with the help of a booming world economy, achieved "the Miracle on the Han River." This rapid economic growth, in turn, boosted national pride, and a symbiotic relationship between economic growth and nationalism continued under the authoritarian regimes. Urban middle-class and working-class citizens temporarily acquiesced to the dictatorship and authoritarianism for the sake of "the historic modernization mission of the time." Many accepted the government's stand that Korean society did not have the luxury of choosing both economic development and liberal democracy (Choi 1993). Interestingly, reciprocal enforcement between nationalism and the economy also extended to anticommunism under authoritarianism. The aim of Park's economic policy, for example, was "to accelerate our economic growth, to modernize our fatherland, and to achieve peaceful unification of our country" (cited in Shin 2006, 104). The rapid growth in the South was seen as the victory of a capitalist economy over communism. Nationalism, economic growth, and anticommunism were organically harnessed to support the regime.

Education was the most effective way to inculcate the government's version of nationalism in its citizens. Park introduced a daily nationalistic ceremony in every school and public office, and promoted the memorizing of the Charter of National Education that starts: "We are born to this country, bearing the historic mission of regenerating the nation." The curriculum promoted nationalism and anticommunism. South Korean history textbooks emphasized on national independence movements but wiped out the entire history of the communist independence movement. The government also promoted nationalism through other channels, including public campaigns, the media, and policy propaganda. Somewhat reminiscent of the ancient Roman policy of Bread and Circuses, sports nationalism played an important role in uniting citizens and diverting their attention from politics. It is well known that Chun, after the coup and bloody suppression of thousands of protestors, created a professional baseball league to divert the public attention from politics. The 1986 Asian Games and 1988 Olympics in Seoul ignited nationalist fervor and increased support for the Chun and Roh administrations.

Nationalism played a still significant but different role under Kim Dae Jung and Roh Moo Hyun. Kim pursued a conciliatory policy toward North Korea, known as "the Sunshine Policy" and slowly increased communication, humanitarian aid, and economic cooperation with the North. Unlike the previous anticommunist nationalism, Kim promoted peaceful coexistence with the North. Important joint projects were advanced, including tourism, a railway connection, and a special economic zone. The policy led to two historic summits: between Kim Dae Jung and Kim Jong Il in 2000 and Roh Moo Hyun and Kim Jong Il in 2007. Confrontational nationalism had changed into conciliatory nationalism and the government no longer considered North Korea as "the main enemy of the state." However, confrontational nationalism strangely found other targets under the Kim and Roh administrations: the United States and Japan. The rise of anti-Americanism began with the end of the Cold War and reached its peak with the death of two teenage schoolgirls who where run over by a U.S. tank in 2002. In addition, tensions with Japan intensified during this period over reparation issues, a territorial dispute over Dokdo, the slanted content of Japanese history textbooks, and the Japanese prime minister's visit to the Yasukuni Shrine (where several Japanese war criminals are buried).

Democracy

The modern discourse on democracy started with the *Gapo* peasant uprising (1894) triggered by a revolutionary indigenous cult called *Donghak* (Eastern Learning). It was the first nationwide popular movement and was a political awakening for the peasants who traditionally remained acquiescent subjects to authority (Kim 2000, 28). *Donghak's* tenets had "populist and protodemocratic inspirations" (Oh 1999, 15) and seriously challenged the Joseon dynasty. The revolutionary and egalitarian notions such as *innaecheon* (human and the God are one) and *sainyeocheon* (treat others as though they are heaven) were a grave threat to the existing class system. The peasant uprising, internally, was a struggle to destroy the abusive socioeconomic order maintained by the landed class and corrupt officials, and internationally, was a resistance movement against foreign powers and their market forces. In order to overcome these challenges, the Joseon dynasty initiated important political and socioeconomic reforms, including the *Gapo* social reforms of 1894, and created a constitutional monarchy in 1897.

Since then, democracy has been the key basis for challenging the consecutive dictatorial and authoritarian regimes. Institutional democracy and democratic values such as freedom, equality, human rights, and justice have always competed with other values such as national security, anticommunism, and economic growth. The first triumph of democracy over competing values occurred in 1960. The legitimacy of the Rhee administration was seriously damaged in 1954 when Rhee and his party amended the constitution to allow Rhee a lifelong presidency. Intellectuals, students, and the urban middle class quickly withdrew their support for Rhee (Lie 1998, 25). An ardent desire for democracy exploded in 1960 when citizens found out that the government was involved in election fraud and the police killed a high school student protestor during a peaceful rally and tried to cover it up. Rhee finally stepped down and the series of political events that ensued in April 1960 is referred to as the 4.19 Revolution.

The Second Republic, created by the 4.19 Revolution, based its legitimacy exclusively on the principles of democracy. The new state adopted the parliamentary system in order to minimize the exploitation of presidential power; it protected basic civil and political rights and promoted human rights, and decentralized political power by strengthening self-governing functions of local governments and councils. Democracy was the single most important source of political legitimacy for the new government. In addition, the first official effort was made to address the civilian massacres committed by the Rhee administration during the Korean War. It was a period of revolutionary change and, as is so often the case, was also a period of some confusion and disorder.

However, democracy lasted only a year until General Park Chung Hee staged a coup in May 1961. Park skillfully maintained his rule (1961–1979) by justifying his "extraordinary" seizure and exercise of power on grounds of national security, anticommunism, nationalism, and modernization. Despite the continuous challenge to his rule by dissidents and political opponents, the elites and public generally acquiesced to the dictatorship and accepted Park's claims of political legitimacy. The support for Park rapidly declined after a constitutional amendment was passed in 1969 allowing him to run for a third term. After a close win against Kim Dae Jung, Park staged a coup in 1972 by dissolving the legislative and judiciary branches and creating an extremely powerful presidency, elected indirectly in secret. Students, intellectuals, workers, and churches started to vocally oppose Park's rule. At the same time, the international political and economic environment was unfavorable to Park: two oil crises slowed down the economy, challenging economic performance as a source of legitimacy; détente in the 1970s threatened Park's emphasis on anticommunism; and U.S. president Carter with his focus on democracy and human rights seriously challenged Park's dictatorship. The protests started in Busan and Masan and were on the brink of exploding into national uprising. However, all these movements suddenly stopped when Park was assassinated by his close subordinate in October 1979.

A brief period of democratization known as the Seoul Spring followed. After 18 years of Park's dictatorship, opposition leaders and citizens all were eager to welcome the much-awaited democracy. However, a clique of army officers led by General Chun Doo Hwan and Roh Tae Woo staged a coup in 1979 and seized power, basing their legitimacy on national security, anticommunism, and economic stability. The most violent challenge to yet another military rule occurred in Gwangju. Student demonstrations soon turned into a massive student-worker-citizen uprising and the military opened fire against civilians. Democratic challenges against the new authority faced brute force and the national demand for democracy soon subsided. After ruling for seven years, Chun started to pave the way for a long-term seizure of power by amending the constitution to favor his reelection and obstruct the united opposition party. The constitutional amendment and the death of a university student from drowning during torture united civil society against Chun. Prodemocracy demonstration initiated by students and opposition leaders spread to the general public, including workers, farmers, churches, and the urban middle class. Due to public pressure, Roh Tae Woo, Chun's proclaimed successor, agreed to have direct presidential elections and Roh himself was elected president.

The Roh administration was a transition period from authoritarianism to democracy. Certainly the arrival of institutional democracy, which allowed the free, fair, and direct election of the president and other key state offices, was an important change. Despite the formal transition to democracy, however, Korean society had not changed much under Roh. The police, military, and intelligence agencies were as powerful and obtrusive as during the Chun regime and incumbent politicians and public officials maintained their positions. Roh first sought to justify his political legitimacy by half-heartedly holding Chun responsible for the 1980 massacre, in which Roh himself was heavily involved. Roh also started to transfer power from the central government to local governments and councils by reviving the regional self-governing system of the Second Republic. However, Roh, due to the lack of a democratic source of legitimacy, later focused more on foreign affairs. Roh established diplomatic relations with former communist states like Hungary, China, and the Soviet Union ("Northern diplomacy"); significantly improved military, social, and cultural relations with the North, and joined the UN at the same time as North Korea in 1990.

The end of the Cold War brought a significant reduction in anti-communism and confrontational nationalism. Moreover, economic growth lost its significance as the pace of economic development slowed. Political discourse over the economy had by then turned to the issue of distribution of wealth, which is closely related to the democratic values of justice and equality. Under the Kim Young Sam and Kim Dae Jung administrations, democracy served as the key source of legitimacy. However, both leaders had seriously damaged their reputations as proponents of democracy and reliable leaders by the time they took the presidency. First, both failed to achieve a united candidacy against Roh Tae Woo in the 1987 election, thus bearing the responsibility for prolonging authoritarianism. Second, Kim Young Sam merged his political party with the ruling party of the old authoritarian regime in order to get elected as president in 1992. Third, Kim Dae Jung retired from politics after he was defeated by Kim Young Sam in the 1992 presidential election but later reneged on his promise to remain out of politics by running in the 1997 election and winning.

While having somewhat different foci, the central theme of each administration was to consolidate democracy through various reforms. Kim Young Sam focused on eradicating corruption in public office, eliminating the possibility of future military coups by dissolving any private and secret organizations within the military, and holding Chun and Roh accountable for their involvement in the 1979 coup and 1980 Gwangju massacre. In addition, he pursued internationalization (*segehwa*) as one of his key policies and pushed for neoliberal economic reforms and financial liberalization in order to join the Organisation for Economic Co-operation and Development (OECD). Despite all this, hasty and unprepared economic liberalization made the Korean economy vulnerable to international speculators and South Korea ended up becoming a victim of the Asian financial crisis in 1997.

Kim Dae Jung spent the first two and a half years of his presidency regenerating the Korean economy through reforms and by paying back the loan from the International Monetary Fund (IMF). Economic recovery was the key agenda for his administration and Kim successfully avoided the possibility of state bankruptcy. Once the economy stabilized, Kim focused on two issues: first, improving the relationship with North Korea, and second, addressing past human rights violations. As mentioned, Kim transformed confrontational nationalism into conciliatory nationalism by emphasizing on peaceful and prosperous coexistence with the North. He substantially increased humanitarian aid to the North on the basis of key democratic values such as human rights, justice, and equality. In addition, Kim focused on breaking from the past legacy of human rights violations by investigating and redressing the widespread abuse of state power under the military and authoritarian regimes. To that end he instituted a permanent human rights commission as an independent agency of the administration to protect and promote human rights.

Conclusion

My study confirms the three general findings of the editors of this volume. First, a single basis of political legitimacy is not sufficient to fully justify holding power. In South Korea, a combination of at least two sources of political legitimacy has always been needed to sustain a regime. Even the most effective justifications (national security and anticommunism) required the addition of either nationalism or economic development. Second, the legitimation process is precarious and easily affected by political and socioeconomic factors in the society. Although economic development was the most important ground for political legitimacy under the Park administration, this was contingent upon the global economy. In addition, economic growth contained the seeds of its own destruction as a source of legitimacy (e.g., discontented farmers who become the urban poor, the labor movement, and the educated middle class). Similarly, a regime may be stable internally but regional and international events can shake the basis of legitimacy. A good example is Park's regime in the 1970s. Although Park secured his long-term rule with the 1972 constitutional amendment, international politics (détente, oil crises, U.S. president Carter) could easily destabilize the firm ground of his legitimacy. Third, coercion is never sufficient to secure a regime. The most coercive regime in Korea's history was the Japanese colonial authority. In the first phase, the authority was a sheer manifestation of Japanese imperial ambition and brute force was used exclusively to make Koreans submit to their rule. However, all this changed with the 3.1 Movement and various softer policies and ideologies were used to gain support for the regime. Coercion is certainly neither a sufficient nor a stable ground for political legitimacy.

In addition to these three findings, two further conclusions can be drawn from the South Korean experience. First, sources of legitimacy dynamically affect each other, both positively and negatively. In South Korea, different leaders and administrations relied on diverse combinations of security/ideology, economics, nationalism, and democracy. Sometimes, different sources of legitimacy worked in combination to strengthen each other (e.g., nationalism and anticommunism under Rhee; nationalism and economic growth under Park; democracy and conciliatory nationalism under Kim Dae Jung) and at other times, one source of legitimacy critically undermined another (e.g., security/ideology overpowering democracy under Rhee, Park, and Chun; the overwhelming focus on economic growth at the expense of democracy under Park and Chun; the excessive advancement of internationalization and its detrimental effect on the economy under Kim Young Sam).

Second, outside actors, especially the great powers and markets, played a decisive role in the legitimation process in South Korea. The mere presence of the communist North has, even up to the present day, been a critical element shaping the security discourse in South Korea. In a similar vein, modern and contemporary Korean nationalism cannot be explained without the Japanese context. The United States also played a decisive role in sustaining the military and authoritarian regimes during the Cold War, thus undermining the political ground for democracy. However, this role of the United States later backfired with the move to democratization. Roh Moo Hyun, known as the first populist politician, effectively and skillfully used confrontational nationalism with Japan and the United States to secure public support for his policies. At the same time, capital and market forces outside the country also played an indispensable role in boosting or ending the economic basis of political legitimacy.

In sum, before 1987 South Korean authoritarian regimes relied heavily on national security, anticommunism, economic growth, and confrontational nationalism for legitimization. With the end of the Cold War, the reliance on these sources of legitimacy significantly decreased as much more attention was given to democracy, conciliatory nationalism with the North, confrontational nationalism against the United States and Japan, and wealth redistribution. However, with the inauguration of Lee Myung Bak, the trend seems to be reversing. Despite his known faults, Lee was elected president based on his promise to generate a 7% annual growth rate based on his successful CEO experience. In addition, with the two recent unprovoked attacks by North Korea (the sinking of the vessel *Cheonan* with a missile and the bombardment of the island of Yeongpyeong) security and anticommunism has come once again to the forefront of South Korean politics. In some circumstances, the government limits some of the core values of democracy (e.g., human rights, freedom of association, and freedom of expression) for the sake of national security and economic growth. Whether the current trend will continue depends on the 2012 presidential election, in which, according to recent opinion polls, Park Geun Hye, Park Chung Hee's daughter, is shown to have an overwhelmingly lead over the other candidates.

Notes

1. Poggi (1978, 101–102) similarly defines legitimacy as "the moral grounds for obedience to power, as opposed to grounds of self-interest or coercion." Others also share this understanding of legitimacy as a belief in political authority (Lipset 1984, 88; Weber 1964, 382).
2. Some scholars still hold this view. For example, Kateb (1984, 180) sees politics as "the natural home of the concept of legitimacy" and argues that one must look to basic political principles in order to understand the conditions of legitimacy. Likewise, White (2005, 3) states: "Legitimacy is specifically and provably political rather than vaguely socio-economic."

Reference

Alagappa, Muthiah, ed. 1995. *Political Legitimacy in Southeast Asia*. Stanford, CA: Stanford University Press.

Amsden, Alice. 1989. *Asia's Next Giant: South Korea and Late Industrialization*. Oxford: Oxford University Press.

Barker, Rodney. 1990. *Political Legitimacy and the State*. Oxford, UK: Clarendon Press.

Bleiker, Roland. 2009. *Divided Korea: Toward a Culture of Reconciliation*. Minneapolis, MN: University of Minnesota Press.

Choi, Jang Jip. 1993. "Political Cleavages in South Korea." In *State and Society in Contemporary Korea*, edited by H. Koo, 13–15. Ithaca, NY: Cornell University Press.

Habermas, Jurgen. 1984. "What Does a Legitimation Crisis Mean Today? Legitimation Problems in Late Capitalism." In *Legitimacy and the State*, edited by W. Connolly, 134–155. Oxford, UK: Basil Blackwell.

Henderson, Gregory. 1968. *Korea: Politics of the Vortex*. Cambridge, MA: Harvard University Press.

Jeon, Yoong-Deok, and Young-Yong Kim. 2000. "Land Reform, Income Distribution, and Agricultural Production in Korea." *Economic Development and Cultural Change* 48: 253–268.

Kateb, George. 1984. "On the 'Legitimation Crisis'." In *Legitimacy and the State*, edited by W. Connolly, 180–220. Oxford, UK: Basil Blackwell.

Kim, Sunhyuk. 2000. *The Politics of Democratization in Korea: The Role of Civil Society*. Pittsburgh, PA: University of Pittsburgh Press.

Koo, Hagen. 1984. "The Political Economy of Income Distribution in South Korea: The Impact of the State's Industrialization Policies." *World Development* 12: 1029–1037.

———. 2002. "Engendering Civil Society: The Role of Labor Movement." In *Korean Society: Civil Society, Democracy, and the State*, edited by C. K. Armstrong, 73–94. London: Routledge.

Lie, John. 1998. *Han Unbound: The Political Economy of South Korea*. Stanford, CA: Stanford University Press.

Lipset, Seymour Martin. 1984. "Social Conflict, Legitimacy, and Democracy." In *Legitimacy and the State*, edited by W. Connolly, 88–103. Oxford, UK: Basil Blackwell.

Moon, Chung-in, and Sunghack Lim. 2001. "The Politics of Economic Rise and Decline in South Korea." In *Understanding Korean Politics: An Introduction*, edited by S. H. Kil and Chung-In Moon, 201–230. Albany, NY: State University of New York Press.

Oh, John Kie-chiang. 1999. *Korean Politics: The Quest for Democratization and Economic Development*. Ithaca, NY: Cornell University Press.

Pak, Ki Hyuk. 1956. "Outcome of Land Reform in the Republic of Korea." *Journal of Farm Economics* 38: 1015–1023.

Park, Won Soon. 1994. *Gukgaboanbeop Yeongu 1: Gukgaboanbeop Byeoncheonsa* [A Study of National Security Act 1]. Seoul: Yoksa Bipyung.

———. 2006. *Yaman Sidaeui Girok: Gomunui Hankuk Hyeondaesa* [History of Barbaric Era: Modern Korean History of Torture], 3 vols. Seoul: Yoksa Bipyung.

Poggi, Gianfranco. 1978. *The Development of the Modern State: A Sociological Introduction*. Stanford, CA: Stanford University Press.

Robinson, Michael E. 2007. *Korea's Twentieth-Century Odyssey*. Honolulu, HI: University of Hawaii Press.

Seo, Jung Seok. 1999. *Cho Bongam gua 1950* [Cho Bong Am and 1950s], vol. 2. Seoul: Yoksa Bipyung.

Shin, Gi-Wook. 1998. "Agrarian Conflict and the Origins of Korean Capitalism." *American Journal of Sociology* 103: 1309–1351.

———. 2006. *Ethnic Nationalism in Korea: Genealogy, Politics, and Legacy*. Stanford, CA: Stanford University Press.

Weber, Max. 1964. *The Theory of Social and Economic Organizaiton*. New York: Free Press.

White, Lynn T. 2005. "Introduction—Dimensions of Legitimacy." In *Legitimacy: Ambiguities of Political Success or Failure in East and Southeast Asia*, edited by L. T. White, 1–28. Singapore: World Scientific.

CHAPTER 12

Democratization as a Legitimacy Formula: The KMT and Political Change in Taiwan

Naiteh Wu and Tun-jen Cheng

The story of Asian economic development and its political consequences in the long postwar era has been told many times, but rarely has the tale been woven around political legitimacy. Taiwan, and for that matter South Korea—the other widely cited newly industrialized economy and young democracy—modernized according to a series of well-sequenced national projects: a successful agrarian reform that laid the ground for rapid and sustained export-led industrialization under a developmental authoritarian regime within a liberal capitalist international order; in due course the rise of new middle class that pushed for democratic change, to which the regime, shored by strong economic credentials, responded positively; leading, upon democratization, to a shift of focus to an affordable social policy that drew warning lessons from the overdeveloped welfare states in some European nations.[1] Yet this benign pattern of transformation can also be analyzed in terms of changing legitimacy formulae. Till its recent democratization, Taiwan had been under Nationalist (Kuomintang or KMT) authoritarian rule for around four decades. Although it initially faced no formidable challenge to its rule, the regime undertook a long search for a new legitimacy basis to justify its continuing monopolization of political power.

It may be fair to say that the authoritarian KMT regime in Taiwan needed a higher degree of legitimacy than its counterparts elsewhere.

First of all, its ruling group had emigrated from mainland China and hence lacked social and political connection with the local society, which had been under Japanese colonial rule for half a century. Second, an island-wide uprising occurred less than two years after the KMT took over the island, and the repression and killing of many native intellectuals, scholars, and artists aroused strong hostility among islanders toward the new regime. Although public mention of the event was a political taboo during the four decades of authoritarian rule, the story of the uprising and repression became a "hidden transcript" passed to the new generation and used as a weapon of the weak against the regime. It was only after the democratic transition that the national trauma was openly addressed, with a long overdue apology of wrongdoings from KMT leaders.

Obviously, attempts by authoritarian regimes to "update" their legitimacy bases are not unique to Taiwan. Few regimes rely on coercion alone, as suppression is simply not cost-effective over time. Ideological justification, security projects, economic performance, and even a good excuse may allow a nondemocratic regime to justify its monopoly of political power to an acquiescent majority of the ruled for long periods. The intriguing question is why some formerly authoritarian regimes choose democratization as their prime legitimacy factor. The Taiwan case is an especially challenging puzzle, as its prior regime was an authoritarian one under a hegemonic party. As Barbara Geddes (2003) shows, hegemonic party regimes have been more enduring than other types of authoritarian regimes such as personal dictatorships and military dictatorships.[2] The political longevity of Taiwan's KMT regimes was particularly pronounced, managing to perpetuate its rule for around eight decades (if we include the KMT's rule on the mainland prior to 1949 when it relocated to Taiwan)! Highly institutionalized itself, and so comfortably positioned to monopolize state power, the hegemonic KMT regime was not expected to permit, much less initiate, democratic transition. Yet it did. What then led the KMT regime to pursue democratic reform?

This chapter shows that the KMT regime, composed mainly of minority Chinese mainlanders ruling a populace of majority native Taiwanese, had been pretty astute in maintaining and reconstituting its legitimacy basis. All its existing options for legitimation, however, lost effectiveness over time. Eventually, as shown in the first part below, democratization became the principal focus for the regime, the society, and indeed for Taiwan's main external supporter. We attribute the KMT regime's choice to pursue democratic change in the late 1980s to its confidence in its ability to compete favorably in a new and open electoral market. As shown in the second part, decades of local elections and sound economic performance had done much to elevate the level of the party's self-confidence.[3]

Our contention—that the KMT regime undertook democratic reform because it had built up enough confidence to engage in competitive elections—may sound redundant to analysts who regard democracy as being a matter of course for this particular regime.[4] Democracy was indeed one of the three goals for national development stipulated in Dr. Sun Yat-sen's doctrine (the other two being nationalism and people's livelihood), and it had been espoused by the KMT ever since its predecessors staged a revolution toppling the dynasty in China in 1911. It might, therefore, seem that democratization was on the road map from day one, as the regime moved from military rule through tutelage to democracy. It could be argued that the experiment with parliamentary democracy in the 1910s, and democratic tutelage of the 1930s, and the making of a liberal constitution in 1947, all marked the KMT regime's successive attempts to follow this road map. In that case, political change in the 1980s could be construed as the inevitable consummation of a preconceived march, halting as it had been, toward democracy.

There may be some element of truth to this "original intent" thesis. However, we caution against using it as the main explanation for democratic change in Taiwan. First, it is nearly impossible to verify or refute such a thesis. A lofty goal can remain merely a goal for an extended period of time, and commitment to it without a timetable can be a good device for perpetuating the status quo and deferring change indefinitely. We need to explain why a goal long upheld on paper was at some point assiduously pursued. Second, it is hard to know whether democratic change is done out of necessity or out of ideological commitment. Third, the litmus test for commitment to a goal should be deed rather than word. Democracy as a lofty goal—embraced wholeheartedly by the KMT—was in fact handled very gingerly so as not to undermine the regime's sure grip on political power in postwar Taiwan. The regime deployed a battery of justifications to extend the decree of martial law and to prevent full-scale national elections. It also silenced all dissident voices, individual or collective, using imprisonment and even executions by martial courts. During its four decades of rule, all attempts at reform (even one by Chiang Kai-shek's close loyal follower to form a moderate opposition party with a liberal-democratic ideology) were crushed. These facts tend to discount the value of the "original intent" thesis.

Shifting Legitimacy under Constant Duress

The KMT regime—formally the Republic of China (ROC)—retreated to Taiwan in 1949 after losing the civil war to the Chinese Communist Party (CCP) that established the People's Republic of China (PRC). From day one, recovering the mainland and eliminating the bandit CCP regime became a sworn goal, a national exigency and a historical mission. The newly installed 1946 constitutional framework was, therefore, suspended, emergency power given to the president, his term limit extended (subsequently removed), and national elections postponed indefinitely until they could be held on the continental scale. Representatives to the legislature, the national assembly (a presidential electoral college and a constitutional-making or amending body), and the Control Yuan (an oversight body) were exempt from renewing their mandate periodically. New press and new political parties were banned. National exigency, or rather national mission, thus became the dominant, if not the only, theme in the regime's propaganda in the first couple decades of its rule in Taiwan. The slogan "Recovering the Mainland" was painted on the walls of public buildings and classrooms everywhere around the country. The theme was also included in students' textbooks.[5] The mere existence of a PRC regime that swore to bathe Taiwan in blood—a promise made real by its blockade and heavy artillery bombardment of the Quemoy Islands for six weeks in 1958—conflated the issues of national survival and the legitimacy of the KMT regime. It was meant to be self-evident that, in extraordinary times, political power could and should be exercised outside the realm of normal democratic processes for the sake of national survival.

But as national survival was in fact secured by military defense from the United States, this legitimation tactic needed to be complemented by another—Chinese nationalism—that was introduced in the early decades and never absent from official propaganda thereafter. Chinese nationalism as a formula for legitimation served several purposes. First of all, it was intended to reduce hostility to the émigré regime, perhaps even create loyalty, among the native Taiwanese. It was hoped that ethnic cleavage and Taiwanese identity would largely diminish if all conceived themselves as Chinese. The cleavage between ruling Chinese mainlander and ruled native Taiwanese would be (re)defined as a difference in local origins. Thus the ruling group was not to be conceived as composed of Chinese emigrants ruling Taiwanese; the two groups merely came from different provinces of the Republic of China, of which Taiwan was one. This emphasis on local (provincial) origin was institutionalized in the form of a personal identification card, the first column of which registered the provincial origin of the cardholder. It was only in 1992, when Taiwanese identity was becoming dominant and ethnic cleavage surfaced in the country's politics, that the provincial origin column was replaced by the cardholder's birth city/county in an attempt to foster the ethnic unity.

Other practices were also implemented to engender Chinese identity. Many streets in Taipei city were renamed for cities in mainland China to help create Chinese consciousness in people's everyday lives. Taiwanese dialect, forbidden on official occasions and schools, was limited to a minimum in radio and television programs, and used mainly for weather forecasts for agriculture and fishery.[6] But the most important of all practices for fostering Chinese identity was the exclusion of Taiwan's history from the school textbooks and curricula. It was calculated that Taiwan's history and geography constituted less than 5%, in terms of pages, of high school textbooks on history and geography, and even in those scarce materials, the focus was on the close historical connection between Taiwan and China. Half a century of colonization by the Japanese, an important era for Taiwan's development, was totally ignored, except for a few words on local rebels against colonial rule.[7] As culture is often the base for national identity, the KMT regime's effort to engender Chinese nationalism also went into the sphere of culture.[8]

The second function of Chinese nationalism was to justify the freezing of national representative organs and the presidency, securing the personal dictatorship of Chiang Kai-shek and later his son. As the KMT regime was held to be the legitimate government of all China, it followed that the national representative organs should not be renewed through elections by the populace of Taiwan alone. This argument was greatly strengthened by the international context. After the outbreak of the Korean War in 1950, the KMT's confrontation with the CCP regime fit well in an international geostrategic landscape dominated by Cold War bipolarity. The United States cemented a security pact with the ROC on Taiwan, seen as a frontline state for the Western liberal camp. The United States and many of its allies supported the KMT regime's claim to be the legitimate government of China and its representation at the United Nation and on the Security Council. Even in 1971, the year Taiwan lost its seat at the UN, quite a few Western nations still maintained diplomatic ties with the ROC in Taiwan rather than with the PRC on the mainland. Indeed the United States held out till 1979. But when international politics changed in the Chinese Communists' favor, this legitimation formula was no longer effective.

It is important to point out that advocacy for the renewal of national representative organs burst out immediately following the expulsion of Taiwan from the UN. As Taiwan's government now represented only the people in Taiwan, it was argued that it should institute political reform to adapt to the new situation. The importance of the newfound public voice of college students and intellectuals at this time cannot be overestimated. Made in an atmosphere of "white terror" and before the emergence of a democratic movement, this first open challenge to the status quo was a breakthrough in the country's transition process. It was a voice the regime could hardly suppress.

This analysis of legitimacy formulae is not intended to downplay the importance of social policies and political institutions used by the regime to create popular support. As an émigré regime, the KMT had to nurture support from its only territorial base, the local society (especially after they had alienated this society by a February 28, 1947 incident that decimated the local elite) (Myers and Lai 1991). Land reform programs implemented in the mid-1950s and local elections held around the same time provided the regime with highly effective mechanisms to penetrate and incorporate society. As detailed in the next section, twin policy initiatives—electoral and agrarian—greatly enhanced the KMT regime's ability to manage electoral processes. Land reform created rural political support and an economic surplus for the regime, while local elections—which were real and competitive despite the frequent exclusion of political opponents—permitted it to co-opt and control local elites, new or old. Land grants to farmers also presented a vivid contrast with agrarian collectivization on the mainland, while local elections allowed the regime to put on a democratic face. The twin policies thus helped the KMT regime to secure international support for its claim to be the legitimate government of China. They thus enhanced its main legitimacy claim regarding its historical mission to retake the mainland.

Postreform agricultural development also proved to be instrumental to industrialization later on, as the regime was in a position to redeploy resources generated in the agricultural sector to the labor-intensive industrial sector (a story that was meticulously detailed in former president Lee Teng-hui's [1971] doctoral dissertation). Economic projects, agricultural or industrial, were initially assessed not on their merits alone, but on their compatibility with the overriding goal of retaking the mainland.[9] Neither were local elections allowed to undermine social mobilization for the regime's historical mission. Public discourse and electoral campaigns were not supposed to discredit the regime's legitimacy.

This legitimacy formula became harder and harder to use, however, as the hope for returning to the mainland via military operations dimmed at the turn of the 1960s. Developing the Taiwanese economy and building Taiwan as a model for the mainland became the new, urgent tasks used to justify the KMT's hegemonic power and the suspension of constitutional democracy. As the economy took off in the 1960s and the 1970s, Taiwan and Korea became the two most cited models for emulation in the developing world. The KMT regime subtly downplayed its role in the history of modern China, while increasingly taking pride in Taiwan's economic achievement. In the meantime, international support for the regime's claim to represent the whole of China was rapidly evaporating.

Yet after two good decades of rapid economic growth, continuous export success, educational expansion, and other achievements, socioeconomic development no longer served to deflect public attention, especially that of new generations, away from the long-delayed promise to deliver democracy. Certainly, economic affluence and political stability had strong appeal for the generation of Chinese mainlanders who had lived through the turbulent politics and economic scarcity of World War II and Civil War. As for the old generation of native Taiwanese, economic development based on labor-intensive industrialization had brought not only economic security but, more importantly, investment opportunities they had never experienced even under Japanese colonial rule. Many took advantage of their educational attainment in the colonial era and engaged energetically in business. If Chinese mainlanders, mostly employed in the government sector, enjoyed job security and generous welfare programs provided exclusively for the government employees, the native Taiwanese were busy becoming entrepreneurs, large and small. The number of business establishments increased from 200,241 in 1961 to 505,378 in 1982, a growth of almost 250% in two decades. As the adult population for the latter year was less than 10 million,[10] this meant that 1 in 20 adults was running his or her own business. The real wage of their employees was nearly doubled in the decade from 1970 to 1980 (Haggard 1990, 230). Life could not be better, if one stayed away from politics, which included not talking about them in the workplace or at home. Yet with the advent of a new generation, political apathy and fear began to subside. The babyboomers—born after World War II and coming of age in the 1970s—had never experienced economic hardship or political repression. This generation, Chinese mainlanders and native Taiwanese alike, found political silence and submission unbearable and began to challenge the authoritarian rule of the KMT.

Just as the babyboomer generation loomed large, Taiwan's geostrategic standing began to erode. As mentioned above, the international security environment had been most benign for the KMT in the 1950s, allowing the party to be an Asian champion of the anticommunist camp even while under a martial law decree. Once détente set in, however, Taiwan's international political capital declined. As China pursued economic reform and adroitly turned outward, Taiwan quickly lost its presence in major international organizations and its diplomatic voice regarding China. Moreover, on the state-to-state level, China (the main source of threat to Taiwan) and the United States (Taiwan's security provider) were developing parallel interests vis-à-vis the Soviet Union, a development that had serious fallout for Taiwan (Mann 2000). One way to prevent Taiwan from becoming totally isolated by the Western community and from being victimized by Sino-American rapprochement was for Taiwan to turn into a full liberal democracy (deLisle 2008). Democratic reform would not only meet the aspiration of a new political generation in Taiwan, it could also improve Taiwan's international political status. Reform would make it harder for a human-rights-touting and democracy-promoting United States to sacrifice Taiwan's interests while partnering with China to rein in the soon-to-be defunct Soviet Union. The regime was not, however, swift in adopting this strategy. Native Taiwanese opposition movement activists, on the other hand, especially those advocating Taiwanese independence in the United States, were most astute in exploiting the situation by informing the U.S. policy community, especially on Capitol Hill, about Taiwan's human rights and democracy violations. As a security consumer, the KMT regime was most sensitive to U.S. congressional hearings on these issues, either in general terms or over specific cases (such as the murder of Taiwanese political dissidents on American soil).

As the existing legitimacy formulae (national exigency, Chinese nationalism, and economic development) began to lose their spell, the regime first retreated to coarse propaganda but then turned to social science literature to fend off demands for democratic reform. The year 1971 saw the loss of Taiwan's membership in the United Nations and mounting cries for democratic reform. The KMT party's official newspaper, *The Central Daily*, thus began in 1972 to publish a series of articles entitled *The Voice of a Little Citizen*, the themes of which were in accordance with what Hirschman (1991) called the threefold "rhetoric of reaction." The articles argued that revolution/reform would produce contrary results (the perversity thesis), that nothing good for society would come from vocal advocacy for reform (the futility thesis), and that reform would endanger what had already been achieved, namely stability and prosperity (the jeopardy thesis). The articles were soon printed in book form and distributed all around the country to high school students, who were required to write reports on it. Several years later, in 1977, following the emergence of a democratic opposition, the regime propagated another wave of propaganda. *The Central Daily* again published a series, this time a more mystic and nonsensible one, entitled *A Blood Letter from the South Sea*, which, the anonymous author claimed, was found on a deserted island by the author's brother when fishing in the South Sea. The letter was allegedly written with human blood on a shirt, which was hidden in a snail, lying amid 13 human bones and skulls. It accused the champions of democracy in South Vietnam of causing the country to fall into the hands of communists, who then turned stability and prosperity into living hell. This was also published soon as a book and distributed to every high school student.

But the most interesting phenomenon, for social scientists at least, was the use of contemporary social science literature to justify authoritarian rule and fend off the demand for democratic reforms. To be sure, the essays and political commentaries written by conservative scholars, intellectuals, and pundits were not commissioned by the regime as coordinated propaganda. They were, however, the only views allowed to be published, often in the conspicuous spots of the main newspapers. In general, these discourses did not challenge the desirability of democratic reforms, but used the detour strategy of addressing the timing, conditions, and most appropriate way of achieving democracy. One of the most cited theories for this purpose was modernization theory (especially Lipset 1983). Many essays and commentaries argued that, as liberal democracy needs economic development first, democratic reform had to wait till the country's economy was fully developed. They never specified, however, the exact stage of economic development that is good for democratic reform, nor how that development would bring forth democracy.

Another often cited theory was the "cultural requisite of democracy," inspired by Gabriel A. Almond and Sidney Verba's (1963) work. This argued that democracy needs some kind of civic culture to sustain it, and that Taiwan was still too strongly under the influence of traditional culture. Even some renowned Chinese liberal-inclined scholars teaching at American universities openly subscribed to this view. One American scholar joined the camp by arguing that "democracy is very much a product of the particular political culture engendered in the West...It is impractical to assume that democracy can be separated from its culture and transplanted in China.... Those who advocate democracy need to examine its cultural dimension.... It is unwise to demand democracy without first considering this issue" (Metzger 1983). In addition to the above two theories, Samuel P. Huntington's (1968) theory of political decay, which was actually antithetical to modernization theory, also gained popularity in the conservative public discourse of the time. The Huntingtonian thesis that mass participation without political institutionalization resulted in political decay was used to discredit the nascent democratic movement and discourage public rallies and protests. Later on, when the opposition began to demand the lifting of the ban on new political parties, Seymour M. Lipset was cited to support an argument that democracy did not require free competition among political parties and that democracy indeed could be sustained in a one-party system.[11] Many Taiwanese advocates of the rhetoric of reaction were renowned scholars, including several academicians of the Academia Sinica, which held the most prestigious academic positions in the country. Since no activist in the democratic movement was well-trained in social sciences, and few scholars stood with the opposition, the effects of the rhetoric when cast in the form of social science theories were considerable. As Hirschman (1991, 45) said, such rhetoric could leave "the promoters of change humiliated, demoralized, in doubt about the meaning and true motive of their endeavors."[12]

Yet by the 1980s, the spinning of the existing legitimation formulae could no longer contain the mounting demands for democratic reforms or dent the growing strength of political opposition forces. Nor was the momentum of the democratic movement arrested by the high profile trial and imprisonment of around 40 democracy activists in 1979, following a riot during a public rally in the southern industrial city of Gaoxong organized by the opposition. Two decades earlier, the first postwar democratic movement had been thoroughly crushed and its participants paralyzed in the wake of the arrest and court-martialing of its leader, Lei Zhen. In the 1980s, the new democratic movement—mainly a baby boomer project—grew ever stronger with each round of suppression. For the leaders of this new movement, the politics of fear was replaced by a politics of commitment, which was in line with a Chinese intellectual tradition. As the frontline leaders were court-martialed, their spouses, relatives, and defending attorneys stepped forward to participate in elections. Their stunning electoral successes were widely construed as a denunciation of political purges and an effective defiance of the authoritarian regime. Facing this new political context, the KMT seemed to have only two alternatives. One was to arrest more people on illegitimate grounds, which would nurture more leaders and activists for the movement and instill a greater passion for democracy, thereby risking being toppled by mass protests. The other path was to use the formula of democratic reform to legitimize its ruling position. But for the regime to adopt this alternative, one condition needed to be fulfilled: the KMT must feel confident that it would not lose its ruling position by democratic reforms.

Conditions for Legitimation by Democratic Reform

Huntington (1991, 57) points out in his seminal work on third-wave democratization that one way authoritarian regimes may confront the erosion of their legitimacy is to take the lead in introducing democracy. Huntington (128) contends that there must be reformers in the regime who believe, among other things, that they can not only renew their legitimacy by restoring democracy but also win the election. The prototypical cases in which ruling authoritarian elites used this formula are Spain and Brazil. In their study of these two cases, Share and Mainwaring (1986) list several conditions that must be met for ruling elites to adopt a strategy they call democratic "transition through transaction." Those conditions are that the authoritarian regime is well established and widely supported, capable of controlling subversive threats, and headed by skillful leadership. It is also crucial that the democratic opposition accepts limits and rules set by the regime and that there be a limited level of mass mobilization (194–199). But all these conditions seem secondary to the most important: the ruling elites must be confident that they can survive the democratic reform.

The essential task is to explain what gives elites this confidence. Elections in authoritarian regimes, if there are any, are often not free and equal so the rulers generally do not have accurate knowledge of their level of popularity. And as the mass media are usually controlled and the opposition repressed or harassed in elections, they have no way of telling how strong the opposition will grow if authoritarian control is loosened. Not knowing if they will survive democratic reform, they are likely to resist using democratic measures to renew their legitimacy. After all, as Huntington (1991, 174–178) points out, there are many cases in which the confidence of ruling elites has proved to be unfounded. This may be one of the reasons why there were few cases of transition through transaction in the third wave of democratization.

As far as the case of Taiwan is concerned, many factors helped build confidence among the ruling elites that they would perform well in open and fair elections. One of those important factors was the regime's impressive performance in economic development. The annual economic growth rate from 1960 to 1985 averaged 8.8%, while the GDP per capita for the same period rose from $164 to $3,290, a twentyfold growth in only 20 years. No less important is the fact that this tremendous economic growth was accompanied by a relatively equal distribution of income. The latter was largely an effect of Taiwan's particular mode of industrialization based on labor-intensive production, which not only created nearly full employment but also allowed the workers a larger share of the profits, compared to other developing countries, through continually increasing wages. Land reform and the government's commitment to education may also have contributed to more equal income distribution (Haggard 1990, 223–229). The ratios of the average income of the richest quintile to that of the poorest one stayed around 4.2–4.5 from 1976, the first year for which we have data, to 1985. Measured using the Gini Index, equality of income distribution stayed as low as around 0.28 during the decade of 1970s. The figure for Brazil in 1980 was as high as 0.57.

If rapid economic growth greatly contributed to the material-based legitimacy of the KMT's rule, the equity accompanying that growth had the effect of insulating the regime from the challenge of working-class mobilization or poor people's movements. It is true that the government tried very hard to suppress leftist literature and thought during the four decades of authoritarian rule; those found owning or reading such material risked being imprisoned. But even without government censorship, it is doubtful that a leftist movement could ever have thrived. Around the time of political liberalization in the late 1980s, a Labor Party led by an opposition legislator made its appearance in the political arena, followed by a Workers' Party led by a famous union leader. A few years later both parties disappeared without trace. The union movement fared no better. Around the same time, many attempts were made by workers and intellectuals to organize new unions or to replace the existing ones, which previously were under a hierarchical corporatist framework controlled by the ruling party. Many did succeed in taking control of the shop unions and also gained concessions from management in terms of wage raises and year-end bonuses. The reason for their easy success was explained by the fact that these independent labor "movements" mostly occurred within public enterprises such as China Petroleum and Taiwan Power. The managers of public enterprises, themselves public employees, had the least incentive to repress union activities. They were also willing to make concessions to workers' demands at public expense.

After unions in many public enterprises gained their independence, the independent union movement died out within a few years.

Working-class mobilization contributed greatly to democratic transition in some countries (Collier 1999). In others, such as South Africa and El Salvador, the transition was arguably also facilitated by insurgent movements (Wood 2000). But we would argue that the nonexistence of working-class mobilization in Taiwan had the beneficial effect of facilitating transition by transaction. Democratic reform can hardly solve problems of economic inequality and income distribution, and hence cannot help an inegalitarian regime to improve its legitimacy. Because the relatively equal income distribution of Taiwan had prevented the rise of class politics, democratic reform became the only game in town. The only players were a moderate opposition on one side, mainly composed of people with middle-class backgrounds, and the ruling elites on the other. This situation gave the authoritarian elites the confidence and security they needed to launch democratic reform from above, depriving the opposition of their only weapon or at least reducing the force of their appeal. The elites could then compete comfortably on the record of their performance using the powerful organizations they had built over the past four decades.[13]

In those four decades of KMT rule, regular and continual elections were held at all levels of local government despite the fact that martial law remained in force until the late 1980s. The Constitution of the Republic of China, promulgated in 1947, lays out a liberal democratic framework. The tenets of liberal democracy were also embodied in the official ideology of the KMT and in the doctrines of Three Principles of the People proposed by the founder of the Republic and leader of the party, Sun Yat-sen. The regime could never simply discard the Constitution nor its own official ideology. The Constitution could be amended, but not wholly rewritten. Thus, the article limiting the president of the Republic to two terms was frozen to allow Chiang Kai-shek to serve in the position till he died. Also frozen was the renewal of the national representative organs, nearly all members of which were elected in China in 1946. Despite these amendments to, or rather infringements of, the Constitution, elections were held from 1946 on at all levels of local government, from the grassroots level of village head and village council, head of township and town council, to mayor and city/county council and the highest level of the Taiwan Provincial Assembly.

Native Taiwanese, many of whom had been sociopolitical elites under Japanese colonial rule, eagerly participated in these elections. Among the city/county councilmen of the whole country elected in the 1946, close to half had held appointed or elective political positions in the former colonial regime. Other elective organs also witnessed a high degree of continuity of political elites. The "February 28 Uprising" in 1947 and the subsequent slaughter by the regime of Taiwanese elites, however, alienated many native Taiwanese. In the first city/county council election held after this political repression, in 1950–1951, 66.2% of incumbents countrywide declined to run for political positions of any kind at any level and retired from politics. About 20% of incumbents were reelected. In other words, around 80% of native Taiwanese elites were replaced in local positions by a new group of politicians, the greatest turnover in Taiwan's history. Even the Land Reform launched a couple of years later, which was supposed to wipe out the political influence of the landlord class, did not have as great an impact on elite turnover.[14] The overall effect was the consolidation of the KMT regime. The vacancies left by the retired traditional social leaders, who were mostly from the educated landlord class, were filled by a new group of *nouveau puissant*. Because this new group benefited from the new political situation, its members were more willing to support and cooperate with the authoritarian regime. It was also at this time that electoral politics began to be plagued by widespread vote-buying practices, which the traditional social elites had not needed or were above doing.[15]

The regime did not hesitate to ally with this new class of native Taiwanese politicians. The national ruling elites in the first few decades of KMT rule were composed of nearly all Chinese mainlanders, who had little social connection with the local society. The use of an iron fist by an ethnic minority ruling a native majority could bring only submission, not active support. The KMT regime needed local politicians to secure popular votes, and the local electoral success of native Taiwanese politicians served an important function in creating a façade of democracy. In order to secure their collaboration, the regime provided many favors for the native politicians. The favors were variegated, but the most profitable were licenses for local public utility businesses, such as gas companies, bus companies, and credit unions. These credit unions latter were just as, or even more, important for Taiwan's economy because they provided capital for the small and medium enterprises that were the main contributor to the country's economic development. (Most loans from public banks went to big enterprises.) Local politicians greatly benefited from profits from the credit unions and from social connections with, or even loan patronage of, local businessmen (Wu 1987, 228–231). A study found that 81 of the total 89 local factions in the country were given at least one credit union or bank license, while 18 of them were given licenses of local bus companies (Chen and Chu 1992).

Aided partly by such financial resources and partly by political and legal protections from the national ruling elites, these politicians energetically engaged in local electoral politics. Informal organizations built and led by them emerged in every locality for electoral mobilization. The authority structure and working practices of this informal political organization, commonly called the "local faction," was quite similar to the clientelist social network of developing countries and the political machine of urban local politics in democracies.[16] First, it was based on the personal following of a top politician in the locality, whose surname often became the name of the faction. (Sometimes color—for example, black, red—would be used if the builders of opposing factions in the same locality had the same surnames.) The leader often occupied or competed for the highest position in the constituency. He distributed economic benefits to his followers. He also had a great say in who (generally one of his offspring) would succeed him when he retired. As for electoral mobilization, the leader provided services to voters and lower level leaders in the faction in exchange for their votes and loyalty. These services included extralegal favors and contracts from local government, handling personal grievances with the local government, free legal aid, and sometimes even employment. The other category of service provided was social privilege, such as the local political leader appearing and making speeches at weddings and funerals. Yet these services and favors alone were seldom enough to get local politicians elected, especially when there were candidates from a rival faction competing for votes. Cash transactions were, therefore, added to the mix, and vote-buying became a common practice.

Regime opponents trying to enter local electoral politics were often harassed by such frauds and vote miscounts, sometimes by arrests without trial, yet the regime did allow free competition between local politicians who were all under the banner of the ruling party. As a result, two different local factions often appeared in the same constituencies of every locality, allowing the regime to adopt a strategy of divide-and-rule. It generally arranged things so that two competing factions took turns running for city/county mayor while the rival faction held the position of assembly speaker for check and balance. When occasionally one faction grew too strong and showed signs of disobedience, the regime would either purge the leader using corruption or vote-buying charges, or nominate the leaders of the opposing faction for important positions to create a balance of power and influence. In those places where there was only one faction, the regime would deliberately create another to compete with it.

These energetically engaged local factions performed an important function for the regime. Although all factions operated on the city and county level, with the whole city and county as their constituency, they also penetrated down to the lower township and village levels, forming a pyramidal power/mobilization structure. Top leaders would be city/county majors or assembly speakers while their lieutenants might serve as town/township heads or leaders in social organizations such as the farmers' associations. The latter provided services and favors to their own voters, supporters, and followers and mobilized votes for themselves and the faction as well.[17] These deep-penetrating electoral machines had the effect not only of securing popular votes for the regime but also of blocking ideological opponents of the regime when they occasionally emerged on the slates. In elections for the Provincial Assembly, the highest level elective position before the democratic transition, the ruling KMT always acquired around 80% of the seats. Most of the remaining seats went to "independents" who never challenged the regime on ideological grounds. The party's domination was even greater at the lower levels of the representative organs, reaching as high as 90% at town and township level. Even in the election of the Provincial Assembly in 1977, in which a countrywide democratic opposition first made its appearance with strong popular support, the ruling party still acquired more than 70% of the seats (table 12.1).

The strong showing of the ruling party during the authoritarian era gave it solid confidence that it might continue this dominance in electoral politics after the democratic transition, thus depriving the opposition of the only appeal it had (namely, to democracy). The two would then compete on the basis of ruling experience and the power of local electoral machines, areas in which the ruling party certainly had an edge. Indeed the KMT's optimistic expectation seemed very much realized in the elections after the democratic transition. In the first post-transition Legislative Yuan election of 1992, in which the whole body of the national representative organ was to be renewed, the ruling party gained 96 of the total 153 seats in a genuinely free and open contest, against 51 seats gained by the opposition DPP. To the present day, the KMT still enjoys a comfortable majority in the Legislative Yuan. As for the presidency of the Republic, the most important position in the democratic regime, the KMT has also performed quite well there since the transition. The opposition Democratic Progress Party would not have won even the presidential election in 2000, causing the

Table 12.1 Seats and Votes Gained by the KMT in Elections, 1950–1995
# of Seats / Total (% of Votes)

	Legislative Yuan	Provincial Assembly	City/County Mayors	City/County Councilmen	Town/ Township Heads
1950	–	–	–	522/814	–
1950–1951	–	–	–	–	256/360
1951	–	41/55	16/21	–	–
1952	–	–	–	642/860	–
1952–54	–	–	–	–	300/360
1954	–	47/57	19/21	697/928	–
1955–1957	–	–	–	–	325/360
1957	–	53/66	20/21	–	–
1958	–	–	–	762/1025	–
1959–1960	–	–	–	–	290/313
1960	–	58/73	19/21	–	–
1961	–	–	–	747/929	–
1963	–	61/74	–	–	–
1964	–	–	17/21	746/907	295/319
1968	–	60/71	17/21	638/847	267/313
1969	8/11*	–	–	–	–
1972	45/51	58/73	20/20	–	–
1973	–	–	–	626/850	288/313
1975	30/37	–	–	–	–
1977	–	55/77	16/20	711/857	292/313
1980	83/97	–	–	–	–
1981	–	59/77 (86.9)	15/19 (80.3)	–	–
1982	–	–	–	599/799	295/312
1983	86/98 (70.5)	–	–	–	–
1985	–	59/77	17/21	–	–
1986	83/100 (69.9)	–	–	705/837	297/309
1989	100/130 (60.1)	54/77 (61.8)	14/21 (52.7)	–	–
1990	–	–	–	588/842 (61.9)	263/309 (71.7)
1992	95/161** (64.7)	–	–	–	–

continued

Table 12.1 continued

	Legislative Yuan	Provincial Assembly	City/County Mayors	City/County Councilmen	Town/ Township Heads
1993	–	–	15/23 (50.6)	–	–
1994	–	48/79 (53.0)	–	542/883 (61.4)	220/319 (69.0)
1995	106/164[***] (59.0)	–	–	–	–

[*]*From 1969 to 1989 the "supplementary elections" for the Legislative Yuan were held to renew only those members elected in Taiwan Province. The number of seats representing Taiwan has been incrementally increased during these years.*

[**]*The first year the Legislative Yuan, the national representative organ, was fully renewed.*

[***] *The figures include the New Party, which split from the KMT.*

KMT to lose power for the first time in Taiwan's history, if the KMT vote had not been split. In that election the DPP's nominee received only 39.3% of the total votes cast while the KMT's nominee gained 23.1%. Another candidate, a popular politician who had served as a KMT government official all his life but failed to be nominated by the party, gained 36.8% of the votes.

Conclusion

The first Chinese democracy was made possible by various factors and the contributions of many actors. We have focused in this chapter on the factor of legitimation through appeal to different formulae in different international and domestic contexts. While democracy was enshrined in Dr. Sun Yat-sen's doctrine of the Three Principles of the People, and espoused by the KMT regime all along, democracy as a (now *the*) legitimacy formula for Taiwan did not come into being according to the regime's ideological script. Rather, it was sidelined for decades during which communist insurgency and threat, nationalism, and economic development formed the justifying basis of KMT authoritarian rule. Democratic reform as a formula for legitimation was adopted only after all other formulae were invalidated or rendered useless. The adoption of democratic reform, indeed, has made Taiwan one of the few cases of "transition by transaction."

But before the ruling elites could choose the democratization formula, they had to be confident that they would not be replaced in free, full, and open elections. We have discussed the factors that gave the ruling elites in Taiwan this confidence. Good economic performance, governing experience, and a moderate liberal-inclined opposition were among those factors. But we have argued that the most important one was that the regime had already built strong electoral machines that penetrated deeply into society. During the four decades of authoritarian rule, the regime permitted local elections that were real and quite competitive, notwithstanding the practices of vote-buying and harassment of the opposition. Although local elections were originally intended to provide a façade of democracy, the regime did gradually enhance its organizational capacity in managing electoral processes. As preexisting legitimacy claims wore thin, losing value and credibility in new international and domestic environments, the KMT regime nevertheless grew confident enough to face the challenge of democratic reform.

Democratic transition is a great human drama that involves many different actors, both domestic and international, evoking moral passions and rational calculations that inspire supreme human efforts that can have both intended and unintended consequences. Such was indeed the case with Taiwan's transition. Yet it may be regarded as an irony of fortune that Taiwanese democratic reform was in large part the result of the authoritarian party's search for new legitimacy to consolidate its own rule.

Notes

The authors are grateful to John Kane for his many invaluable comments on this essay.

1. Regarding these transformations, Haggard and Kaufman (1995) in two volumes, one on democratic change, the other on the evolution of the welfare state, masterfully put East Asia (South Korea and Taiwan most notably) in vivid contrast with Latin America (especially the Southern Cone nations) and East and Central Europe. See Stephan Haggard and Robert Kaufman (1995), and their subsequent work Haggard and Kaufman (2008) .

2. Barbara Geddes' (2003) database shows that personal dictatorship has an average life span of 18 years, the average military junta lasts 12 years, while authoritarian party regimes persist for about 34 years.

3. Elsewhere, we have dwelt on how the civil society and political opposition pushed for democratic change. See Cheng (1989); Wu (2000).

4. See, for example, Chao and Myers (1998).

5. The present authors still remember vividly that when they were in primary school, the last paragraphs of their compositions were always connected to this theme, whatever the subject they wrote about.

6. With political liberalization in the 1980s, a movement emerged in public discourses to protest the discrimination against the Taiwanese dialect and to advocate "speaking the language my mother taught me." Later, when the Taiwanese identity became the mainstream, many mainlander politicians struggled to learn the dialect and would intentionally speak a few sentences in public rallies, no matter how awkwardly.

7. Research cited in Wang Fu-chang (2005, 63). One of the present authors, Wu, has to admit embarrassedly that although he attended the high school, in the 1960s, cofounded by the most renowned and respected leader of the anticolonial movement, Lin Xian-tang, whose bust located by the main gate of the school he passed for six years, he never knew who he was. And this was less than 20 years after Lin's prime in the anticolonial struggle, 15 years after Lin's self-exile to Japan. It was as if an African American schoolboy did not know of Martin L. King in the 1970s.

8. See generally Chun (1996).

9. Some KMT elites were concerned that the construction of the largest dam in Taiwan might have frozen capital resources needed for a military counterattack on the mainland.

10. Executive Yuan of ROC, *Statistical Yearbook of the Republic of China*, 1984.

11. See King (1982, 71–72). We, however, could not find this argument in the work of Lipset (*The First New Nation*) that he cited.

12. For a detailed discussion of the authors and contents of these discourses, see Wu (2001).

13. For decades-long party building under local elections, see Cheng and Lin (2008, 161–183).

14. For a full presentation of continuity and turnover of native Taiwanese political elites, see Wu and Chen (1993).

15. As James C. Scott (1972, 104–105) points out, in new nations when political leaders can no longer rely on the traditional social deference for support, competition among leaders will encourage the wide spread use of concrete, short-run material interests.

16. See generally Eisenstadt and Lemarchand (1981); Schmidt et al. (1977).

17. For a detailed and very informative study on the process of voting buying and vote mobilization on the grassroots level of the KMT machine, see Wang Jin-shou (1997).

References

Almond, Gabriel A., and Sidney Verba. 1963. *The Civic Culture*. Princeton: Princeton University Press.

Chao, Linda, and Ramon Myers, 1998. *The First Chinese Democracy*. Baltimore: Johns Hopkins University Press.

Chen, Ming-tong, and Yun-han Chu, 1992. "Monopoly of Local Economy, Local Factions, and the Provincial Assembly Election: Analysis of the Background of Provincial Assemblymen" [in Chinese]. *Journal of Humanities and Social Sciences* 2: 77–97.

Cheng, T. J. 1989. "Democratizing the Quasi-Leninist Regime in Taiwan." *World Politics* (July 1989): 471–499.

Cheng T. J., and Gang Lin, 2008. "Competitive Elections: Experience in Taiwan and Recent Developments in China." In *Political Change in Taiwan and China*, edited by Larry Diamond and Bruce Gilley, 163–183. New York: Lynne Rienner.

Chun, Allen. 1996. "From Nationalism to Nationalizing: Cultural Imagination and State Formation in Postwar Taiwan." In *Chinese Nationalism*, edited by Jonathan Unger. New York: M. E. Sharpe.

Collier, Ruth. 1999. *Paths toward Democracy: Working Class and Elites in Western Europe and South America*. New York: Cambridge University Press.

deLisle, Jacques. 2008. "International Pressures and Domestic Pushback." In *Political Change in China: Comparisons with Taiwan*, edited by Bruce Gilley and Larry Diamond. Boulder: Lynne Rienner.

Eisenstadt, Shmuel. N. and R. Lemarchand, eds. 1981. *Political Clientelism, Patronage, and Development*. Beverly Hill: Sage.

Geddes, Barbara. 2003. *Paradigms and Sand Castles: Theory Building and Research Design in Comparative Politics*. Ann Arbor: University of Michigan Press.

Haggard, Stephan. 1990. *Pathways from the Periphery: the Politics of Growth in the Newly Industrialized Countries*. Ithaca: Cornell University Press.

Haggard, Stephan, and Robert Kaufman. 1995. *The Political Economy of Democratic Transition*. Princeton: Princeton University Press.

———. 2008. *Development, Democracy, and Welfare States: Latin America, East Asia and Eastern Europe*. Princeton: Princeton University Press.

Hirschman, Albert O. 1991. *The Rhetoric of Reaction: Perversity, Futility, Jeopardy*. Cambridge, MA: Harvard University Press.

Huntington, S. P. 1968. *Political Order in Changing Societies*. New Haven: Yale University Press.

———. 1991. *The Third Wave: Democratization in the Late Twentieth Century*. Norman: University of Oklahoma University.

King, Ambrose Yeo-chi. 1982. "Construction of Chinese Democracy" in [in Chinese]. In *Predicament and Development of Democracy in China*, 71–72. Taipei: China Times..

Lee Teng-hui. 1971. *Intersectoral Capital Flow in the Economic Development of Taiwan, 1895–1960*. Ithaca: Cornell University.

Lipset, Seymour M. 1983. "Some Social Requisites of Democracy: Economic Development and Political Legitimacy," in *Political Man: The Social Bases of Politics*. London: Heinemann.

Mann, James. 2000. *About Face*. New York: Vintage.

Metzger, Thomas A. 1983. "Ethics of Responsibility and Democratic Culture" [in Chinese]. *China Times*, February 8,.

Myers, Ramon, and Lai Tse-han. 1991. *A Tragic Beginning: the Uprising of February 28, 1947*. Stanford: Stanford University Press.

Scott, James C. 1972. *Comparative Political Corruption*. Englewood Cliffs: Prentice-Hall.

Schmidt, Steffen W., Laura Guasti, Charles H. Lande, and James C. Scott. 1977. *Friends, Followers, and Factions*. Berkeley: University of California Press.

Share, Donald and Scott Mainwaring, 1986, "Transition through Transaction: Democratization in Brazil and Spain," ed. Wayne A. Selcher, *Political Liberalization in Brazil: Dynamics, Dilemma, and Future Prospects*. Boulder: Westview.

Wang Chin-shou. 1997. "The Making and Operation of a KMY Candidate's Vote-Buying Machine" [in Chinese]. *Taiwan Political Science Review* 2 (December 1997): 3–62.

Wang Fu-chang. 2005. "Why Bother about School Textbook?" In *Culture, Ethnic, and Political Nationalism in Contemporary Taiwan*, edited by John Makeham and a-Chin Hsiau. New York: Palgrave.

Wood, Elisabeth Jean. 2000. *Forging Democracy from Below: Insurgent Transitions in South Africa and El Salvador*. New York: Cambridge University Press.

Wu, Naiteh. 1987. *Politics of a Regime Patronage System*. Dissertation submitted to the Political Science Department at the University of Chicago, 1987.

———. 2000. "Impact of Moral Values in Historical Transformation: Explaining Democratic Transition in Taiwan" [in Chinese]. *Taiwanese Political Science Review* 4 (December 2000): 57–104.

———. 2001. "Social Sciences and Rhetoric of Reaction: Defending Taiwan's Authoritarianism" [in Chinese]. *Taiwan Historical Research* 8, 1 (June 2001): 125–162.

Wu, Naiteh and Ming-tong Chen. 1993. "Elites Circulation and Regime Transformation" [in Chinese]. In Jeh-han Lai, edited by *Taiwan History during the Early Post-war Period*. Taipei: Sun Yat-sen Institute for Social Sciences and Philosophy.

CHAPTER 13

Justice and the Problem of International Legitimacy

John Kane and Haig Patapan

What is legitimacy? Barker (1990, 11) defines political legitimacy as the belief in the rightfulness of the state, in its authority to issue commands, so that "the commands are obeyed not simply out of fear or self-interest, but because they are believed to have moral authority, because subjects believe they ought to obey." Legitimacy, on this view, concerns the right to rule, a right admitted by those who are ruled. Barker thus ties legitimacy explicitly to "the state," although the concept has much wider application to the perceived validity of any political role or action. Yet it is true that it is with the rise of the modern state that political legitimacy comes most strongly into focus as an issue of importance and contention. In the modern milieu it is not just the legitimacy of a particular ruler that is at stake, but the legitimacy of the state itself and of the regime that operates it. Moreover, the legitimacy or illegitimacy of a state and its regime is a matter of consequence, not just for its citizens, but for the international community of states as well. Indeed the two perspectives, internal (or domestic) and external (or international), are dynamically interlinked, as the studies in this book attest.

Those studies also reveal that legitimacy within states is at once fundamental but always contestable and frequently contested, a necessary but mutable basis for government, forever in need of reinforcement and manifest in protean and often subtle ways rather than ever being simply given. The essential complexity of legitimacy, however, has largely been overlooked within the international arena, where discussion has tended to reduce the issue to two broad and contradictory alternatives. In this chapter we label them the *first* and *second moments of legitimacy*. In the *first moment*, legitimacy is traced to legality understood positivistically, so that the mere fact of stable government, no matter what its stripe, is enough to earn the label "legitimate." In this moment the "monopoly of violence" and citizen obedience ensure stability, and stability overrides any other possible bases of legitimacy. In the *second moment*, citizen consent is argued to be the true basis of legitimacy, with the result that any regime other than the genuinely democratic is regarded as illegitimate.

Neither of these conceptions appears politically or morally sufficient. The first regards all stable regimes as equally legitimate and deserving of respect and recognition, and thus leads to moral relativism (or the amoral "realism" of international relations). The second regards all nondemocratic regimes, however stable, secure, and prosperous, as illegitimate and thus risks declining into democratic imperialism. Taken together, they are limited in their (1) scope (only two forms of political structures are covered); (2) implications for international relations (quietism versus moral evangelism); and (3) capacity to take into account the internal politics of nations.

We argue for the desirability of recognizing a *third moment of legitimacy* that incorporates but exceeds the claims of the first and second by admitting the actual complexity of legitimacy claims and contests as they occur in particular polities. We call this moment *legitimacy as justice*, understood as a concern for the common good of a society and its component members. Justice as the common good acknowledges the need for stability and thus the concerns of the first moment, and also comprehends, *without being limited by*, the requirement of consent of the second moment. Assessments of the relative justice of regimes traverse domestic and international politics and provide room for properly prudential judgments in international relations, thus avoiding the twin dangers of moral absolutism and relativism.

We begin by exploring the origins, rationales, and shortcomings of the first and second moments of legitimacy. We then outline the idea of legitimacy as justice that we argue provides a more satisfactory account of state legitimacy and a sounder basis for policy.

Moment One: The State

Political legitimacy first appeared as a distinct modern issue with the rise and institution of the state as the primary form of political organization in Europe. The Peace of Westphalia of 1648, which ended the confessional and dynastic wars that had devastated Europe from the mid-sixteenth to mid-seventeenth centuries, established certain pragmatic principles aimed at ensuring peace and stability. It settled boundaries between principalities and recognized de jure the sovereign independence of each, thus laying the legal foundations for the modern international system of independent sovereign states. The latter were defined as territorially distinct units enclosing settled populations under a stable government. States, however large or small, were considered formally equal and, under a principle of nonintervention, equally entitled to govern themselves as they chose particularly in matters of religion, although the principle could be extended to all internal arrangements. For the sake of peace and stability, state legitimacy was deliberately divorced from questions of internal regime or system of governance, thus producing what we here call the *first moment of modern legitimacy*.

The most influential theoretical formulation of the new idea of state central to this moment was Thomas Hobbes's *Leviathan*, published three years after the Westphalian Peace. Starting from materialist premises and using a "scientific" deductive method, Hobbes presumed to reveal universal political truths whose understanding would secure the internal peace of a state and allow it to prosper. Hobbes's state was a human artifact that ensured stability and order, thereby liberating the peaceable desires for domestic prosperity and commodious living that could be achieved through science, trade, commerce, and manufacturing. Political decisions that led to endless civil disputes and quarrels—especially on issues of justice and religion—were entrusted wholly to the sovereign. This revolutionary conception of the state overthrew all previous conceptions of law (classical, common law, Natural Law, traditional) in the name of individual natural rights (as opposed to duties), which could be secured only by the establishment of an overwhelming Leviathan state capable of enforcing general obedience.

Hobbes personally favored monarchy but was theoretically indifferent to regime type so long as rulers possessed sufficient power to ensure internal peace and stability. The question of a state's legitimacy was thus divorced from that of its internal form and exhausted in its *effectiveness* in overawing the population and preserving stable peace. According to Hobbes's materialist account of human will and action, a contract secured by fear was morally equivalent to one secured by any other passion. It followed that a Commonwealth gained *by acquisition*—that is, by force, with the multitude authorizing the conqueror from fear of death (*Leviathan* XX)—was no different to a Commonwealth created *by institution*—that is, authorized by a covenant rationally agreed among equal bearers of individual rights. The Hobbesian state, founded on the proper use of fear or violence, does not distinguish between compulsion and free consent, or between de facto power and justified authority, nor, therefore, between democracy and tyranny. There exists no "external" standard of justice by which the sovereign and its actions may be judged, for justice comes into being only after sovereignty is established: "before the names of just, and unjust can have place, there must be some coercive power, to compel men equally to the performance of their covenants" (*Leviathan* XV). Justice does not precede, but *proceeds from* the sovereign power, so that force and justice are effectively conflated.

Hobbes's positivistic view still informs modern studies of legitimacy, largely because Max Weber's account, which follows Hobbes, is taken as the usual starting point (see, for example, Beetham 1991, 121; Gilley 2009, 8). In his *Theory of Social and Economic Organization*, Weber provided a hugely influential definition of the state (repeated in *Politics as a Vocation*) as that political entity whose "administrative staff successfully upholds a claim on the *monopoly* of the *legitimate* use of violence in the enforcement of its order" (emphasis added; 154). By "legitimate" Weber seemed to mean not much more than that those possessing the monopoly always claimed to hold it legitimately. In *Economy and Society*, Weber depicts a distinctly Hobbesian brutish state of nature in which dominion is established by sheer coercion—of men over other men, and over women in general—although naked power is often cloaked by religion and ceremony. A "political community" thus formed is defined as "forcible maintenance of orderly dominion over a territory and its inhabitants" (Weber 1978, 901). In Weber's view, simple coercion becomes genuine legitimacy (i.e., the admission by inhabitants of the community's *right* to punish them for nonfulfillment of obligations) only by the use of violence against outsiders, whether in aggression or defense, creating "a community of destiny or fate" in which individuals concede the right of the group to expect them to sacrifice themselves for the whole.

Weber's account of legitimacy, therefore, does not differ significantly from the first Hobbesian moment in which effective power *equals* legitimate authority. This remains a tempting equation for modern scholarship because it is difficult to distinguish citizen attitudes formed through effective power from those formed by other, purely internal processes. Schaar (1981), for example, argues that it is impossible to disaggregate a population's acceptance of a regime's legitimacy from other subjective attitudes like obedience through compulsion, habitual conformity, or mere acquiescence, making the concept useless for purposes of social scientific measurement. Yet on such reasoning a regime may be counted legitimate merely because it is not significantly contested by its subjects, which is to come close to adopting Hobbes's moral claim that contracts based on fear are valid.

This first moment of legitimacy continues to influence and shape international politics and our understanding of relations between states. Note, for example, the "customary international law" definition of a state provided by Article 1 of the Montevideo Convention on the Rights and Duties of States (1933): "The state as a person of international law should possess the following qualifications: (a) a permanent population; (b) a defined territory; (c) government; and (d) capacity to enter into relations with the other states." And note further the solemn declaration of UN Resolution 2625 (XXV): "Declaration of the Principles of International Law Concerning Friendly Relations and Cooperation among States 1970" of "The principle concerning the duty not to intervene in matters within the domestic jurisdiction of any State, in accordance with the Charter." Because no relevance is attached to the nature of the government for the purposes of admission to the community of mutually non-intervening states, a universal standard originally designed to preserve international peace has become definitive for determining the question of legitimacy domestically. International recognition, founded upon perceptions of state stability, becomes the proof of domestic legitimacy, at least as externally regarded. The price of accepting universalism seems to be an amoral stance toward the internal arrangement of states.

Moment Two: Democracy

This is a price, however, that many have been unwilling to pay, preferring to adhere to an alternate account of state legitimacy propounded by political philosophers other than Hobbes.

These other philosophers did not abandon the core Hobbesian conceptions of sovereignty, power, natural rights, and social contract; rather, they put their main focus on the *moral basis* of the contract. John Locke's (1992) conception of constitutionalism in his *Second Treatise* revealed the direction in which an alternate justification for the state would be developed. Locke's core idea was to transform the moral ambivalence of a state founded upon fear into the moral legitimacy of a state founded upon freely given consent. Consent provided justification for parliamentary institutions of representative government to exercise scrutiny over the executive, an executive that was no longer all powerful, but strictly limited. After Rousseau (1978) translated free consent into the idea of "popular sovereignty," the politics of the state began to move in a more democratic direction.

Although the question of how to tell whether consent, explicit or implied, was or was not freely given was as philosophically problematic as that of legitimacy itself, the idea of consent persisted as a rhetorically powerful foundation of state legitimacy. To be sure, this more comprehensive moral understanding came at a certain price, as Locke himself indicated when he noted its potential to create instability: natural rights and consent could now justify dissent and popular rebellion should a government prove tyrannical. Locke, however, thought this danger was outweighed by the greater stability that would be achieved by requiring that a ruler's moral authority be secured through popular consent. The major political consequence of this Lockean transformation of legitimacy was that modern political thought came to regard only democracies as truly legitimate (Kaufmann 1997). Kant raised the stakes in international relations by originating the idea of the "democratic peace," insisting that perpetual peace would be possible between nations—a peace of comity and amity rather than one dependent on the mutual restraint of distrustful neighbors—only when all states become popular "Republics" dedicated to maximizing individual freedom (Kant 1891). Kant also influenced attitudes by his transformation of Hobbesian and Lockean natural rights into human rights, which became a new *lingua franca* of legitimacy.

The historical advance of democracy among nations was piecemeal and gradual, yet the basic question regarding a state's legitimacy would be increasingly unequivocal: "Is it a democracy?" This *second moment of legitimacy* provided a universal standard for evaluating all states, but in doing so it challenged the status of the state per se as a legitimate political actor. Stability alone could not secure legitimacy. States were either democracies or they were not, and if not they were either democratizing or resisting democratization or perhaps degenerating from democracy. For many, the new focus on internal arrangements became the measure of the international legitimacy of a state, just as surely as the first moment's indifference to regime type became, contrarily, a measure of domestic legitimacy.

This inevitably gave rise to questions about the criteria to be used to determine whether a state was or was not democratic. The initial emphasis on contract and consent tended to favor general definitions based on procedural requirements, particularly the procedure of voting. Soon, however, the importance of specific institutional arrangements—such as the separation of powers, rule of law, and "transparency"—were also emphasized. Democratization was a matter of appropriate institution and nation building, and legitimacy could be measured by the suite of institutions introduced into a democratizing state.[1] Since it was widely assumed that these institutions of liberal democracy also provided the best protection for Kantian human rights, the latter became a further convenient standard that democracies could use to criticize nondemocratic states.

Indeed, one of the questions raised by casting democracy as central to state legitimacy was what to do with unquestionably nondemocratic and, therefore, definitionally illegitimate states. This issue became more pressing as democracies found themselves in increasing economic and political intercourse with such states. A policy of toleration and coexistence seemed inadequate if it was deemed desirable that all seemingly atavistic states be transformed into enlightened democracies, thus moving toward the Kantian ideal of a world federation of peaceful republics. The insistence on democracy inevitably encouraged a certain missionary spirit among "free peoples." Perhaps, on the way to world peace, states that refused to become democracies could, in the spirit of Rousseau's "general will," be legitimately "forced to be free." Such an approach has been a persistent temptation among democracies, especially but not exclusively in the United States, even though ex-president John Tyler had forecast as early as 1849 where such dangerous passions would lead: to a determination to advance with the sword the doctrines of republicanism under a banner that proclaimed, *"there is but one form of govt. upon the earth which we will tolerate and that is a republic"* (cited in Hendrickson 2009, 189; emphasis in original). More recently John Ikenberry has noted a danger that even "enlightened interventions" to defend human rights under an assumed responsibility to protect run the risk of turning into a form of imperialism (Ikenberry et al. 2008, 23).

The second moment of legitimacy thus seemed superior in capturing a moral dimension that the concept of the state had sought to omit. It denoted the preparedness to look into the state, its institutions, rule and practices to see if it could be judged truly legitimate. Yet it also raised doubts about the possibility of peaceful coexistence of democracies and nondemocracies, encouraging the perception of a duty to help or compel nondemocratic states to change for the sake of both their citizens and a more peaceful world.

The Third Moment: Justice

There are clearly significant obstacles in a practical diplomacy that seeks to take its bearings from the second moment of legitimacy, not least of which is the need to have a concerted democratic response to international problems that do not threaten the already suspicious non-democratic world. Yet falling back on "realism" of the kind preached in international relations theory is hardly more helpful, albeit the natural tendency of those recoiling from the dangers of a "Wilsonian" foreign policy. Thus Robert Kaplan (2009) writes that, after two decades of optimistic interventionism based on the "humanistic" assumption that all barriers between human beings were surmountable, the "rehabilitation of realism" has begun.

Such oscillation between "idealism" and "realism" is really an oscillation between the two moments of legitimacy, illustrating the perennial inadequacy of both. Together they seem to yield only a battle of false alternatives, in which self-interested calculation is pitted against starry-eyed humanitarianism or, alternatively, grave ethical concern is pitted against hard-headed indifference to moral questions. We are presented again with a false choice between accepting all states as legitimate or differentiating them on a basis that makes all nondemocratic states equally illegitimate. Yet one must ask whether it is sensible or useful to judge that there are no relevant differences between say, China and North Korea, or Vietnam and Burma. Every actor on the international stage knows that there are important differences and acts accordingly, yet what defensible criteria for differentiation can be espoused that combine genuine ethical discrimination with solid realism?

It should go without saying that the prospect of successful action or negotiation in the international realm requires a prudent realism—not IR theory realism, indeed, but a more commonsense form that implies a soberly realistic assessment of not just what *should* be done, but of what *can* and *cannot* be done, and of the necessary *means* to achieve anything. A prudent realism is an intelligently informed realism that eschews hubristic pride and calculates with care the limits as well as the possibilities of action—but also one that does not indulge in the fantasy of ethical indifference. The operation of such realism might be described as "pragmatism," and pragmatic it certainly must be. But thorough-going pragmatists are likely to be accused of too readily betraying principles for immediate ends or cheap bargains, or even of possessing no deeply held principles at all. A properly ethical realism must have some defensible principle that refutes such charges, and this implies the need for one that transcends those embodied in the first two moments of legitimacy (namely the principle of state and the principle of democracy respectively).

Both these moments sought to furnish universal standards for evaluating the political arrangements of different countries. The standards they impose, however, fail to take into account obvious as well as subtle political facts and circumstances that inevitably confront those engaged in political action. No space is left for the genuinely prudential choices and judgments that politics demands. The options presented turn on foundational opinions regarding the relative place of stability and morality in politics, and once one or the other is selected, the consequences are inevitable, irrespective of the specific political circumstances of any country under assessment. There is thus a curious and seemingly unwarranted abstraction in both moments of legitimacy.

The division created by the two moments is also reflected among students of legitimacy. Studies tend to be *either* normative *or* empirical, that is, conducted either by political philosophers trying to determine universal norms or social scientists attempting to understand how legitimacy functions in particular societies that employ different, often contradictory, criteria for legitimating power (Beetham 1991, 5–6). The former seem to issue in judgments that are too indiscriminately universal to apply to the actual world, the latter seem to imply a practical attitude of permissive relativism. The trouble is that any assertion by a scholar that a regime is legitimate or illegitimate seems automatically to imply certain normative attitudes toward it that may feed into practical policy. This systematic ambiguity is the real reason that some political scientists argue that legitimacy should be replaced with something more morally neutral and potentially measurable, like "political support" (O'Kane 1993). Such a suggestion can only evade the real issue, however, if political support always depends significantly on citizen judgments of the rightness (i.e., legitimacy) of existing political arrangements. Accurate description of political reality thus requires close understanding of this irreducibly normative dimension of all politics.

Dissatisfaction with this situation is evident in various attempts made to overcome the two moments by means of synthesis. Beetham, for example, tries to combine "normative" and "descriptive" aspects by distinguishing the concept of popular sovereignty as the core premise of legitimacy and then positing an historical, evolutionary process that demonstrates the natural "superiority" of societies informed by it-in effect, taking the second moment of legitimacy and putting it into Darwinian motion (progress being, according to Beetham, by no means teleologically foreordained but nevertheless indicative: 1991, 127–128, 248–249). This and other attempts to resolve the two moments of legitimacy are compelled by the obvious need to acknowledge and give due weight to the moral and practical complexities that confront any thoughtful attempt to assess political regimes.[2]

We would like to suggest here a third moment of legitimacy founded, not solely on facts of stability or consent, but on a wider notion of justice that is frequently occluded or simply assumed. It is worth noting at the outset that the first and second moments of legitimacy were also, in their own way, concerned with justice. The first, Hobbesian moment regarded justice as impossible until the Leviathan state imposed its order on a disorderly multitude, with the implication that it conceived the state positivistically as being not just the provider of the necessary foundations for justice, but the *author* of justice and thus itself beyond critique on the basis of justice. Hobbes, as we saw, was indifferent to regime type provided only order (and, therefore, justice so understood) was enforced. The second, Lockean moment corrected this defect by emphasizing the moral foundation of the state's authority in consent, but the long-range effect was to allow that only a single type of regime could be counted as just, the liberal democratic one.

In our third moment we seek to go further by, in effect, going back to an Aristotelian view of justice based on the common good. Aristotle (1984) made a moral distinction between regimes that were or were not devoted to the common good, yet allowed that different types of regime could be just (*Politics* III, 7, 1279a, b). In his famous categorization of six regime types, three were virtuous because looking to the common good—monarchy (rule by one), aristocracy (rule by few), and polity (rule by many)—while three were "degenerate" forms of these— tyranny, oligarchy, and democracy—because they looked only to the good of a particular individual or class at the expense of others. Justice was a disposition to render unto each person and class their proper due, which none of the degenerate forms did.[3]

Justice, in its determination to give all their proper due, assumes that there exists a common good in which all have a share, even if, given the inevitable inequalities of social life, this is not an equal share. Thus the test of a state's legitimacy becomes less a question of regime-type than of the regime's determination to render, under whatever particular circumstances it finds itself, justice within a common good framework. Focusing on justice, then, rather than simply on either stability or democratic form, allows us to make more subtle, comprehensive, and politically relevant discriminations between states, thus escaping the impasse between the amoral first moment and the morally dogmatic second moment of legitimacy. It will allow us to name certain regimes out-and-out tyrannies, whether soft or brutal, and to treat them accordingly, while distinguishing them in a principled manner from "authoritarian" or "autocratic" states that can be judged, all in all, as guided by some, albeit limited or truncated, conception of the common good.

Of course, given what Kant called the "crooked timber of humanity," no state will ever be judged absolutely just, our own no more than any other. It is worth noting here that even advanced democracies have not escaped charges of illegitimacy for being insufficiently democratic; judged according to ever more ambitious criteria, no actual state could possibly meet.[4] Critics have argued that representation is skewed toward particular groups or classes while others are ignored, that the voices of individual citizens are seldom heard except at election time and even then imperfectly, that governments are remote, arrogant, and elitist, and so on. Western democracies are said to be suffering a "legitimacy crisis," bringing into question the authenticity of democracy and "the degree to which democratic control is substantive rather than symbolic, and engaged by competent citizens" (Dryzek 2000, 1). Unhappy with minimal or aggregative versions of democracy, theorists and activists have pursued more deliberative and participatory approaches, hoping to make the democracy more democratic (Fung 2007, 448–449). At an extreme is the view that true consent and democratic inclusion is not possible, and that all regimes are, therefore, strictly speaking, illegitimate; democratic justice could be hoped for, or held up as an unrealizable but nevertheless salutary ideal, but not actually practiced (see, for example, Derrida 1992).

Democracy as an absolute standard for judging legitimacy is, therefore, inherently problematic, which is exactly why a focus on justice that rejects all absolutes enables better discrimination. It allows us to moderate the claim that only democracies can be valid or just, and enjoins us to take serious note of the actual diversity of regimes. Assessing the disposition of a regime toward its citizens and the wider world requires that we exercise great care to understand what is and is not possible in the particular situation before making judgments of legitimacy or illegitimacy. We are encouraged to evaluate the peculiar problems and challenges a regime might face before insisting precipitately on change and transformation that may be neither feasible nor beneficial in the circumstances. Focusing on justice opens up space, in other words, for the exercise of the practical wisdom that is the heart and soul of good political practice.

It may be objected that justice is always contested, either because there is no consensus as to its meaning or because any consensus that exists is inevitably shaped by a particular historical horizon. Such an argument misses the mark but in doing so concedes much. The fact that justice is always contested—often vigorously contested—demonstrates its importance in shaping political discourse and in criticizing particular exercises of power. Claims regarding justice will inevitably be influenced by disparate factors unique to each regime, including history, culture, religion, and so on. The point is that all political claims, no matter how unique or specific to each polity, will inevitably be formulated in terms of justice because that is the primary political phenomenon. Contestation as such is not proof that there is no justice; merely that there is dispute in specific cases as to its meaning or as to what is required to meet its demands. Justice takes us to the specific case, and in doing so gives weight and substance to actual political debate. It brings the level of analysis down to street level, so to speak, enabling greater accuracy and discernment.

What are the practical consequences of judging legitimacy through the lens of justice and, in particular, of justice understood in terms of the common good? By taking seriously specific arguments of justice made by participants in each context and noting the extent to which they contend with other demands, we may discern in domestic and international struggles a unique mix of might and right. A demand for redistribution of income or political authority by a minority group, for example, will reveal the status of that group within the regime, and the extent to which it thinks it can legitimately make a claim on the regime. Such justice claims, varying in extent and duration and with variable regime responses, will allow a balanced assessment of the nature of the regime. Resorting to violence and rebellion will reveal the fundamental claim of justice that a section of society believes is not being addressed.

Such rebellion may portend a crucial rift in the regime, but it would be hasty to assume that such a regime is thereby rendered "illegitimate"— was the Sri Lankan government rendered illegitimate by the quarter century rebellion of the Tamil Tigers? Certainly the Tigers by their actions challenged the legitimacy of the regime with regard to Tamil aspirations, but any just assessment must include not only a judgment of the justice of the Tamil cause but of the means that the Tigers took to pursue it. The justice of the Sri Lankan case, as of most others, is much more complex when viewed from every necessary angle of assessment. The larger picture of country conditions, complexities, and challenges will always demand attention if a just estimation is to be made, including some idea of the basic intent of both the regime leaders and the insurgents, as well as the attitudes and opinions of a majority of citizens (whether expressed through formal consent mechanisms or not).

The true nature of a regime is revealed, moreover, not only in its internal policies and actions but in its external stances and ambitions. Indeed the two are generally intimately connected. In this sphere it is necessary to assess the justice of the regime's intentions, ambitions, and dealings with other states and with the international community in general. Assessments of the justice and injustice of either internal or external actions are never simple or easy, but that, of course, is the point. It is because they are complex, and possibly never final, that they provide a superior approach to that which reduces matters to mere questions of stability or the existence or absence of democratic forms. In interpreting the problem of legitimacy as a problem of justice, we acquire more subtle political access to the interplay of ideas, institutions, history, and culture, without abandoning the requirements of rigor. We become attentive to the political and moral landscape of all politics.

Scholars who have attempted to overcome the limitations of the first two moments of legitimacy by offering a broader and more dynamic account have, we contend, implicitly turned to an Aristotelian conception of justice, regime, and the common good. Alagappa, in *Political Legitimacy in Southeast Asia* (1995), starts with Weber but goes beyond the first moment to show the important moral dimension of legitimacy. He argues that political legitimation is "an outcome of an interactive process between ruler and ruled" so that legitimacy is "contingent, dynamic and continuously defined" (29). He uses multifarious bases of legitimacy to show the complexity of the phenomenon as it operates in the region under study. Such diversity of foundations suggests that the question of legitimacy in particular cases can never be simply settled, but requires the sort of fine-grained approach that Alagappa adopts in his final discussion (293–334). In trying to do full justice to each regime—which is to say to determine the extent to which the regime itself does justice by its citizens—he inevitably employs an implicit understanding of a complex but genuine common good.

A similar argument can be made with respect to Bruce Gilley's *The Right to Rule* (2009), which also starts with a Weberian concept of the state and its attendant principles of coercion and dominance yet soon reaches beyond this to claims of right or "rightfulness." Gilley argues that rightfulness contains three underlying dimensions—legality, justification, and consent—and notes that, while political philosophy is concerned with the ethical uses of power, "the empirical study of legitimacy can be important to widen the understanding of different types of reasoning *to inform judgments about alternative pathways to legitimate rule*" (xiii; our emphasis). He employs his categories to conduct a rigorous empirical measure of legitimacy in 72 states and uses these measures to "examine the attributes of legitimate and less legitimate states" in a manner that avoids absolutist judgments and produces some surprising results (ibid.). Even states with poor human rights records enjoy modest levels of legitimacy on this scaling, although, as Gilley comments, no doubt in spite of rather than because of those records (220).

Gilley's relativistic measures of legitimacy argue for more variegated attitudes and more prudent responses among both policy analysts and political leaders. Emphasizing good governance and state performance as much as rights, he places at the heart of his analysis a common good not reducible to an aggregate of individual interests. As he puts it, "citizens must trust one another, they must believe in the common good, and they must be sufficiently educated and informed to make judgments about the performance of their states and leaders" (xiv). Where there are very significant disagreements over the common good, Gilley observes, for instance, in deeply divided states racked by mutual animosities, "legitimacy is impossible" (4).

Such a view casts an interesting light on the recently advanced principle of a "responsibility to protect," whose intention was to modify and moralize the first moment of legitimacy. Initiated by Kofi Annan after the atrocities in Rwanda, Bosnia, and Kosovo and developed by an International Commission on Intervention and State Sovereignty (ICISS), the responsibility to protect recharacterized sovereignty in terms of both internal and external duties: internally, a state had a responsibility to respect the dignity and rights of its citizens; externally, it had a responsibility to respect the sovereignty of other states. The latter responsibility did not preclude an international humanitarian intervention in a state that failed drastically to meet its former responsibility (ICISS 2001). On what premises of legitimacy other than ad hoc ones, however, did this first, newly devised responsibility rest? On a principle of justice, on the other hand, it is the clearly obvious grave injustice being done to a section of the community that destroys legitimacy and may justify intervention. Of course, interventions even to prevent great atrocities will depend not merely on what is right but on what is judged feasible.

Alagappa and Gilley provide examples of scholars who have apprehended the inadequacy of the first two moments of legitimacy and endeavored to move beyond them. In providing a more expansive moral vocabulary grounded in practical and empirical confrontation with debates, facts, and opinions, their research reaches toward a political scholarship that takes legitimacy as justice seriously. It also allows us, incidentally, to admit our own limitations without relinquishing the responsibility of ethically weighing the misdeeds of others. The search for justice is always an ongoing affair in any regime, and remembering this may prevent self-righteous occupation of an imagined moral high ground that the mere fact of democratic forms supposedly affords.

The Need for Prudent Realism

No one need deny that stability is a value that ought to be respectfully regarded, and even, in very difficult circumstances, at the expense of other values. No one committed to the virtues of democratic procedure and consent need feel they are relinquishing these by accepting the legitimacy of some nondemocratic regimes. All that is claimed is that judgments of what justice requires, both in our own case and that of others, will keep us on the one hand from moral indifference to the condition of others and on the other hand from self-righteous high-handedness. It is the very difficulty of such subtle judgment— the recognition of the limitations both of our own faculties of accurate assessment and of our abilities to achieve well-intentioned goals—that recommends it to people who must deal on a practical level with the world as it is, as well as however we might wish it to be.

The prudent realism of this approach is in any case the mainstay of men and women who have the responsibility for understanding countries as media commentators, area specialists, and policy analysts, and with those who must deal with various countries as diplomats and ambassadors. By removing procrustean templates, both amoral and moralistic, in order to reveal the true nature of politics, our approach merely acknowledges, in a theoretical way, what such people are already doing. The focus on justice, we argue, is more realistic than the realism of power or the hopefulness of blind idealism, and provides a true insight into the problem of modern legitimacy.

Notes

1. For an overview of the scholarship, especially the 1970s and 1980s separation of democratic transition and consolidation, the emphasis on process, and subsequent shift from structural to cultural and political economy concerns see Grugel (2002). More generally see O'Donnell et al. (1986); Huntington (1991); Przeworski (1991); Rueschemeyer et al. (1992); Diamond (1999).

2. Alagappa (1995, 15) includes among his criteria to establish a "right to rule" both proper and effective use of power and consent of the governed, an attempt to combine Hobbesian and Lockean moments. Others, aware of the limitations of synthesis, seek to liberate themselves from these categories altogether. Waller and Linklater (2003), for example, have turned to the concept of loyalty. Coleman (1988) and Putnam (2000 and 2002) have proposed "social capital" or norms of reciprocity and networks of civic engagement to understand better the nature of political stability and change.

3. Aristotle was, however, all-too-familiar with the unending quarrels, especially between rich and poor, that marked most Greek regimes, which he argued arose from people's partial understanding of justice and their consequent tendency to push their own just claims too far. He, therefore, recommended a model of a mixed polity combining all three elements of rule that would ensure both justice and stability (*Politics* IV, 11, 1295a).

4. See, for example, the critiques of advanced liberal democracies by the UN Human Rights committees, as well as general surveys, such as Freedom House (http://www.freedomhouse.org).

References

Alagappa, Muthiah, ed. 1995. *Political Legitimacy in South East Asia: The Quest for Moral Authority*. Stanford: Stanford University Press.

Aristotle. 1984 [350 BC]. *Politics*, translated by Carnes Lord. Chicago: University of Chicago Press.

———. 1985 [350 BC]. *Nicomachean Ethics*, translated by Terence Irwin. Cambridge, IN: Hackett.

Barker, Rodney S. 1990. *Political Legitimacy and the Sta*te. Oxford: Oxford University Press.

BBC. 2009. "Obama Interview: The Transcript." *BBC World Service*, http://www.bbc.co.uk/worldservice/news/2009/06/090602_obama_transcript.shtml.

Beetham, David. 1991. *The Legitimation of Power*. London: Macmillan.

Derrida, Jacques. 1992. "Force of the Law: The 'Mystical Foundation of Authority'." In *Deconstruction and the Possibility of Justice*, edited by Drucilla Cornell, Michel Rosenfeld, and David Gray Carlson. New York: Routledge.

Diamond, Larry 1999. *Developing Democracy-Toward Consolidation*. Baltimore: Johns Hopkins University Press.

Dryzek, John S. 2000. *Deliberative Democracy and Beyond: Liberals, Critics, Contestations*. Oxford: Oxford University Press.

Fishman, Robert M. 1990. "Review: Rethinking State and Regime: Southern Europe's Transition to Democracy." *World Politics* 42: 422–440.

Fung, A. 2007. "Democratic Theory and Political Science: A Pragmatic Method of Constructive Engagement." *American Political Science Review* 101: 443–458.

Gilley, Bruce. 2009. *The Right to Rule.* New York: Columbia University Press.

Grugel, Jean. 2002. *Democratisation: A Critical Introduction.* Houndmills, UK and New York: Palgrave.

Hendrickson, David C. 2009. *Union, Nation, or Empire: The American Debate over International Relations, 1789-1941.* Lawrence: University Press of Kansas Press.

Hobbes, Thomas. [1651] 1968. *Leviathan,* edited by C. B. Macpherson. Harmondsworth, England: Penguin.

Human Rights Watch. 2009. "Obama Mid-East Speech Supports Rights, Democracy." June 4, http://www.hrw.org/en/news/2009/06/04/obama-mid-east-speech-supports-rights-democracy.

Huntington, Samuel P. 1991. *The Third Wave: Democratization in the Late Twentieth Century.* Norman: University of Oklahoma Press.

ICISS (International Committee on Intervention and State Sovereignty). 2001. "The Responsibility to Protect." http://iciss.ca/report-en.asp.

Ikenberry, John G., Thomas J. Knock, Ann-Marie Slaughter, and Tony Smith. 2009. *The Crisis of American Foreign Policy: Wilsonianism in the Twenty-First Century.* Princeton, NJ: Princeton University Press.

Kant, Immanuel. 1965 [1796]. *The Metaphysical Elements of Justice,* translated by John Ladd. Indianapolis: Bobbs Merrill.

———. 1891 [1784]. "Kant's Principles of Politics, Including His Essay on Perpetual Peace. A Contribution to Political Science," translated by W. Hastie. Edinburgh: Clark. http://oll.libertyfund.org/?option=com_staticxt&staticfile=show.php%3Ftitle=358&chapter=56096&layout=html&Itemid=27.

Kaplan, Robert D. 2009. "The Revenge of Geography." *Foreign Policy* May/June.

Kaufmann, Alexander. (1997). "Reason, Self-Legislation and Legitimacy: Conceptions of Freedom in the Political Thought of Rousseau and Kant." *The Review of Politics* 59: 25–52

Locke, John. 1992 [1689]. *Two Treatises on Government,* edited by Peter Laslett. Cambridge: Cambridge University Press.

O'Donnell, Guillermo, Philip C. Schmitter, and Laurence Whitehead, eds. 1986. *Transitions from Authoritarian Rule—Comparative Perspective.* Baltimore: Johns Hopkins University Press.

O'Kane, Rosemary. 1993. "Against Legitimacy." *Political Studies* 41: 471–487.

Peter, Fabienne. 2007. "Democratic Legitimacy and Proceduralist Social Epistemology." *Politics, Philosophy & Economics* 6: 329–353.

Przeworski, Adam. 2000. *Democracy and Development: Political Institutions and Well-Being in the World, 1950–1990.* New York: Cambridge University Press.

Putnam, Robert D. 2000. *Bowling Alone: The Collapse and Revival of American Community*. New York: Simon & Schuster.

———, ed. 2002. *Democracies in Flux: The Evolution of Social Capital in Contemporary Society*. Oxford: Oxford University Press.

Rousseau, Jean Jacques. 1978 [1762]. *On the Social Contract with Geneva Manuscript and Discourse on Political Economy*, edited and translated by R. Masters. New York: St. Martin's Press.

Rueschemeyer, Dietrich, Evelyne Huber Stephens, and John D. Stephens. 1992. *Capitalist Development and Democracy*. Cambridge: Polity Press.

Schaar, John H. 1981. *Legitimacy in the Modern State*. New Brunswick: Transaction Books.

Waller, Michael, and Andrew Linklater, eds. 2003. *Political Loyalty and the Nation-State*. London: Routledge.

Weber, Max. 1964. *Theory of Social and Economic Organization*, edited by Talcott Parsons. New York: Free Press.

Contributors

Greg Barton is Herb Feith Research Professor for the Study of Indonesia in the School of Political and Social Inquiry, Monash University.

William Case is a Professor in the Department of Asian and International Studies and Director of the Southeast Asia Research Centre, City University of Hong Kong.

Tun-jen Cheng is Professor in the Department of Government, the College of William and Mary.

Björn Dressel is Senior Lecturer at the Crawford School of Economics and Government, Australian National University.

Heike Holbig is Professor of Political Science with a focus on Chinese and East Asian Area Studies at the Department of Social Sciences, Goethe University in Frankfurt.

Xunming Huang is a doctoral candidate in political science in the Department of Political Science, the University of Toronto.

John Kane is Professor in the Department of Politics and Public Policy, Griffith University.

Hun Joon Kim is Research Fellow in the Griffith Asia Institute and the Centre for Governance and Public Policy, Griffith University.

Hui-Chieh Loy is Assistant Professor in the Department of Philosophy, National University of Singapore.

Stephen McCarthy is Senior Lecturer in the Department of International Business and Asian Studies at Griffith University.

Noel M. Morada is Executive Director of the Asia Pacific Centre for the Responsibility to Protect at the University of Queensland.

Haig Patapan is Professor in the Department of Politics and Public Policy, Griffith University.

Haruko Satoh is Research Fellow in the Osaka School of International Public Policy, Osaka University.

Carlyle A. Thayer is Emeritus Professor in the School of Humanities and Social Sciences, the University of New South Wales.

Benjamin Wong is Associate Professor with the Policy and Leadership Studies Academic Group at the National Institute of Education, Nanyang Technological University.

Naiteh Wu is Research Fellow in Academia Sinica.

INDEX